This is the first introduction to rhythm and meter that begins where students are: as speakers of English familiar with the rhythms of ordinary spoken language, and of popular verse such as nursery rhymes, songs, and rap. *Poetic rhythm* builds on this knowledge and experience, taking the reader from the most basic questions about the rhythms of spoken English to the elaborate achievements of past and present poets. Terminology is straightforward, the simple system of scansion that is introduced is suitable for both handwriting and computer use, and there are frequent practical exercises. Chapters deal with the elements of verse, English speech rhythms, the major types of metrical poetry, free verse, and the role of sense and syntax. *Poetic rhythm* will help readers of poetry experience and enjoy its rhythms in all their power, subtlety, and diversity, and will serve as an invaluable tool for those who wish to write or discuss poetry in English at a basic as well as a more advanced level.

Poetic rhythm

Poetic rhythm

An introduction

DEREK ATTRIDGE

The University of York

CAMBRIDGE
UNIVERSITY PRESS

CAMBRIDGE UNIVERSITY PRESS
Cambridge, New York, Melbourne, Madrid, Cape Town, Singapore,
São Paulo, Delhi, Dubai, Tokyo

Cambridge University Press
The Edinburgh Building, Cambridge CB2 8RU, UK

Published in the United States of America by Cambridge University Press, New York

www.cambridge.org
Information on this title: www.cambridge.org/9780521423694

First published 1995
Eighth printing 2008

A catalogue record for this publication is available from the British Library

Library of Congress Cataloguing in Publication data
James I, King of England, 1566–1625.
Attridge, Derek.
Poetic rhythm: an introduction / Derek Attridge.
   p.   cm.
ISBN 0 521 41302 8 (hardback) – ISBN 0 521 42369 4 (paperback)
1. English language – Verisfication.   2. English language – Rhythm.
3. Poetics.   I. Title.
PE1505.A86 1995
821.009 – dc20   94-33191 CIP

ISBN 978-0-521-41302-2 Hardback
ISBN 978-0-521-42369-4 Paperback

Transferred to digital printing 2010

For Edward Weismiller

Contents

Preface

The approach to rhythm and meter in this book broadly corresponds to the one I set out at length in *The Rhythms of English Poetry* (Longman, 1982). Readers who wish to follow up the introductory discussion here in more detail should turn to that book, in which a fuller account of the complexities of rhythmic movement in verse is presented. I have changed the notation used in that book, partly because of the advent of the personal computer since it was written: the symbols used here are easy to write by hand and to produce on a computer. (A simple macro will make any symbol a matter of one or two keystrokes.) However, there is no difficulty in converting these symbols to the ones used in *The Rhythms of English Poetry*, and vice versa. The only substantive difference is that I now distinguish between successive stressed beats separated by a perceived offbeat (a "virtual offbeat") and those separated by nothing more than the necessary pause induced by the linguistic rhythm (an "implied offbeat," though I do not use the term in this book). This change makes possible a clearer distinction between the movement of stress verse and that of syllable-stress verse.

Chapter 8, on phrasal movement, is indebted to the work of Richard D. Cureton, notably his *Rhythmic Phrasing in English Verse* (Longman, 1992), though I take full responsibility for the adaptation and simplification of his arguments. Not all readers will wish to enter the little-explored realm of phrasing, but my hope is that many will be persuaded of the importance of this young branch of prosodic study.

This book owes a great deal to others who have committed themselves to the movements of poetic language, whether in writing poetry or writing about it, and if it were another kind of book it would be studded with references to their publications. One debt I am especially happy to acknowledge – to someone whose commitment to poetry has been of both kinds – is signaled in the dedication.

Many people have contributed time and expertise to this project in a more direct way. The book has benefited enormously from the careful reading of the manuscript at different stages of its evolution by Tom Furniss, John Gouws, George Kearns, and Suzanne Hall. The readers for Cambridge University Press were both generous and scrupulous in their comments. Richard Cureton counseled me on phrasing, and Bruce Tucker gave me just the right advice about rap. Laura and Eva Attridge have reminded me how important, and how pleasurable, the experience of rhythm and meter is in our earliest years.

The writing of *Poetic Rhythm* was made possible by a Summer Stipend from the National Endowment for the Humanities and a fellowship from the John Simon Guggenheim Memorial Foundation, and by research funding from Rutgers University. I gratefully acknowledge this support. My family's contribution goes far beyond the assistance already mentioned, not least in making home – wherever it may be – the best possible place I could have to work in.

Cambridge, New Brunswick,   D.A.
and Pietermaritzburg

Acknowledgments

Quotations from published texts (listed here in order of their appearance in the book) are taken from the following sources:

Denise Levertov, from "Matins," in *The Jacob's Ladder*, New Directions Publishing Corp., 1961; William Carlos Williams, from "The Dance," in *Selected Poems*, New Directions Publishing Corp., New York, 1968; Wallace Stevens, from "Peter Quince at the Clavier," in *The Collected Poems*, Random House Inc., New York, 1982; Philip Larkin, from "Church Going," in *Collected Poems*, ed. Anthony Thwaite, The Marvell Press, Faber and Faber, and the Noonday Press, 1988; H. D. (Hilda Doolittle), from "The Flowering of the Rod," in *Trilogy*, New Directions Publishing Corp., 1973; Theodore Roethke, from "Frau Bauman, Frau Schmidt and Frau Schwartze," in *Collected Poems of Theodore Roethke*, Faber and Faber, 1968; James Joyce, from *A Portrait of the Artist as a Young Man*, Penguin Books (Viking Critical Library), 1977; John Ashbery, from "The New Spirit," in *Three Poems*, The Viking Press, 1972; Flannery O'Connor, from "Good Country People," in *The Complete Stories*, Farrar, Straus and Giroux, New York, 1979, taken from *A Good Man is Hard to Find*, – acknowledgment made to Harcourt Brace Jovanovitch, Inc.; Langston Hughes, "Motto," from *The Panther and the Lash* by Langston Hughes, copyright 1951 by Langston Hughes, reprinted by permission of Alfred A. Knopf Inc. and Harold Ober Associates Incorporated; William Butler Yeats, from "Into the Twilight" in *Collected Poems*, Macmillan and Company Ltd, London, 1963; Louis Untermeyer, from "Song Tournament: New Style," in *Burning Bush*, Harcourt Brace Jovanovitch Inc., 1928; Robert Frost, from "The Thatch," in *Complete Poems*, Jonathan Cape, 1951; W. H. Auden, from "The Age of Anxiety," in *Collected Shorter Poems*, Faber and Faber, 1968; from "The Seafarer," translated by Michael Alexander, in *The Earliest English Poems*, Penguin Books, 1966; from *Sir Gawain and the Green Knight*, translated by Marie Borroff, New York: W. W. Norton & Company, 1967; E. Sermon and P. Smith, from "It's My Thing," in *Rap: The Lyrics*, ed. Lawrence A. Stanley, Penguin Books, 1992 – acknowledgment made to Paricken Music, administered by WB Music Corp.; Matt Dike, Mike Ross, Tony Smith, and Marvin Young, from "Wild Thing," in *Rap: The Lyrics*, ed. Lawrence A. Stanley, Penguin Books, 1992 – acknowledgment made to

Varry White Music (ASCAP); E. Fletcher, S. Robinson, C. Chase, M. Glover, from "The Message" in *Rap: The Lyrics*, ed. Lawrence A. Stanley, Penguin Books, 1992 – acknowledgment made to Sugar Hill Music Publ., Ltd. (BMI); Karl Shapiro, from "Elegy Written on a Frontporch," in *Selected Poems*, Random House, 1968; Thom Gunn, from "Blackie, the Electric Rembrandt," in *Selected Poems 1950-75*, Faber and Faber, 1979; John Betjeman, from "Church of England Thoughts Occasioned by Hearing the Bells of Magdalen Tower," in *Collected Poems*, John Murray, 1970; W. H. Auden, from "Lullaby," in *Collected Shorter Poems 1927-57*, Faber and Faber, 1966; W. H. Auden, from "In Memory of W. B. Yeats," in *Collected Shorter Poems 1927-57*, Faber and Faber, 1966; Robert Lowell, from "Mr Edwards and the Spider," in *Robert Lowell's Poems: A Selection*, ed. Jonathan Raban, Faber and Faber, 1974; W. B. Yeats, from "A Dialogue of Self and Soul," in *Collected Poems*, Macmillan and Company Ltd, London, 1963; Sir John Betjeman, from "Slough," in *Collected Poems*, John Murray, 1970; W. B. Yeats, from "Among School Children," in *Collected Poems*, Macmillan and Company Ltd, London 1963; W. B. Yeats, from "Meditations in Time of Civil War," in *Collected Poems*, Macmillan and Company Ltd, London, 1963; W. H. Auden, from "Shorts" (1940), in *Collected Shorter Poems 1927-57*, Faber and Faber, 1966; W. B. Yeats, from "On a Political Prisoner," in *Collected Poems*, Macmillan and Company Ltd, London, 1963; W. H. Auden, "Precious Five," in *Collected Shorter Poems 1927-57*, Faber and Faber, 1966; Ezra Pound, from "The Return," in *Selected Poems*, Faber and Faber, 1975; T. S. Eliot, from "Marina," in *Collected Poems 1909-1962*, Faber and Faber, 1963; William Carlos Williams, from "The Descent of Winter," in *Selected Poems*, New Directions Publishing Corp., 1968; John Berryman, from "I'm scared a lonely," poem 40 in *The Dream Songs*, Farrar, Straus, and Giroux, New York, 1969; Susan Howe, from "Pythagorean Silence 3," in *Language Poetries: An Anthology*, ed. Douglas Messerli, New Directions, 1987; Adrienne Rich, "Night Watch" and the lines from "Novella," "Women," and "Burning Oneself In" are reprinted from *THE FACT OF A DOOR-FRAME, Poems Selected and New, 1950–1984*, by Adrienne Rich, by permission of the author and W. W. Norton & Company, Inc., copyright © 1984 by Adrienne Rich, copyright © 1975, 1978 by W. W. Norton & Company, Inc., copyright © 1981 by Adrienne Rich; F. T. Prince, from "The Old Age of Michelangelo," in *Collected Poems*, Sheep Meadow Press, New York, 1979; D. H. Lawrence, from "Mountain Lion," in *Complete Poems*, ed. Vivian de Sola Pinto and F. Warren Roberts, The Viking Press Inc., 1964; Elizabeth Bishop, from "A Cold Spring," in *The Complete Poems 1927-1979*, Farrar, Straus, and Giroux, New York, 1983; Ogden Nash, "The Turtle," from *Verses from 1929 On* by Ogden Nash, copyright © 1940 by Ogden Nash, renewed, reprinted by permission of Curtis Brown, Ltd., and of Little Brown and Company; Oswald Mbuyiseni Mtshali, "Boy on a Swing," from *Black Poets in South Africa*, ed. Robert Royston, reprinted by permission of Mbuyiseni Oswald Mtshali and Ad. Donker (Pty) Ltd.; Robert Graves, "The Impossible," from *Collected Poems 1975*, copyright © 1975 by Robert Graves, reprinted by permission of Oxford University Press, Inc. and A. P. Watt Ltd on behalf of the Trustees of the Robert Graves Copyright Trust.

On using this book

The primary aim of this book is to help readers experience and enjoy the rhythms of English poetry in all their power, subtlety, and diversity. A secondary aim is to provide ways of talking and writing about the contribution made by rhythm to the meaning and force of individual poems. These two aims aren't as separate as they may sound, since we recognize and respond to the rhythmic features of poetry all the more fully if we possess some basic tools of rhythmic analysis. No understanding of the history of poetry, or of the place of poetry in history, is possible without an understanding of poetic rhythm. Moreover, a thorough acquaintance with rhythm is essential to the writing of good poetry, and this book is also designed to help poets – and those who wish to become poets – to develop that necessary familiarity.

This book does not, however, offer a metrical *theory,* in the strong sense of the word. It does not attempt to formulate rules that would enable a reader (or a computer) to decide if a given line is an acceptable example of a given meter. No successful metrical theory in this sense has yet been produced, though there have been many attempts. The approach in this book is different: bearing in mind that poetry is a matter of hearing and experiencing meaningful sounds and not calculating with abstract symbols, it introduces the reader to the basic ingredients of rhythm and meter and shows how they function in the most common types of verse.

What is offered here is just a first step. There is space for only a limited number of examples, and nothing like a full account of the intricacy and expressive potential of poetic movement is attempted. Just as students of music need to know the elements of harmony and counterpoint before proceeding to more complex analytical, critical, and comparative tasks, students of poetry need to become familiar with the elements of rhythmic form. But it is not enough just to know the conventions that govern the use of rhythm and meter. This book attempts to *explain* the features that it describes: why are certain metrical forms common in English poetry and others rare, why do certain variations in the line cause major disruptions while others don't, how do the movements of English verse spring from the characteristics of the language we speak? In coming to understand the reasons for the particular choices made by poets down the centuries, we appreciate more fully the poems they wrote.

The organization of chapters reflects this approach. After an initial chapter on rhythm in poetry, chapter 2 presents an outline of the significant rhythmic features of the English language out of which all verse is crafted. Chapter 3 introduces the workings of meter, especially in its familiar four-beat version. Chapter 4 builds on the foundation of the previous two chapters to consider stress meter, the most common type of English meter outside the literary canon. Chapters 5 and 6 examine syllable-stress meter, the major literary form of meter in English. Free verse is the subject of chapter 7, and chapter 8 discusses the role of syntax and meaning in poetic movement (with further consideration of free verse). Each chapter except the first includes a number of exercises, which offer a small sample of the many ways in which the tools of analysis may be deployed. Chapters are followed by brief summaries of their more technical points.

There are four appendices: the first summarizes the activity of *scansion* that is crucial to the development of sensitivity to rhythm, the second is a *glossary* of terms used in the study of rhythm and meter (including terms not employed in this book), the third lists the *sources* of the quotations given throughout the book, and the fourth provides suggested *responses to the exercises* where these involve scansion of examples.

Most of the poetry discussed in this book is in regular meters, even though the majority of poets writing in English today use some form of free verse. There are a number of reasons for this emphasis. First, in the history of English poetry, free verse represents a relatively recent preference, and the great bulk of existing verse is written in metrical lines. Second, free verse is usually written, and gains by being read, in relation to this tradition, which it resists and embraces in varying degrees. And third, becoming familiar with the working of regular meter is a good way to gain an understanding of the rhythms of spoken English, upon which all verse, free or metrical, is based.

In discussing rhythm and meter some technical terms are necessary; and it's an unfortunate fact that the field of prosody, as the study of rhythm and meter has traditionally been called, presents a dizzying array of such terms, without very much agreement about their precise meanings. It has been said of the most traditional method of analyzing meter – in terms of "feet" – that it works only for those who already know what is going on and are able to make the vague gestures which others who also know what is going on can understand. This book tries to avoid such elitism by using the simplest terms available and keeping close to their commonest meanings, and it ignores the fact that many of these terms have been the subject of lengthy disputes. Readers should be prepared to find different terms in other books on poetry, as well as some of the same terms being used with different meanings. Appendix 2 will help to relate the vocabulary used in this book to that found in other studies of verse. Much of the traditional terminology of prosodic study in English was originally derived from Greek prosody, and since these terms – however misleading – are in wide use they are explained in chapter 5, in the section on "Foot-scansion."

This book contains numerous examples of poetry scanned to show how they might be read. Examples are numbered, and those that are not invented are identified in Appendix 3. Lines that have been rewritten to illustrate a point about their rhythm are indicated by a letter after the number, thus: (7a). (Where appropriate, older spellings have been modernized.) No poem has only one correct mode of rhythmic delivery; on the contrary, the study of prosody makes it clear that poems on the page allow for a number of alternative realizations, much as a musical score allows for a variety of different performances. The value of poetry lies partly in these multiple possibilities. The test of a system of scansion, therefore, is not that it should fix the manner in which lines are read, but that it should provide a way of clearly showing alternative readings. In the discussions that follow, however, it will often be necessary to choose one option and therefore impose one interpretation, and all readers are bound to experience moments of resistance to some of these choices. As long as allowances are made for individual preferences, these moments should not affect the exposition of the argument.

Scanning a poem – especially if it involves attention to phrasal movement as well as to the rhythm of stressed and unstressed syllables – has its own value, as a way of becoming intimate with it, hearing it with the fullest possible attention. But it is only one element in appreciating a poem, and this book offers no recipe for moving from a particular metrical or rhythmic feature to an interpretive or critical commentary. The same feature has very different effects in different poems, and even in the same poem may be interpreted very differently when it appears in dissimilar contexts. Though I have included as many examples of the critical usefulness of rhythmic analysis as space has allowed, the major emphasis in this book is on hearing and understanding the movements of the language themselves. Whatever critical approach to poetry a reader wishes to use will benefit from accurate and responsive dealings with rhythm and meter.

Chapter 1

The rhythms of poetry: a first approach

Reading poetry

Poetry is as old and as widespread as human culture. Just to possess a language is enough, it seems, to arouse the desire for utterances more vivid and more memorable than those of daily speech, a need to treat the productions of language as sequences of sounding words rather than strings of inert symbols whose only function is to point to their encoded meanings. What is distinctive about poetry is its exploitation of the fact that spoken language *moves*, and that its movements – which are always movements of meaning and emotion at the same time as movements of sound – achieve a varied onward momentum by setting up expectations that are fulfilled, disappointed, or deferred. These sequences suggest connections with other meaningful movements, in literature, in daily talk, in the world outside language. Speech always *happens*, as a process of unfolding sounds and significations, echoing and anticipating each other, and poetry aims at a precision that makes every word count as something experienced meaningfully through the body at the same time as it is understood by the mind.

The engine that drives this sonorous and meaningful activity is *rhythm*: the continuous motion that pushes spoken language forward, in more or less regular waves, as the musculature of the speech organs tightens and relaxes, as energy pulsates through the words we speak and hear, as the brain marshals multiple stimuli into ordered patterns. To understand and enjoy poetry means responding to, and participating in, its rhythm – not as one of a number of features that make up the poetic experience, but as the heart of that experience.

Read the following sentence – the opening of William Wordsworth's 8,500 line poem *The Prelude*, which I have set out as if it were prose – like the beginning of a long novel, silently, aiming to get the gist of it as efficiently as possible:

(1)   O there is blessing in this gentle breeze that blows
        from the green fields and from the clouds and from
        the sky: it beats against my cheek, and seems half-
        conscious of the joy it gives.

Now read it aloud, slowly, letting the sound and movement of the words carry you along, pausing briefly at the ends of the lines signaled on the page:

```
(1a)      O there is blessing in this gentle breeze
          That blows from the green fields and from the clouds
          And from the sky: it beats against my cheek,
          And seems half-conscious of the joy it gives.
```

What is the difference between these two experiences? In the second reading, each line *takes place* as an occurrence with its own integrity and emotional quality. At the end of the first line we pause to comprehend and respond to the opening announcement – the speaker's happiness, and the belief that it comes from the "gentle breeze" – before we move on to discover and take pleasure in the sources of the breeze in the line that follows. The line after this enacts the overflowing exuberance of the speaker's feeling as yet another natural source is added to the list. The movement then halts in mid-line, before starting again with a new description of the physical action of the breeze, rendered verbally as it happens experientially. The final line, like the previous lines, is not simply a statement but is a movement of thought – a far-fetched yet emotionally justifiable speculation. Only in the second of our two readings can the lines be said to function *as poetry*, enacting for us as we speak the words an experience, a happening in time, that is physical and emotional and mental all at once.

Poems are made out of spoken language. A very few of the millions of poems that have been written have an existence only as visual artifacts, but even these derive some of their impact from the *impossibility* of reading them aloud. This is not to say that in all other poems the visual aspect is unimportant. On the contrary, once poems started to be circulated in print as well as recited from memory or from a precious manuscript, their look on the page became significant, and the history of English poetry could be written as a history of the gradually increasing importance of its visual dimension – but always as this interacts with its aural dimension. The commonest way we now experience poetry is not by listening to a reciter or reader, but by reading it on a page in front of us, and we shall see that much poetry, especially recent poetry, capitalizes on this situation.

Of course, we can't always read poetry aloud. If we read on trains or in libraries or shared rooms we have to compromise, but it is still possible to shape the words in silence and to feel the rhythm coursing through the lines as we do so. (We manage this by means of minute muscular movements that are enough to suggest the larger movements that take place in actual speech.) Reading poetry requires *time*; each word needs to emerge and fulfill itself before we go on to the next. A poem is a real-time event. Our habit of skimming for sense when we read a newspaper or a novel, of barely noticing the little words that take us from one kernel of meaning to the next, is a great asset in modern civilization, but it doesn't stand us in good stead when it comes to poetry, which simply cannot work *as* poetry if it is read in this way. This is not because poetry is only or primarily sound, but because it is *in* sound – and above all in sound in movement – that its meanings are produced and performed. To remember a poem is not the same as remembering a fact or an experience; it's to remember words spoken in a certain order – and one of the best ways of becoming sensitive to the possibilities of poetic rhythm is to memorize poems in different rhythmic forms.

The first rule in appreciating rhythm and movement – a requisite for appreciating poetry – is therefore a simple one: read poems aloud whenever you can (and have others read to you as well). Do this often enough for it to become an automatic impulse whenever you pick up a poem. Then if it's *not* possible to read aloud, you will find yourself enunciating the poem under your breath slowly and with full attention, allowing it to take the same time it would demand if you were using your voice. It's worth remembering that although we talk of someone "reading a poem," it's never simply a matter of a person doing something to a passive textual object. What happens is that the "reader" sets in motion a two-way process, keeping just enough control to carry out the interpretive activity that is necessary, but as far as possible letting the language take charge, having its way, springing its surprises and offering its satisfactions.

Some basic terms

During the course of this book, a number of terms will be introduced, discussed, and exemplified. Here are some preliminary comments on a few of the most important of the terms that will be used. (For a full list of terms and brief definitions, see Appendix 2.)

1. Rhythm

Rhythm is one of the most familiar experiences of our daily lives. We are all constantly making and encountering rhythms. Whenever the muscles of your body engage in a repeated activity a rhythmic movement is set up, and when you watch someone else engaged in such an activity – or hear the sounds that are produced by it – you naturally respond to it rhythmically, sometimes with movements of your own body. Breathing, walking, running, talking: these are all rhythmic activities. *Rhythm is a patterning of energy simultaneously produced and perceived; a series of alternations of build-up and release, movement and counter-movement, tending toward regularity but complicated by constant variations and local inflections.* Rhythm can be both produced and perceived by a single person, as when you sing a song or read a poem aloud; or the production and perception can be separate, as when someone sings a song or reads a poem to you. Although strictly speaking the idea of "movement" implies travel in *space*, rhythm is what makes a physical medium (the body, the sounds of speech or music) seem to move with deliberateness through *time*, recalling what has happened (by repetition) and projecting itself into the future (by setting up expectations), rather than just letting time pass it by. Rhythm is *felt* as much as it is *heard* or *seen*.

All languages have their distinctive rhythms, their own ways of harnessing the energies of the body as they unfold in time. The job of the rhythm in any language is to economize on that expenditure of energy by imparting a degree of regularity to it. And poetic rhythm is a heightening and an exploitation of the rhythm of a particular language. To be able to speak English, therefore, is to be familiar with the rhythms that English poetry uses. The further back you go in history, of course, the more likely you are to encounter words that have to be pronounced with somewhat different rhythmic qualities from those we give them today. But even as far back as Shakespeare this applies to only a few words, and with a little practice it's easy to become responsive to the rhythms of the verse written by Chaucer some six hundred years ago. Different accents and dialects produce no major difficulties either. Although a very detailed analysis of rhythm would show up discrepancies, the fundamental features that we will be looking at are common across a wide range of varieties of current English.

The rhythm of the English language is fundamentally a matter of *syllables* and *stresses*, and we will come back to these terms in chapter 2. The point I want to emphasize now is that simply being able to speak and understand English means being able to handle both of these, whether we are conscious of this ability or not. Operating together, syllables and stresses give spoken English the rhythmic drive it needs to keep going: like all rhythms, that is, it enables the muscular movements to happen with a certain evenness and predictability. (Imagine what it would be like trying to saw through a log if the arm and hand muscles, instead of working rhythmically, moved in irregular spasms.) Poems harness that rhythmic drive to their own ends, but they do so by exploiting the language's own potential, not by imposing arbitrary rules on it.

More important than settling on and memorizing a definition of rhythm is learning to read poetry in such a way as to *experience* its rhythm. Poetic rhythm is not a secret property that only the initiated can appreciate; it is the most open and immediate of qualities. If we sometimes miss it, it's because we've learned *not* to hear it in our rush to attend to other things.

2. Verse

Almost all poetry is written in verse, as opposed to prose. Prose follows only the rules of the English language, but verse introduces some additional principle or principles that heighten our attention to its rhythms. A few poems have been written in prose, and we might also want to apply the word "poetry" to parts of some novels – James Joyce's *Ulysses*, for instance – on the basis of their attention to the movement and sounds of language. But in this book we are concerned with poetry written in verse, of which there are two major types, metrical verse and nonmetrical, or free, verse. (Freedom is, of course, a relative matter, and there is no reason why free verse shouldn't be as carefully controlled as metrical verse.) "A verse" can mean either "a line" or "a stanza"; because of the ambiguity, the term is not used in this book.

3. Free verse

Free verse, which became common in the twentieth century after some isolated earlier examples, is, in one sense, the simplest kind of verse. It uses a very straightforward device to bring about a focus on the movement of the language: the introduction into the continuous flow of prose language, which has breaks determined entirely by syntax and sense, of another kind of break, shown on the page by the start of a new line, and often indicated in a reading of the poem by a slight pause. When we read prose, we ignore the fact that every now and then the line ends and we have to shift our eyes to the beginning of the next line. We know that if the same text were printed in a different typeface, the sentences would be broken up differently with no alteration in the meaning. But in free verse, the line on the page has an integrity and function of its own. This has important consequences for the movement and hence the meaning of the words.

Here are two examples of free verse, by Walt Whitman and Denise Levertov, each consisting of one descriptive sentence from a longer poem:

```
(2)  The big doors of the country barn stand open and ready,
     The dried grass of the harvest-time loads the slow-drawn wagon,
     The clear light plays on the brown gray and green intertinged,
     The armfuls are pack'd to the sagging mow.
```

```
(3)      The new day rises
         as heat rises,
         knocking in the pipes
         with rhythms it seizes for its own      4
         to speak of its invention -
         the real, the new-laid
         egg whose speckled shell
         the poet fondles and must break          8
         if he will be nourished.
```

What these two examples show is that the category "free verse" (like the category "metrical verse") embraces widely differing uses of rhythm. The first example uses long lines that correspond to the main divisions of the sentence, while the second cuts up the sentence at places where we wouldn't normally pause, resulting in a very different rhythm. All kinds of free verse depend on the intrinsic rhythmic characteristics of spoken English, but they exploit it in a variety of ways.

4. Meter and metrical verse

Most rhythms – whether in language or elsewhere – are not organized into longer repeated units. They begin, project themselves forward, peter out, change, or stop, but they don't fall into regular patterns made up of groups of rhythmic pulses. I walk forward, slow down, break into a run, come to a sudden halt; the muscles of my body go through a series of rhythms, working with and against one another in complex relationships, without any sense that I could *count* the movements I make, or if I could, that the numbers would be significant. I read aloud from a newspaper, and my speech obeys the rhythmic norms of the English language, determined entirely by the sentences I read and not by any system of repeating sequences. The free verse lines just quoted are given their rhythm by the interaction between the rhythms of the language itself and the line-divisions marked on the page; there is no further principle of organization or subdivision.

If, however, you read the following lines by William Blake aloud, letting their individual rhythm emerge, you will find that they develop a swing of their own. A different impulse of rhythmicality emerges to mesh with that of the language itself, and perhaps even alter it (by making you read the last two words more deliberately than in prose, perhaps):

```
(4)      Never pain to tell thy love,
         Love that never told can be;
         For the gentle wind does move
         Silently, invisibly.
```

The words have been chosen by the poet in such a way that the rhythm which is produced when they are read with their normal pronunciation falls into a pattern of repeating units, a *meter.* The word suggests the measuring that is implicit in such units: the units are countable, and the number is significant. *Meter is an organizing principle which turns the general tendency toward regularity in rhythm into a strictly-patterned regularity, that can be counted and named.*

We don't have to do any work to *make* Blake's lines metrical; the poet has already done the work in his arrangement of words, his placing of syntactic boundaries, and his organization of lines, and we merely have to follow his lead. If the sense seems to require a pause, or a quickening, we can provide either of these without fear that the metrical pattern will dissolve – it is built into the words, and will continue to make itself felt. For instance, you may feel that although the first sentence goes on after the first line, the meaning demands quite a long pause after the first "love." Read it in this way, and you will find that the rhythmic pattern is merely postponed, not broken. Equally, you might want to read straight on from the third to the last line; again, the organization of the rhythm does not suffer. Meter is not a metronome ticking away while we read; it is a quality of the poet's chosen language, both emerging from and having an effect on that language.

As with the free-verse poet, part of what the poet has done is to divide the sentence up into lines on the page. This is less significant here because the language itself sets up a metrical pattern that divides at those places – which are also signaled by rhymes. We can show the difference by rewriting this example and one of the earlier free-verse examples without the line-breaks:

(4a) Never pain to tell thy love, love that never told
      can be; for the gentle wind does move silently,
      invisibly.

(3a) The new day rises as heat rises, knocking in the
      pipes with rhythms it seizes for its own to speak
      of its invention - the real, the new-laid egg whose
      speckled shell the poet fondles and must break if he
      will be nourished.

We would be unable to reconstruct the line-divisions in the second example, but it would be an easy task in the first – and not only because of the rhymes.

Though not all meters are as clear-cut as the one Blake uses in this example, it is always the case that the units into which metrical verse is divided are determined by its own internal structure, whereas the units of free verse are determined by the layout on the page. The less clearly marked the meter, the more the responsibility falls on the reader to indicate the line-ends in pronunciation. Different readers do this in different ways, and only the slightest of modifications to a normal reading – such as a slowing-down on the final syllable or a brief pause after the last word – will usually be enough.

Like rhythm, meter is not limited to a single medium. In principle, any rhythmic movement can be made metrical: if I push the saw with extra vigor on every fourth stroke I am setting up a simple meter. (Even the alternation of stronger forward and weaker backward strokes in normal sawing might be called a meter, of a very elementary kind.) Meter is, of course, a fundamental feature of most Western music. It is signaled by the time-signature at the beginning of a piece of music, and by the bar-lines that divide up the work, but more importantly it emerges from the structure of notes and rests – patterns of duration, melody, dynamics, and harmony – that make up the texture of sound. Meters can also be produced in a number of languages whose physical properties are very different from each other.

Although in theory any principle of organization based on the counting of units could be considered a meter, we are concerned only with those systems that produce an *intensification and regularization of the normal rhythm of the language* – and as we shall discover, only a very few of the theoretically possible systems of meter achieve this result. The lines by Blake just quoted are an example of one of the most common of such systems, and the fact that a reader can tell they are in a meter without having to do any counting shows how well it does its job of intensifying and regularizing. What we experience is precisely the rhythm of spoken English becoming more insistent and more even in its pulses (two aspects of the same process).

Most of the basic metrical patterns that occur over and over again in English poetry can be found in the poetry of many other languages, and in much of Western music. It must be stressed that meter is not abstract or theoretical, although sometimes it is talked about as if it were; it is not *opposed* to rhythm but is a way of *organizing* rhythm. But while the meter of the poem is something it shares with other poems, rhythm involves many factors besides meter, and is unique to a particular poem. We will find that the field of meter is classified according to a number of overlapping categories: meter in general; stress meter and syllable-stress meter; duple and triple meter; four-beat and five-beat meter; and so on. These different metrical possibilities give rise to different kinds of *verse*: stress verse and syllable-stress verse, duple and triple verse, and so on for all the other types of meter. *Versification* is the art of writing in verse; *metrics* or, more traditionally, *prosody*, is the study of that art.

The fact of a poem's being written in a meter doesn't mean that it enters a realm of special difficulty: far from it, since the majority of the meters used by poets are fundamentally very simple and very familiar. The bulk of English verse is metrical, and this includes both literary epics and folk ballads, sonnet sequences and nursery rhymes. Readers who turn to literary verse are almost always already proficient at reading popular verse, and therefore have a solid foundation on which to build. The most valuable way of doing this is by reading as much poetry as possible in a variety of meters, trying to bring out the rhythmic structure (chanting the lines, if necessary) so that the metrical patterns and possibilities of English verse become second nature.

5. Beat

The most fundamental feature of any rhythm that is organized as a meter is the *beat*, a burst of energy that is part of a repeating and structured pattern. *Metrical language is language written in such a way as to make possible the experiencing of beats.* It would be less accurate to say the "hearing" of beats, because it is an important fact that beats are not just heard: what makes a particular sound a beat is the way that it engages with the body and not just the ears and brain. We say that a stretch of language has beats when, on hearing it or reading it aloud, we sense an impulse to move at regularly occurring places – to bring down the hand, to nod the head, to tap the foot. The oldest meaning of the word "beat" is "strike repeatedly," and its later use in discussions of music and poetry still carries something of that sense of repeated physical action. What was described as the "swing" of the Blake lines quoted earlier is the effect of the beats that emerge as we read it. It's important to note that a beat never exists in isolation – it is always part of a patterned series, since it is only in such a series that beats can be produced.

In between two beats there is invariably a lull, a moment of slack often felt as either an after-effect of the previous beat or a build-up of tension leading to the next beat. This moment can be just a pause, or it can have a pulse (or sometimes more than one pulse) of its own – and if it does, we refer to the weaker pulses as *offbeats*. An offbeat is a kind of beat, but it is clearly distinguishable from a full beat by being less powerful, and by being rhythmically linked to a full beat before or after it. The alternation of beats and offbeats gives rise to a much stronger rhythm than a simple series of beats, and is the basis of all English meter. As we shall see, different types of offbeat play an important role in giving meters their specific character.

6. Some other terms

All poems (apart from prose poems, which we are not dealing with here) are divided into *lines*. The lines may be continuous, or divided into *stanzas* (groups of lines, usually with the same pattern of line-lengths and often the same pattern of rhymes). When a continuous poem is divided into irregular subdivisions, these are called *verse paragraphs*. If the end of a line coincides with a break in the syntax (usually, though not always, indicated by punctuation), it is called an *end-stopped line*. If the syntactic unit carries on over the end of the line into the next one, it is called a *run-on* line. All the lines in example (2) above are end-stopped; most of the lines in example (3) are run-on.

The names of the commonest metrical lines in the literary tradition are taken from Greek prosody (though their meanings when applied to English verse are different). The two most common lengths of line are the four-beat line, or *tetrameter* (from the Greek prefix tetra-, four), and the five-beat line, or *pentameter* (from the Greek prefix penta-, five). Other names will be defined later in the book.

Rhyme is a familiar phenomenon, involving the repetition of the stressed vowel of a word and any sounds that follow it, combined with a difference in the consonant immediately preceding it: "bee"/"free"; "lake"/"take"; "dressy"/"messy"; "kick it"/"stick it." It is used as a structural device in English verse to mark the end of metrical units or lines. A *rhyme-scheme* is a pattern of rhymes. To represent a rhyme-scheme in shorthand, every different rhyme is given a different letter of the alphabet: *aabbccdd* (couplets), *abab* (a quatrain with alternating rhymes), *abbaabbacdecde* (one type of sonnet).

When a poetic line runs smoothly because it fulfills the demands of the meter in the most straightforward way, it displays *regularity* or *simplicity*. We could also simply say that it is *highly rhythmical*. When it diverges from the simplest pattern of alternation enshrined in the meter there is an increase in *irregularity* or *complexity*. We can also describe this variation in terms of the degree of *relaxation* or *tension*, since meter is built out of readers' expectations, and when expectations are only partly met the language seems to be pulling away from the anticipated patterning.

To identify the meter of a poem by means of a system of visual symbols is to *scan* it, thus producing a *scansion*. The main purpose of scansion is to indicate clearly the basic rhythmic structure of a line or group of lines. It is not an attempt to represent a specific reading with all its nuances (though a scansion will often suggest one kind of reading in contrast to other possible readings). We can make a scansion more or less detailed, depending on the specific purpose it is being used for. One of the difficulties in analyzing meter is that the terms and symbols we use and the diagrams we draw tend to suggest, quite erroneously, that meter is largely a matter of space and of seeing. We need to bear in mind constantly that what we are dealing with is primarily a matter of *the movement of meaningful sound through time* – psychological time, especially – and that our employment of a visual, spatial vocabulary is forced on us by necessity. (See also Appendix 1, *Scansion*.)

Types of meter

There are a number of ways of classifying the meters of English poetry, none of which produces absolutely watertight categories. This book is organized according to a basic distinction between *stress meter* and *syllable-stress meter*, which differ in the way they use the fundamental building-blocks of the language. (A third type of meter, *strong-stress meter*, is discussed in conjunction with stress meter, to which it is more closely related.) But other categorizations cut across this one: the distinction between *duple* and *triple* meter, for instance, occurs in both stress meter and syllable-stress meter.

It is also useful to consider every metrical poem as falling into the category of either *four-beat verse* or *non-four-beat verse* (the most usual form of the latter being five-beat verse). As we shall see, the distribution of these categories is not symmetrical. Four-beat verse occurs in all types of meter, whereas non-four-beat verse occurs almost exclusively in syllable-stress meter; or, to put the same thing the other way round, stress verse and strong-stress verse are almost always in four-beat meter, whereas syllable-stress verse can be in both four-beat and non-four-beat meters. Since our perception of a meter is the product of a number of factors (which will be outlined in chapter 3), a given poem can be classified in a number of ways – its phrasing, its use of stressed and unstressed syllables, its layout on the page, its line-lengths, its transitions from one line to the next, its rhyme-scheme, and so on. We shall be dealing with many of these in the chapters that follow.

Functions of rhythm in poetry

All poetry in English exploits the rhythmic potential of the English language, but this does not mean that it does so for only one purpose. The functions of rhythm in poems are many and varied, though it is difficult to separate them out in any specific example because they work together so closely. It is also important to remember that the way rhythm works in poetry is a product of the literary culture in which it is written and read; these functions are not "inherent" qualities of rhythm, but modes of understanding that have developed through the history of English literature. They have changed in the past, and will no doubt do so in future – largely through the inventive practice of poets themselves. Any particular poem could be said to rediscover the functions of rhythm, and may exploit them in unanticipated ways.

In the chapters that follow, we shall consider many samples of poetry in English in which a number of the functions of rhythm are exemplified simultaneously. The following list is an initial, and somewhat arbitrary, classification of the major purposes which rhythm can serve in a poem. It is divided into two kinds of function: those which relate to the working of the poem as a whole, and those which relate to local effects at particular points in the poem.

1. The poem in general

(a) Heightened language

A poem's use of rhythm is one important way in which its language is heightened; that is to say, it is made to seem a special language demanding special attention. In poetry, language is rendered less haphazard, less ephemeral, less a product of the moment than in other utilizations. In free verse, this arises from the lines that divide up the continuous movement of the language, and their relation to syntactic and semantic structures. In metrical verse, the meter itself acts as a continuous principle of organization, and in its stricter forms it conveys the feeling that *every syllable counts*.

Although rhythm in poetry can often work effectively as an imitation of the spoken voice – and we shall turn to this function in due course – the heightening of language also produces a certain *impersonality*. When language, usually assumed to be the product of a single individual and a single mind, takes on the garb of some conventional order such as figures of rhetoric or oral formulae, it becomes to that extent trans-individual. The rhythmic forms of poetry – especially metrical poetry – furnish utterances with a public quality, even when they seem most personal and intimate. Interpretation may be a matter of responding to a range of possibilities held in suspension rather than identifying the inflections of a single "authentic" voice.

(b) Consistency and unity

A poem is usually experienced as a single entity, and one reason for this is its rhythmic consistency. Metrical verse remains in the same meter (with the same kinds and degree of rhythmic variation), and free verse keeps to the same kinds of line-length (which may mean the consistent use of very varied line-lengths) and the same relation of the line to syntactic units. By the same token, a poem that contravenes these expectations can convey a strong sense of internal change or fragmentedness. In achieving unity, rhythm works hand-in-hand with other features of the poem, of course, such as diction and imagery.

(c) Forward movement and final closure

Related to the consistency of a poem is the sense that during its course it is moving forward and that at its end it reaches a point of finality, rather than just stopping. Metrical form contributes to this aspect of poetry by providing larger structures which poems fulfill, both over short spans (syllables, stresses, lines) and long ones (stanza forms, fixed poetic forms). The existence of metrical expectations produces sequences of tension and relaxation, and these, too, provide a forward drive, especially when they are counterpointed against the units of grammar and meaning. Finally, phrasal movement – which we shall examine in chapter 8 – is an important factor in onward progress and culminating closure.

(d) Memorability

Because of its heightened and intensified language, poetry lodges itself in the brain more easily than prose. This is particularly true of metrical verse (especially when the rhythm is a strong one), since the physical imprint of the meter acts as a storehouse for the words. It's no accident that rural lore is often passed down in simple rhymes. ("Red sky at night, shepherd's delight; Red sky at morning, shepherd's warning.") This fact in turn gives poetry more potential for the richness that accrues from associations with other poems, since readers tend to come to poems with other poems held in memory (see "Literary associations" below). Another result of the memorability of poetic language is that poems gain in depth as we carry them with us through our lives. Even if we think we have forgotten a poem, it may come to life with greater vividness and richness when we re-encounter it.

(e) Mimetic suggestiveness

In rather general ways, the choice of a particular rhythmic form for a poem can suggest particular physical qualities. A rapid rhythm can be appropriate for a quick-moving subject; a slow rhythm may suit a somber topic. The rhythm of William Carlos Williams's "The Dance," with its one-two-three movement, is clearly representative of its subject:

```
(5)    In Breughel's great picture, the Kermess,
       the dancers go round, they go round and
       around, the squeal and the blare and the
       tweedle of bagpipes, a bugle and fiddles
       tipping their bellies...
```

Such devices don't go very far toward the achievement of a successful poem, but they may be a small part of it. They are certainly not a major justification for poets' attention to rhythm.

(f) Emotional suggestiveness

The choice of a particular rhythmic form can also imply a certain emotional coloring. Though the association of rhythmic qualities and emotional states is no doubt in part a matter of cultural conditioning, it seems likely that there's a physiological connection as well, since emotions manifest themselves directly in the way we expend muscular energy. When we speak, we impart to our words a rhythmic quality expressive of our feelings – light and rapid, heavy and slow, regular, abrupt, smooth, and so on. What's unusual about verse is that it has the capacity to *build in* these qualities, so that they become an inherent feature of the lines.

G. K. Chesterton's "Lepanto," for instance, is imbued with a rhythmic exuberance that implies a voice proclaiming rather than musing over or regretting the events it describes:

```
(6)    White founts falling in the courts of the sun,
       And the Soldan of Byzantium is smiling as they run;
       There is laughter like the fountains in that face of
         all men feared,
       It stirs the forest darkness, the darkness of his
         beard...
```

Wallace Stevens, on the other hand, in "Peter Quince at the Clavier," uses a meter that also has four main beats in each line to convey a meditative, reflective mood:

```
(7)    Just as my fingers on these keys
       Make music, so the selfsame sounds
       On my spirit make a music, too.
```

(g) Literary associations

The rhythm of one poem can allude to the rhythm of others – whether to a specific poem or group of poems or to an entire tradition of poetry. Writers who choose the same meter that Shakespeare and Milton chose know that readers will unconsciously relate their poetry to these earlier works. A poem in Spenserian stanzas can't help referring to Spenser's long poem *The Faerie Queene*, for which the stanza was invented. This process of association is by no means a limitation on the poet's craft; on the contrary, it is one of the available resources, making possible an increase in the richness and suggestiveness of the language.

Even when a poem is written *against* a particular tradition, it is still relying on some prior identification with that tradition. The incomprehension and mild irreverence displayed at the opening of Larkin's "Church Going" is directed not only at the tradition represented by the sacred building that the speaker is entering; its unawed tone and casual diction is equally an act of ironic detachment from the weighty tradition of the chosen meter, Shakespeare's and Milton's iambic pentameter:

```
(8)    Once I am sure there's nothing going on
       I step inside, letting the door thud shut.
       Another church: matting, seats, and stone,
       And little books; sprawlings of flowers, cut      4
       For Sunday, brownish now; some brass and stuff
       Up at the holy end; the small neat organ;...
```

2. Within the poem

(a) Emphasis

Organized rhythm sets up expectations, and any departure from the expected norm is potentially a moment of emphasis. The stricter the control of rhythm, of course, the more powerful the foregrounding which can be achieved when the rhythm of the language diverges from its anticipated course. Thus Milton, in his sonnet "On the Late Massacre in Piedmont," begins two lines with stressed syllables where unstressed syllables are expected in order to fix our attention on the horror of the events he is describing:

```
(9)    Forget not: in thy book record their groans
       Who were thy sheep and in their ancient fold
       Slain by the bloody Piedmontese that rolled
       Mother with infant down the rocks.
```

If we rewrite these lines so that "Slain" and "Mother" fall in the expected places, the emphasis is weakened and the lines lose some of their power:

```
(9a)    Forget not: in thy book record their groans
        Who were thy sheep and in their ancient fold
        Were slain by bloody Piedmontese that rolled
        The mother with the infant down the rocks.
```

Not every departure from the norm will be experienced as an emphatic moment, however; as always, co-operation with other aspects of the poem is decisive.

(b) Articulation

A departure from a norm that has been set up can also mark a shift of subject or tonality, as when a poem moves into a different meter and thereby alters the focus and feeling of a poem. Here's a stanza by Thomas Hardy in which the mood shifts startlingly from nostalgic remembrance to real grief at the sixth line, where a distinctive new rhythm is introduced:

```
(10)    They sing their dearest songs –
        He, she, all of them – yea,
        Treble and tenor and bass,
          And one to play;                              4
        With the candles mooning each face...
          Ah, no; the years O!
        How the sick leaves reel down in throngs!
```

(c) Mimetic effects

A common type of commentary on poetic rhythm involves relating a particular rhythmic sequence in a poem to a quality or event referred to by the words. It's easy to find oneself inventing connections of this kind, so scrupulous attention to the reading experience itself, and comparison with other poems, is necessary. Apparent mimetic effects frequently turn out to be simply the result of a rhythmic emphasis on a particular word or phrase. Mimetic devices that really do imitate movements or sounds are often comic, since they intrude upon the more subtle working of poetic rhythm.

Dryden changes the rhythm of his "Song for St Cecilia's Day" suddenly to suggest the sound of a drum; the device undeniably works, but more as a rhythmic conceit that we enjoy for its cleverness than as a moment of realistic engagement with the physical world:

(11)   The trumpet's loud clangour
            Excites us to arms,
         With shrill notes of anger,
            And mortal alarms.   4
         The double double double beat
            Of the thundering drum
         Cries: "Hark! the foes come;
         Charge, charge, 'tis too late to retreat."   8

(d) Emotional effects

More important than imitations of the world referred to by the words are
the ways in which changes in the mental and emotional state of the imagined speaker of the words are suggested by the rhythm. Just as the whole
poem can be imbued with a certain emotional timbre by its rhythm, so
individual lines or parts of lines can use movement to enhance feelings
expressed in the words. Again, it is difficult to separate out the contribution
of rhythm from that of meaning and syntax; but the capacity that rhythms
have for being smooth or jagged, forceful or hesitant, rapid or slow,
undoubtedly enters into the local effects of emotionally colored poetry.

Listen to the change of rhythm in the third and fourth lines in this
excerpt from Spenser's *Faerie Queene*. The figure of Despair is tempting the
hero to suicide:

(12)   Is not short pain well borne, that brings long
            ease?
         And lays the soul to sleep in quiet grave?
         Sleep after toil, port after stormy seas,
      Ease after war, death after life does greatly
         please.

By manipulating the allowable variations of the meter he is using, Spenser
has created a repeated rocking rhythmic figure that temporarily displaces
the sterner alternating rhythm. In this way, the rhythm evokes the speaker's
lulling tones while at the same time imitating the condition of restfulness he
is so persuasively advocating.

(e) Meaning in process

Because verse heightens the reader's sense of language moving through time,
the poet can suggest meanings that are then modified or contradicted a
moment later (and once a meaning in poetry has been suggested, even con-

tradicting it doesn't expunge the fact that for a time it existed). Although the revision of interpretations as the reader progresses is something that happens in prose as well, poetry possesses a special power to present meaning as a constantly changing process. This power is particularly noticeable at the transition from one line to another, where the reader usually attempts to establish some coherent meaning up to the end of the line before beginning to process the next line.

Since division into lines – and more generally the sense of a continual onward movement which involves repeated beginnings and endings – is a characteristic of all verse, this dimension of poetic meaning is potentially present in any poem, and we shall consider it further as an aspect of phrasal movement in chapter 8. Milton's poetry is full of such effects, one example being the very first line of *Paradise Lost*:

```
(13)    Of Man's first disobedience, and the fruit
        Of that forbidden tree...
```

Taking the first line as a whole, we tend to read "fruit" as meaning "consequence," referring to the outcome of that act of disobedience which is the subject of the poem. But when we read on to the next line, we realize that we are being told not about a metaphorical fruit but a literal one, the actual produce of a tree that grew in the Garden of Eden. However, the first meaning is not eradicated; the poem is about the terrible consequences of Adam and Eve's disobedience, which Milton believes are everywhere visible in his own time.

(f) Connection and contrast

We have considered the general unifying power of organized rhythm; it is also possible for particular parts of a poem to be connected by rhythmic similarities. Each of the first three stanzas of George Herbert's "Virtue" – presenting examples of earthly beauty – ends with the short, grim line "For thou must die"; the last stanza, however, closes with a climactic assertion that gains its power in part from its repetition of the earlier rhythmic units while contradicting their message. Here are the first and last stanzas:

```
(14)    Sweet day, so cool, so calm, so bright,
        The bridal of the earth and sky:
        The dew shall weep thy fall tonight,
                        For thou must die.    4
```

```
Only a sweet and virtuous soul,
Like seasoned timber, never gives;
But though the whole world turn to coal,
            Then chiefly lives.      8
```

"Then chiefly lives" has the same rhythmic outline as "For thou must die" but triumphantly reverses the meaning in a culminating assertion of faith.

It is quite possible for all these functions of rhythm to be at work in a single poem, and an exhaustive commentary on the rhythmic dimension of any poem would be an enormous project (especially if the interrelation between rhythm and the other dimensions of the poem were properly taken into account). In commenting on a poem, it's more likely that you will single out those functions of rhythm that are relevant to the point you are making – but this can only be done if you are aware of all the ways in which rhythm may participate in the experience of reading.

Summary

A. Reading poetry

Poetry *takes place* in time; its movement through time, more or less regular, is its *rhythm*. It should be read aloud whenever possible, and even when read silently it should take up the same amount of time that reading aloud would give it.

B. Some basic terms

Rhythm is the production and perception of patterned energy. It is *felt* rather than *heard*. Every language has its own characteristic rhythm.

Verse involves the introduction of an additional principle into language that heightens the reader's attention to rhythm. In *free verse*, this principle is the division of the language into discrete units by the layout on the page.

Meter is an organizing principle which turns the general tendency toward regularity in rhythm into a strict regularity that can be counted and named. It involves an intensification and regularization of the normal rhythm of the language. Metrical language is language written in such a way as to make possible the experiencing of *beats*, bursts of energy that produce repeated and structured patterns.

Types of meter

Meter can be classified in several ways; this book is organized around the distinction between stress verse and syllable-stress verse. Another important classification distinguishes between four-beat verse and non-four-beat (most often five-beat) verse.

Functions of poetic rhythm

The major *functions* of rhythm in poetry are the following:

1. The poem in general
(a) Heightened language
(b) Consistency and unity
(c) Forward movement and final closure
(d) Memorability
(e) Mimetic suggestiveness
(f) Emotional suggestiveness
(g) Literary associations

2. Within the poem
(a) Emphasis
(b) Articulation
(c) Mimetic effects
(d) Emotional effects
(e) Meaning in process
(f) Connection and contrast

Chapter 2

The rhythms of spoken English

Learning to speak English, as a child or an adult, is not just a matter of learning the sounds of the consonants and vowels, and putting them together in meaningful words and sentences. It also involves internalizing, through imitation and practice, a certain way of using the muscles of the speech apparatus to produce sequences of sounds. One has to learn (as one learns to swim, not as one learns a mathematical theorem) to produce the unique rhythm of English speech, different from the equally unique rhythms of other languages. Out of this unique rhythm the movements of English poetry down the centuries have been fashioned. This is one important reason why the rhythms and meters of English verse have no exact parallel in other linguistic cultures, though they have some similarities with the rhythms and meters of poetic traditions in closely related languages.

The study of English speech rhythm could take us into extremely complex and still rather vexed territory, but fortunately we need to deal with only a few elementary components before moving on to the poetic employment of this rhythm. It is only in recent years that phonologists working on the sounds of English (and related languages) have started to study in detail the rhythmic regularities that underlie our speech, though poets have been exploiting these patterns for centuries.

Syntax

The rhythm of a language is not just a matter of the sounds of its words; equally crucial are their meanings and the way they relate to one another in sentences – what is called *grammar* or *syntax*. It isn't necessary to know a great deal about the technicalities of linguistic analysis in order to appreciate and talk about the function of syntax and sense in poetic rhythm, but it *is* important to have a feeling for the way syntax joins and separates words in longer or shorter units and with different degrees of strength. It is in this way that syntax contributes crucially to our experience of language as movement. Fortunately, this feeling for syntax is part of knowing a language.

The language we speak is divided into coherent units by its syntax. Syntax thus has both a separating and a unifying function. Most obviously, language is divided into sentences; and sentences are often further divided into smaller units, and so on in a hierarchical structure. This structure can be shown graphically. In the following diagram the highest level (labeled 1) shows the main division of the sentence, and each succeeding level shows further (and weaker) subdivisions:

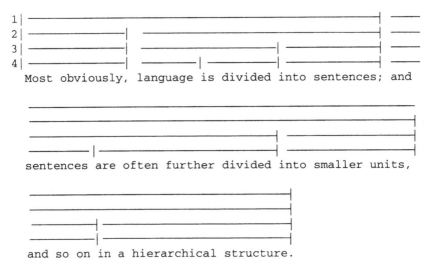

The strongest breaks within the sentence are usually marked by colons and semi-colons, the next strongest ones are often marked by dashes or commas. The space we see on the page between words always marks some degree of break, but this becomes minimal when the words form part of a tightly connected unit. Look at the line-endings in this example:

```
(1)    in the hot noon-sun, I think of the grey
       opalescent winter-dawn; as the wave

       burns on the shingle, I think,
       you are less beautiful than frost;...
```

A comma would be possible at the end of the first line ("the grey, opalescent winter-dawn"), but not the second ("the wave burns on the shingle"). This means that there is a stronger syntactic break at the end of the first line than the second, giving the two moments different rhythmic qualities.

However, the link between "the" and "wave" is even stronger than that between "wave" and "burns." You can feel this if you read a rewritten version:

```
(1a)   in the hot noon-sun, I think of the grey
       opalescent winter-dawn; as the
```

```
wave burns on the shingle, I think,
you are less beautiful than frost;...
```

Here the line-break cuts through a strongly unified phrase, "the wave," and the break is even more marked than in the original.

We sometimes represent a strong syntactic break in speech by either a silence or a pause (that is, by slowing down our reading speed, which usually means extending the last syllable before the break). It's important to understand that this is by no means essential, however. As speakers of the language, we are already familiar with the working of syntax, and we therefore know – not necessarily at a conscious level – when a break is occurring. In reading a poem, we *feel* the occurrence of breaks of different strengths, whether or not we choose to pause or insert a silence when we reach them.

The science of linguistics has developed complex (and competing) systems to describe the operations of syntax, but in this book we will avoid most of its terminology, and rely on the English speaker's sense of the divisions and links that order the language. When they function as part of a poem's movement, these processes are called *phrasing*, and although they will remain relevant throughout our discussion of meter and rhythm they will receive special attention in chapter 8.

EXERCISE

Syntax

(1) Read the following lines, paying attention to the links between the end of one line and the beginning of the next. Rank them by means of numerals, starting with 1 for the strongest link and using the same numeral for those you think are approximately equal:

```
Gone the three ancient ladies
Who creaked on the greenhouse ladders,
Reaching up white strings
To wind, to wind
The sweet-pea tendrils, the smilax,
Nasturtiums, the climbing
Roses, to straighten
Carnations, red
Chrysanthemums; the stiff
Stems, jointed like corn,
They tied and tucked,—
These nurses of nobody else.
```

(Note: chapter 8 will introduce a more sophisticated method of assessing the strength of run-on lines.)

Syllables

English speech is carried on a stream of *syllables*, each one a little articulation of energy produced by the muscles that expel air out of the mouth, shaped by the vocal cords and the organs of the mouth. It's very easy for a speaker of English to gain a sense of the way in which syllables work as a rhythmic motor; all you have to do is read out a sentence in which you exaggerate the syllables by making them into regularly occurring rhythmic beats. (It helps to tap on something with your hand for each beat.) Try it first with a sentence made of monosyllabic words (that is, words with only one syllable), so that all you have to do is give each word the same degree of emphasis – which means, you will find, pronouncing each word at the same pitch:

        This–is–a–test–that–will–not–last–long.

Now do it with polysyllabic words (words of more than one syllable) as well:

        This–ex–pe–ri–ment–will–be–ve–ry–short.

In reading like this, you have brought out the way in which syllables provide a primary rhythmic carrier for the language. Every sound of the language that you utter is a component of a syllable, and each syllable, being a rhythmic pulse, pushes you on to the next one.

It's not so easy to pronounce the *phonemes* – the distinctive sounds of the language – in the same way. Try to separate out the sounds of the word "experiment" as regular rhythmic beats:

        e–k–s–p–e–r–i–m–e–n–t

Phonemes are not produced rhythmically, and it's a strain to pronounce them as if they were. (It's much easier to count the *letters* in "experiment," because each pronounced letter is a syllable: ee—ex—pee—ee—are—eye— em—ee—en—tee.) Even pronouncing *words* as repeated beats involves more effort than doing so with syllables, unless of course they are all monosyllabic words, as in the example above. Try giving the following sentence a regular beat for each word:

        This–experiment–will–be–a–very–undemanding–one.

There is a sense of strain in subjecting words to this treatment.

Although linguists have not been able to come up with an exact physiological explanation of the syllable, it's clear from this kind of reading that syllables have a fundamentally rhythmic basis. Counting syllables – which is sometimes helpful if you are really puzzled by the meter of a line – is easy: just read in this way, counting on your fingers as you go. Don't be misled by spelling; not all vowels are pronounced, and not all syllables have a vowel. Take the word "rhythm" itself: it has no vowels as traditionally understood (though of course "y" often functions as a vowel), but we pronounce it as two syllables ("rith-im"). On the other hand, the last vowel of "danced" and "hoped" does not represent a syllable (except in some older poetry, where it is sometimes marked by an accent: "dancèd.")

Often two vowels are part of a single syllable, even if they are pronounced as a diphthong (that is, using more than one vowel sound): "maid," "steal," "shout." Some consonants can function as syllables: listen to the second syllable of "steeple." In this word it's the "l," not the "e," which constitutes the syllable. An apostrophe can also represent a vowel: "church's" and "class's" have two syllables (though of course "state's" and "text's" have only one). The guide should always be how the word is spoken. Sometimes we exaggerate the syllabic rhythm to make ourselves understood: "I said EX-PE-RI-MENT!!!"

Occasionally, you will encounter words where you can't be certain of the number of syllables. Are the following two-syllable or three-syllable words?

```
dubious   wandering   fiery   conduit
```

The answer is that they may be either, depending on how they are pronounced. Such words are handy for poets writing in meter, who may use them in accordance with either pronunciation. They usually don't pose any problems for readers of poetry, who are guided by the rhythmic expectations set up by previous lines. The general term for the omission of a syllable in pronunciation is *elision* (the syllable is said to be *elided*); we shall discuss some examples in verse in chapter 5.

EXERCISE

Syllables

(2) Mark each syllable in the following extracts with an "s" above its first vowel (or above a consonant if it constitutes the syllable). Underline any words which are capable of being pronounced with one more or one less syllable than you have shown.

(a) A quibble is to Shakespeare what luminous vapours are
    to the traveller: he follows it at all adventures; it
    is sure to lead him out of his way and sure to engulf
    him in the mire.

(b) In life's last scene what prodigies surprise,
    Fears of the brave, and follies of the wise?
    From Marlb'rough's eyes the streams of dotage flow,
    And Swift expires a driv'ler and a show.

(c) The box of pawntickets at his elbow had just been
    rifled and he took up idly one after another in his
    greasy fingers the blue and white dockets, scrawled
    and sanded and creased and bearing the name of the
    pledger as Daly or MacEvoy.

Stress

In bringing out the underlying syllabic rhythm of English by giving each syllable the same emphasis, you suppressed the language's other rhythmic characteristic: the varying degree of *stress* that is carried by syllables. The result, you will have noticed, sounded like some kind of crude machine-produced language. English, like other Germanic languages, is a language in which stress plays a dominant role in speech rhythm. (Stress is sometimes also called "accent," and stressed syllables "accented syllables." Occasionally a writer will reserve the term "accent" for a particular kind of stress, but you can usually assume that it means the same as "stress," which is the term I will use consistently in this book. See Appendix 2 for these and other related terms.)

A stress can be thought of as an intensified syllable. Certain syllables in the words and sentences we speak are pronounced with extra energy, making them louder or longer, or different in timbre or in pitch, or a combination of these. In effect, what you did in bringing out the syllabic rhythm of the earlier examples was to make *every* syllable stressed. (Note that a syllable is a *thing*, or speaking more strictly an *event*: a group of sounds pronounced and perceived as a single unit. Stress, however, is a *feature*, a way of pronouncing a syllable. When we talk of the "stresses" in a sentence, this is only a shorthand way of saying the "stressed syllables.") In uttering a sentence with a great deal of emphasis, you give special weight to the stressed syllables – and in doing so, speak in a highly regular rhythm. You might even beat your hand in time with the emphasized syllables:

```
THIS exPEriment will be VERy SHORT.
```

Knowing which syllables are stressed and which are unstressed in normal speech is no problem for the speaker of English: to be able to speak English is to possess this knowledge already. Developing the ability to mark syllables as stressed or unstressed on the page is just a matter of becoming aware of what you already know, of listening carefully to your own production of speech. We actually utter, and hear, not just stressed and unstressed syllables but a complex hierarchy of stresses; however, in dealing with the major types of meter it is enough to think in terms of two categories of syllable. When we consider how in poetry the actual variations in English stress relate to the simplified model of the metrical scheme, however, we need to allow for other possibilities, and we will touch on these below.

It is quite possible to study the rhythms of English poetry without knowing a great deal about the kinds of stress that occur in English; it is enough to be able to hear what sounds normal in speaking the language. However, in order to discuss the operation of stress in the working of poetry, and to make judgements in tricky cases, it is useful to know some of the basic terms and distinctions. The following summary does not go into the complex details of English stress-patterns, but it will be sufficient for most discussions of poetry. We shall give separate consideration to *word-stress* and *phrase-stress*, since taking words on their own and in the verbal context in which they appear are two different things – both necessary to an understanding of stress.

1. Word-stress

In discussing word-stress, it is useful to make a distinction between two kinds of word: *content words* and *function words*.

Content words are words which operate with a certain degree of independence, conveying a full meaning by themselves. They are

Function words are words that depend on other words for their meaning, usually indicating some kind of relation. They include

nouns ("gold," "caterpillar," "envy"), verbs ("shine," "employ," "swam"), adjectives ("full," "extraordinary," "lazy"), and adverbs ("now," "gently," "lazily"). Most of the words in the dictionary are content words.

prepositions ("before," "into," "of"), articles ("the," "a," "an"), demonstratives ("this," "that," "those"), conjunctions ("but," "however," "when"), pronouns ("she," "they," "anybody"), and auxiliaries (verbs used in conjunction with other verbs – "will," "may," "have" – and adverbs used in conjunction with adjectives or adverbs – "more," "so," "very").

We can consider these types of word separately.

(a) Content words

(i) Monosyllabic content words

Monosyllabic content words ("hole," "stand," "blue") usually take a stress. As we shall see in discussing phrasal stress, they aren't necessarily all *equally* stressed in spoken sentences, and in rapid speech some may lose their stress altogether.

(ii) Polysyllabic content words

Every content word with two or more syllables has one fully stressed syllable, called the *main stress*. Knowing how to pronounce a polysyllabic word in English means knowing which syllable takes the main stress, and English speakers who come across an unfamiliar word in print can usually guess, from its structure, how to stress it.

In the case of uncertainty, a good dictionary will help, as the stressed syllable of polysyllables is always marked (check the front of the dictionary to find out what system of marking is used, as there are several). In this book, stressed syllables will be shown by a *slash* (/) over the syllable (actually over the vowel, or the first vowel, of the syllable):

```
     /           /              /              /
  groundhog hippopotamus unsatisfactoriness investigate

     /      /      /           /            /
  marry freely hopefully delighted catastrophic
```

(When marking words for stress in a word-processing program whose basic font has characters of variable size, it may be useful to switch to a font in which all characters are the same width, such as Courier. The same is true of all scansion that relies on markings above or below the words, where it is important to line up characters on different lines.)

If it is necessary to show *un*stressed syllables, we will use the symbol x:

```
/  x  x  /  x     /   x  x
marry   inventor  hopefully
```

Remember that although we often talk about stressing a word or a phrase, it is, strictly speaking, only on a single *syllable* that a stress can fall. If we want to emphasize a polysyllabic word in speech, we emphasize the syllable that carries the main stress. If you are having any trouble in hearing where the stress in a word falls, imagine saying it with great emphasis, as if you were extremely angry. The syllable where you find yourself putting most emotional force – where you might bang the table – is the one with the main stress. ("I inSIST on being heard!")

Sometimes it's useful to distinguish a degree of stress between fully stressed and unstressed, which we call *secondary stress*. Secondary stress occurs in polysyllabic words on one or more syllables other than the one that carries the main stress. There are no hard-and-fast rules for secondary stress, and it varies across different dialects and modes of pronunciation. (North American English tends to have more secondary stresses than British English, for instance.) Again, dictionaries will usually indicate it with a special symbol. In this book, secondary stress is shown by a *backslash*: \ (to be distinguished from the main stress, which is always a full stress: /).

Secondary stress often occurs on compounds, that is, words constructed out of existing words:

```
/     \      /   \         /        \
groundhog  backslash  spawning-ground
```

The more strongly a speaker feels that the compound has been newly minted, however, the more likely he or she is to give it two full stresses:

```
/      /      /     /
sober-suited  fawn-froth
```

Polysyllables that are not compounds also often take a secondary stress:

```
 \    /       \     /      /   \
hippopotamus  catastrophic  dynamite
```

The presence or absence of secondary stress can be the distinguishing factor between two forms of a word:

```
                  /
It was a deliberate mistake.

                   /   \
The jury might deliberate all night.
```

Occasionally, words with secondary stress can undergo a shift in stress under rhythmic pressure (this happens in speech as well as in poetry). Many speakers of English would find it normal to say:

```
      \   /      /            / \     /    \
   sixteen believers but sixteen anecdotes
```

This stress shift is a way of avoiding the rhythmic awkwardness of successive fully stressed syllables.

Sometimes a phrase of two words will function as a compound word such as "groundhog" or "mailbag." Try out the difference between "Main Street" and "Jones Road," or between "the White House" (where the American president lives) and "a white house" (where you or I might live). The first of each pair is pronounced as a compound, while the second is a normal phrase:

```
    /      \      /      /
  Main Street   Jones Road
    /      \      /      /
  White House   white house
```

Another kind of compound phrase that it's useful to look out for in poetry consists of a verb and an adverb. Here the main stress goes on the *second* word, and the stress on the first word is weakened:

```
    \  /     \    /     \    /
  go out   came home   stood up
```

We absorb these distinctions along with the rest of the English language when we learn it.

Most of the time, secondary stress is accommodated very easily to a metrical pattern. These syllables can function as either stressed or unstressed syllables according to the demands of the meter, and very often the rhythm will accommodate them however they are pronounced. Just occasionally, however, it matters crucially to the metrical movement of a line that a syllable with secondary stress should be weaker than a fully stressed syllable or stronger than an unstressed syllable.

(b) Function words

(i) Monosyllabic function words

Most monosyllabic function words, unlike content words, are unstressed (unless there is some reason why they should be emphasized, a situation we will discuss under "Emphatic phrasing" below). Prepositions, conjunctions, and articles are regularly unstressed, and auxiliary verbs or adverbs are usually unstressed – though note that auxiliaries are often used for emphasis, in which case they are stressed: "I *did* pay the bills"; "He *has* given me the money." Pronouns, however, can vary (they are, after all, not purely function words, but stand in for nouns): some are stressed ("who?," "mine"), and some are not ("I," "she" – unless, of course, they are emphasized).

(ii) Polysyllabic function words

Every polysyllabic function word – such as "before," "under," "therefore" – has a main stress, just like polysyllabic content words, and speakers of English know which syllable to put it on. But in some situations (having to do with the rhythm of the sentence and the speed of the utterance) that stress can disappear. Try saying the following sentence fast, accompanying the strongest stresses with a hand movement:

```
I've worked under pressure before.
```

You'll probably find that you exaggerate the stress on two or more of the words "I've," "worked," "pressure," and "before," depending on the meaning you give to the sentence, but that you don't give any stress to "under."

Some function words, like some words with secondary stress, can shift their stress according to the needs of the rhythm. In the first of the following sentences, "without" is stressed on the second syllable, as is usually the case, but in the second it's possible for the first syllable to take the stress in order to avoid successive stressed syllables:

```
      /        /        /
A home without a hearth.

      /        /        /
A country without justice.
```

The net effect of these properties of polysyllabic function words is that, unlike content words, they are extremely flexible, and can be used by poets with a considerable degree of freedom.

2. Phrasal stress

As we have already begun to see, looking at words in isolation tells only part of the story of stress in English. Two further points need to be made. First, in spoken English, the faster the speech the fewer the stresses; full stresses may become secondary stresses, secondary stresses (and sometimes full stresses) may lose their stress altogether. Since poetry is usually spoken slowly, these effects of rapid speech don't often occur in the kind of language that is the subject of this book, but certain meters or certain contexts do encourage quick articulation.

Second, when words occur in phrases and sentences, their word-stresses relate to one another in a *hierarchical* manner. Once more, this is not something the English speaker has to learn, even though it's usually not the kind of knowledge that is held consciously. We need not go into any details here; all we will note is that one result is that a full stress can be *subordinated* by the syntax and meaning of a sentence to one that precedes it or follows it within a phrase. A subordinated stress is always perceived in relation to another stress, and is felt to be the weaker of the two (even if it is physically the same). As with secondary stress within words, we seldom need to pay special attention to subordinated stress in analyzing the meter of a poem, but it can occasionally be useful in showing just how the contours of the spoken language relate to the metrical pattern.

There are two kinds of phrase, those with a neutral stress pattern and those in which a special emphasis is present.

(a) Neutral phrasing

In neutral phrasing, where there is no special emphasis on any word or words, there is a general tendency for earlier stresses to be subordinated to later stresses. If it is necessary to indicate a subordinated stress we do so by means of the same symbol as secondary stress, to indicate that, although it is a full stress in terms of the structure of the word, it is relatively weak in the sentence. Once again, you can try the experiment of beating with your hand as you say the following sentences with extra emphasis; you'll find that it's quite easy to give only the second syllable in each pair a beat. If you give the first and not the second a beat, however, you will depart from the neutral phrasing and produce a special emphasis:

```
     /               \     /
   I wish I had strong hands.


       /          \    /                 \      /
   It's best to stay cool when you feel cheated.
```

There would be nothing wrong in showing the marked syllables here as all equally stressed, which is how they would be spoken in a slow, careful reading. In scanning poetry, in fact, we usually do not indicate subordinated stresses. Occasionally, however, it is important for the meter that we take advantage of the potential subordination of stresses in reading a line.

(b) Emphatic phrasing

Often when we speak a sentence, or read one out, we don't treat it as a neutral sequence but give special emphasis to one or more words. (It's no accident that we use the same word to refer to the way we pronounce an especially significant word and to the additional importance given to a part of an argument – "Let me stress this point.") These words can be content words or function words:

```
   Where did you get such enormous onions?

   Keep pushing the left button.

   She wanted meat and vegetables!
```

The use of emphatic stress is a common feature of English speech, and it isn't difficult to imagine situations in which these sentences would be spoken. Emphatic stress can indicate which word in a sentence provides the new or important information, can give emotional force to one element in an utterance, or can bring out a contrast.

Although in writing we underline the whole word we want to stress, whether it is a monosyllable or a polysyllable, in speech we usually emphasize only a single syllable. As we have seen, in a polysyllabic word it is the syllable that takes the main stress which receives the additional force. Emphatic stress may fall not only on a syllable that already has word-stress (in the sentences above, "-nor-," "left") but also on one that wouldn't normally carry stress at all ("and"). It also often has the effect of *reducing* the stress on those syllables that would normally receive a strong stress – such as the stressed syllables in the final words of each of the above sentences.

Unless it is indicated by a graphic device such as italics or capitals, emphatic stress is an optional extra in reading aloud a passage or a poem, and we have to remain alert to the writer's concerns in order to place it appropriately. But when there is a *contrast* between two words in a sentence, or in nearby sentences, we have no choice but to give them emphatic stress:

```
I said the left button, not the right button.
```

Here, the word "button" loses much of its normal stress (it would not be inaccurate to mark it as a subordinated stress), and the adjectives "left" and "right" take emphatic stress:

```
       /      /  \              /  \
I said the left button, not the right button.
```

Contrastive emphasis occasionally changes the stress-pattern of a polysyllabic word. Thus the word "undone," normally stressed on the second syllable, has to be stressed on the first to bring out the wry force of the comment which John Donne made in a letter to his wife Anne after their secret marriage had become known:

```
    /          /         /
John Donne, Anne Donne, undone.
```

EXERCISE

Stress

(3) Mark the main stress in the following words with /, any secondary stresses with \, and unstressed syllables with x. In all cases, the symbol should go above the first vowel of the syllable.

```
rocket  divine  tree-root  restful  unhinged  gladly

consign
/ x   x   x /  x    \ x   / x / x   / \ x
terribly  delightful  understand  relation  dog-lover
/ x \ x
topsy-turvy
\ x / x   \ x / x x   \ x / x x
intermission  multiplicity  reprehensibly
/ x \ x x
dairy-manager
```

(4) As in (3), mark the stressing of the following sentence, in a slow and deliberate reading (ignore phrasal stress):

```
Quick thinking on your part saved us from such a

melodramatic end, though: you merely restored the

dimension of the exploratory dialogue, conducted in

the general interest, and we resumed our roles of

progressive thinkers and builders of the art of love.
```

(5) In the following sentence, mark all the possible instances of subordination in successive stresses (put \ above the subordinated stress and / above the full stress to which it is subordinated). Are any of these potential subordinations affected by emphatic stresses?

```
They lingered, half chastened, half glad, in the cool

shadow of the old barn; the day's happenings needed

much thought.
```

Speech rhythms

1. Syllables and stresses

We've seen how the rhythm of spoken English is based on both syllables and stress; that is to say, English speakers use both syllables and stress to move the language along as an orderly sequence of varying expenditures of energy. If we exaggerate either syllables or stresses – say, to count them – we find that the natural tendency is to make them occur at regular intervals of time. In a stretch of language where the stresses are always separated by the same number of unstressed syllables, the two rhythmic principles will work hand-in-hand to create a very even progression:

```
          /  x    x   / x    x   /   x    x   /
    (2) Under the blossom that hangs on the bough

          x   /    x   /  x  /   x   /x      /
    (3) And all that mighty heart is lying still!

            /        /       /
    (4) Break, break, break
```

In each of these lines, the stress-rhythm – the tendency toward the regular occurrence of the stresses – is aided and abetted by the syllabic rhythm. In the first line two unstressed syllables separate the stresses, in the second line one unstressed syllable separates the stresses, and in the third line there are no unstressed syllables at all.

Where the number of unstressed syllables between stresses varies, however, as is usual in prose, the two rhythmic tendencies come into collision. The tendency of the stresses to space themselves out at equal intervals (which is simply the effort made by our muscles to function rhythmically as they produce stresses) is counteracted by the tendency of the syllables to take up their own time in pronunciation.

```
          x   x   x    /     x x / x   x x    / x          x   x
(5)       It is a truth universally acknowledged, that a

          /  x / x   x  / x   x x  /   / x    /    x
          single man in possession of a good fortune must be

          x   /   x  x   /
          in want of a wife.
```

Here the unstressed syllables before and between the stresses number 3, 2, 3, 3, 1, 2, 3, 0, 1, 2, 2. The pressure from the stresses to set up a regular rhythm is countered by the pressure from the syllables to maintain their own rhythmic identity, making the intervals between stresses different in length. The result is that the sentence has no identifiable rhythmic pattern.

But the struggle is not an equal one. Stress, being the result of a stronger muscular effort, can to some extent override the weaker syllabic rhythm, especially if it is given some encouragement (which is what we did in reading "THIS exPEriment will be VEry SHORT"). What happens is that when there are many unstressed syllables in an interval between stresses, we squeeze the syllables so that they each take a shorter time to pronounce, and when there are only a few, we extend them so that they take a longer time. When there are no syllables between stresses, as in "Break, break, break," we use a silence or a lengthening of the stressed syllable to produce a phase of relaxation.

You will find that it's possible to read the following two-stress sentences with the same stress-rhythm (again, tap on the stresses to make sure you keep them at equal intervals – and start fairly slowly):

```
  /      /
Carl tends

 / x    /
Carol tends

 / x x     /
Caroline tends

 / x x   x /
Caroline intends

 / x x   x x /
Caroline interferes

 / x x   x  x  x  /
Caroline is interfering

 /,x x   x  x  x  x  /
Caroline is an interferer
```

What this example shows is that it's possible to compress six unstressed syllables into roughly the same time as is taken by none or one, and that we do this without great concentration or effort, as a natural product of the rhythms we use in speaking English. English is said to be a *stress-timed* language, since it is the stresses that provide the main markers of regular rhythm. As soon as we introduce another stress, it prevents us from compressing the syllables: compare the following, which have the same number of syllables but a very different rhythm:

```
 / x x   x  /
Caroline intends

 / x x     /      /
Caroline Jones tends
```

Although this kind of compression and expansion of syllables is going on in spoken English all the time, it usually happens only to a limited degree. In example (5), for instance, we are not tempted to heighten the stress-timed nature of the language in order to make the stresses fall at equal intervals. In metrical verse, however, the disposition of stressed and unstressed syllables is so controlled that the reader will find regularity emerging of its own accord, and will unconsciously strengthen it and seek to continue it.

The first type of English meter we shall look at, in chapter 4, is one which takes advantage of the greater strength of stress-rhythm over syllable-

rhythm. In chapter 5 we shall look at meters that are designed to effect a
more even balance between the two rhythms.

2. Stress groups

Another feature of English speech rhythm is that every syllable that is
unstressed or carries secondary stress tends to be perceived as attached either
to a preceding or to a following fully stressed syllable. This is because the
muscles that produce stresses use unstressed or weakly stressed syllables, when
they are available, to build up to the burst of energy that produces a full
stress and to subside into a relaxed condition after it. The linkages are syntactic and semantic, and correspond to the speaker's sense of how the language is divided up. For instance, an article, preposition, or conjunction
goes with a following stress ("the book," "off limits," "and everything").
Pronouns, however, can go with preceding or following stresses ("hold him";
"he comes").

A single full stress and any attached unstressed syllables, or syllables with
secondary stress, constitute a *stress group*. A stress group can consist of one or
more words, and can even consist of a single stressed word of one syllable (a
monosyllabic group). If a stress group consists of unstressed or weakly stressed
syllables ending in a stress it is said to have a *rising* rhythm:

```
    x  /    \ x  /    x  x   /     x  x x  /
    allow   overcome  in a trice   to be inside
```

If a stress group consists of a stressed syllable followed by unstressed or weakly
stressed syllables it has a *falling* rhythm:

```
    / x     / x  x    / x x     / x   x
    habit   syllable  happily   mention it
```

(These are purely technical terms, and do not imply anything about the
emotional or mimetic potential of the two types of rhythm.)

Many stress groups combine rising and falling rhythms; we call these
mixed groups. In most stretches of language, whether prose or verse, there is
a great deal of variation among rising, falling, mixed, and monosyllabic
groups. There are more falling words than rising words in the English language, but a rising rhythm predominates in continuous speech, thanks to
the many stress groups which consist of unstressed function words followed
by content words. In the following passage, the stress groups are indicated
above the words:

```
        | x   /  | x  x   /  | x      x / x   |x    /  | x
(6)       So now she is gone,  and the servants are gone,  and

          x   /   |x    /  | x      x  x  / x  | / |  x
          the things are gone,  and there is nothing left but

          x    /  | / | \  | \      / | x    x / x |
          that great bedstead nailed down,  with the canvas

          /   x  | x  /    x  x |
          mattress we found on it.
```

There are seven rising groups, two falling groups, four mixed groups, and one monosyllabic group – a fairly typical combination. Notice that it can be important to show subordinated stress in a phrase, as in "nailed down," where the first word leads into the second within a single stress group. If, on the other hand, we chose to give "nailed" as much emphasis as "down," the result would be two monosyllabic stress groups.

3. Alternation

One final characteristic of English speech rhythm that we need to note is that it has a preference for the *alternation* of stressed and unstressed syllables (a preference that is obviously related to the tendency of English stresses to fall at rhythmically equivalent intervals). This is only a preference, not a rule, and in normal speech it is modified by other characteristics of speech production. But there are many signs of the role it plays, some of which we have noted already, and one of the important advances in recent phonological theory has been the recognition of the impact of such rhythmic preferences on the way languages have developed.

For instance, we tend – without thinking about it – to prefer phrases that are alternating to phrases that contain back-to-back stresses: most people will say "black and sparkling eyes" rather than "sparkling and black eyes," because the first phrase separates the stressed syllables by unstressed ones. As we noted earlier, we may actually pronounce certain words differently in order to avoid successive stresses, like the word "unknown" in the following examples:

```
          /           /                /          /
      the unknown soldier      this unknown clarinetist
```

And the stress-patterns of longer words show some tendency for secondary stresses to be separated from the main stress by one unstressed syllable:

```
    \ x  /        / x  \        \   x / x \
    supersonic   crystalline   electromagnetism
```

Even when there's no reason to stress a syllable that falls between two unstressed syllables, our instinct for alternation can produce a slight stress when we speak (or induce us to hear a slight stress whether it's physically there or not). Listen to – or, more accurately, try to feel – the difference in the word "no" in these sentences, when the last word is emphasized:

```
    Dan is no fool

    Dan is no buffoon
```

In the second sentence, "no" is the middle syllable of three unstressed syllables, and as a result it attracts to itself a suggestion of stress. Rhythm is a matter not of objective reality – the physical features that a measuring instrument would record – but of perception by the human ear and brain of movements with which they are already familiar. An important consequence of this is that there is no need to *pronounce* the syllables of English poetry with an alternating stress-pattern; it is there in the language, and will be heard by those who are themselves speakers of the language.

This preference for an alternating rhythm, oscillating between stressed and unstressed syllables, means that poetry which has such a rhythm will often be felt to be closely related to the spoken language, heightening and clarifying the movements of speech.

EXERCISE

Speech rhythms

(6) Read the following examples, and rank them in order of rhythmic regularity. Then mark stressed and unstressed syllables, and see if your experience of rhythm tallies with the patterning that is revealed. Note any places where the preference for an alternating rhythm encourages a particular stressing. In (c) and (d), mark the stress groups (see example 6 above). Count the number of rising groups, falling groups, mixed groups, and monosyllabic groups. Is there any significance in your findings?

(a) I remember well, that once, while yet my inexperienced hand could scarcely hold a bridle, with proud hopes I mounted, and we journeyed towards the hills: an ancient servant of my father's house was with me, my encourager and guide.

(b) He was gazing at her with open curiosity, with fascination, like a child watching a new fantastic animal at the zoo, and he was breathing as if he had run a great distance to reach her.

(c) Should you ask me, whence these stories? Whence these legends and traditions, with the odors of the forest, with the dew and damp of meadows, with the curling smoke of wigwams, with the rushing of great rivers, with their frequent repetitions, and their wild reverberations, as of thunder in the mountains?

(d) In easy state upon this couch, there sat a jolly Giant, glorious to see; who bore a glowing torch, in shape not unlike Plenty's horn, and held it up, high up, on Scrooge, as he came peeping round the door.

Summary

This chapter sketches the elementary principles of rhythm in spoken English.

A. Syntax

Syntax binds and separates words to produce a hierarchy of units and breaks.

B. Syllables

Syllables are the elementary carriers of the rhythm of the language. In some words, the number of syllables is variable; when a potential syllable is not pronounced it is *elided* (and the phenomenon is known as *elision*).

C. Stress

Stress is the result of an additional expenditure of energy on a syllable. It is shown by a slash (/). An unstressed syllable is shown as x.

Word-stress occurs in words of more than one syllable. In *content words* word-stress falls on one syllable of polysyllabic words, and on the single syllable of monosyllables. Some polysyllabic words also have secondary stress, shown by a backslash (\). In *function words* word-stress is usually absent if the word is a monosyllable; whether or not it falls on one syllable of a polysyllabic function word depends on the phrasal context.

Phrasal stress occurs in sequences of words. In *neutral phrasing*, earlier stresses tend to be *subordinated* to later ones. In *emphatic phrasing*, the neutral pattern gives way to one in which a particular syllable or syllables are given additional stress, producing a different pattern of subordination. If it is necessary to mark subordinate stress, the same symbol is used as for secondary stress (\).

D. Speech rhythm

In English speech rhythm is produced by the arrangement of *syllables* and *stresses*. If stresses are separated by a consistent number of unstressed syllables, the stress rhythm and the syllabic rhythm co-operate to produce a strongly regular rhythm. When there is more variety, the stress rhythm tends to dominate, as English is a *stress-timed* language.

Stress groups consist of a single fully stressed syllable, either on its own (a *monosyllabic group*) or with one or more unstressed syllables (or syllables with secondary stress) before and/or after it. A *rising* rhythm is produced by a stress group that consists of one or more unstressed syllables followed by a stress; a *falling* rhythm is produced by a stress group that consists of a stress followed by one or more unstressed syllables: a *mixed* rhythm is produced by a stress group that both begins and ends with an unstressed syllable.

Alternation between stressed and unstressed syllables is often preferred in English speech rhythms.

Chapter 3

Dancing language

The familiarity of meter

We are all experts in rhythm and meter. To breathe is to control a complicated set of muscles by means of rhythmic neural commands, and to speak a human language, enjoy a piece of music, or dance to a band is to demonstrate familiarity with the rhythmic patterns that underlie the entire tradition of poetry. Rap and reggae, salsa and soul, like all widely popular varieties of music, show a sophistication of meter and rhythm that its listeners respond to without any special training. Rhythmic understanding is something we generally learn very early: before a child can articulate the words of a language, it is mimicking the way patterns of syllables and stresses are produced in that language, and absorbing the metrical structure of the nursery rhymes and songs that it hears. In fact, one of the problems we face in discussing this subject is the deep familiarity we have with the rhythms of poetry, whether we are aware of it or not: it's sometimes difficult to achieve the necessary *distance* from the subject to begin to analyze it.

There is nothing remarkable, therefore, about a two-year-old chanting the following rhyme with perfect metrical placing of the syllables, even if the actual pronunciation of the words is far from perfect:

(1)   Star light, star bright,
        First star I see tonight,
        I wish I may, I wish I might,
        Have the wish I wish tonight.

Our two-year-old will know that the words in the first line have to be pronounced with unusual slowness (an adult might say that each of them carries a beat), whereas the third line moves much faster (every *second* word carries a beat). The other two lines fall between these extremes. We can show this variety by means of a simple scansion, using underlining for the emphasized syllables:

(1)   <u>Star</u> <u>light</u>, <u>star</u> <u>bright</u>,
        <u>First</u> <u>star</u> I <u>see</u> tonight,
        I <u>wish</u> I <u>may</u>, I <u>wish</u> I <u>might</u>,
        <u>Have</u> the <u>wish</u> I <u>wish</u> tonight.

Of course, rhymes like this often come with a tune attached, and the tune helps to bring out the rhythmic regularity of the verse. But it is a striking fact, and one that lies at the heart of English versification, that speakers of English can turn irregular-looking sets of lines like these (they vary in length from four to eight syllables) into regular metrical verse, and do so without thinking twice. What is more, if a group of English speakers are asked to read lines of this kind of meter together, they will use exactly the *same* procedures to achieve rhythmic regularity in pronunciation – even if they have never seen the lines before. We can test this ourselves by means of an invented rhyme based on the model of many familiar nursery rhymes.

```
(2)     Croak, crack, the bride's in black;
        The groom's in white, so he won't come back.
        The baker has baked a cinnamon pie,
        Beneath the bright stars that shine in the sky.
```

To read this little rhyme rhythmically you have to make a number of rather tricky decisions about the speed and emphasis with which every word is pronounced. A computer program that was able to carry out such an operation would be extremely complex, yet anyone who grew up with traditional songs and rhymes will not find it a difficult task, even though this particular set of words has never been encountered before. It is in fact a task that is easier to accomplish by just doing it than by careful analysis, because it is something most people have never had to think about. (In a similar way, we would begin to stumble over our sentences if we became conscious of the complicated grammatical rules – not even fully understood by linguists – that we employ every time we speak.)

If you read our made-up and deliberately nonsensical example aloud a few times, trying a chanted sing-song until the movement seems "right" (you can even imagine the kind of tune it might be sung to), you will actually have applied certain rules to bring out in pronunciation the lines' *potential* metrical structure. And if this exercise is carried out by a group, all reading the lines aloud without a designated leader and trying to do so in unison, the metrical structure will emerge clearly as a consensus shared by the whole group. Upon this foundation – a widely shared ability, from an early age, to find simple rhythms in certain arrangements of words – is built the impressive edifice of the centuries-old English poetic tradition.

What you will probably find when you read the example in an exaggerated chant is that each of the four lines has four places where an emphasis falls, where you tend to speak louder and longer, and where you feel you want to tap your finger or nod your head. These are the *beats* of the meter, each of which falls on a single syllable. *English meter depends on the perception of beats, and when beats are felt in a stretch of language, a meter is present.* Between the beats are stretches of language without this kind of emphasis, where the syllables move more quickly and lightly. (In a couple of places, there's no language at all between the beats.) A simple way of showing where the beats fall is by placing a B under the appropriate syllables (by convention, we usually put the mark under the first vowel of the syllable – remember that when word-processing it may be useful to choose a typewriter-style font such as Courier). Here is the most probable reading:

(2)   `Croak, crack, the bride's in black;`
         ` B     B         B        B`

         `The groom's in white, so he won't come back.`
         `      B        B            B         B`

         `The baker has baked a cinnamon pie,`
         `      B        B     B    B`

         `Beneath the bright stars that shine in the sky.`
         `  B                B          B        B`

Not only is it possible to predict the consensus pattern that will emerge when readers utter these lines, it is also possible to predict where there might be some disagreement – where a group reading might falter a little, and where the language, when we read it aloud, has to be forced slightly to fit the pattern. The adjective "bright" – in the line "Beneath the bright stars that shine in the sky" – has to be read without any emphasis, whereas in an ordinary prose reading we would be bound to give it some weight. All the other syllables that fall between the beats are either whole words function-ing in a supportive role rather than carrying the main meanings ("the," "in," "so," "he," etc.) or they are unstressed parts of longer words ("-amon," "-er," "be-"). So "bright" has to be treated as if it were an unimportant word. If there were a less usual word here than "bright" – which is what we expect stars in a poem to be – we would feel the strain even more, since it would demand some emphasis for itself. Try, for instance, reading the following version of the line (the stressed syllables as well as the beats are shown):

         `    /         /      /          /           /`
         `Beneath the crazed stars that shine in the sky.`
         `  B                B          B        B`

Such shared moments of slight strain show just as clearly as the general agreement on the rhythmic reading of the verse that speakers of English rely on the same principles of metrical form and strategies of performance.

   Let us consider for a moment what the brain and the muscles of the speech organs have had to do to get from the words printed on the page to a rhythmic utterance. One set of processes involves using highly familiar codes to interpret the printed marks as letters, then as words, then as syntactic structures with a certain meaning; all this happens, for the person who can read English, immediately and without effort. As this is being done, another set of codes is being used to interpret the letters, words, and syntactic units as specific *sounds*, arranged in a sequence of syllables with varying degrees of emphasis. All this is necessary just to read the sentences aloud, but already, thanks to the rhythmic characteristics of the language that we have already considered, some rhythmic shaping is taking place. Certain syllables demand strong emphasis (like "Croak," "crack," "bride's," and "black" in the first line), an emphasis which is created by the additional exertion of some of the muscles which produce speech. These muscles, like the muscles we use to walk, or to breathe (which include many of the same muscles, of course), prefer to operate rhythmically – that is, with a tendency for their movements to occur at roughly regular intervals and with roughly equivalent strength. When the stressed syllables get caught up in this kind of rhythm, they function as beats. The first line of the invented rhyme therefore has four beats, each of which is an energy pulse which we experience as part of a larger pattern of such pulses (whereas a stress that is not a beat – like "crazed" in the previous example – does not relate to any larger pattern).

But simply to read these lines as examples of the English language is not enough to read them as an example of a common English meter. They have some regularity and rhythmicality in a normal prose reading, but they need to be adjusted a little before they move with the rhythmic swing that we recognize so easily. Once again, it's a matter of deploying codes with which we are very familiar, even if we haven't learned any way of describing them: we try, as we read, to make the rhythms that emerge from the language itself conform to the simple patterns which we have carried over from all the other rhymes and songs we have heard. The fact that four beats emerge in our reading of the first line (and of the next three lines as well) is no accident: the four-beat line is the commonest metrical line in all popular verse. (We will discuss four-beat rhythm in the final section of this chapter.)

Not every group of lines can be made to conform to a metrical pattern, however; we've seen how there are places in this invented example where there is some strain involved in doing so. In other possible lines, the strain would be greater (we've noticed what happens if you substitute "crazed" for "bright"), and in yet others we would feel that no strategy of reading could produce a meter. Let us rewrite our invented example, keeping the same number of syllables per line:

```
(2a)      Crick, croak, crack, the bride's back;
          The groom all in white garb won't come back.
          The lazy baker has baked a lime pie,
          Beneath the bright stars shining in the sky.
```

If we try to read this as a regular four-beat stanza, we run into trouble. The beats do not fall with rhythmic regularity, nor in clear groups of four, and as we try to manipulate the language to make it conform to such a pattern, we find we are distorting the natural pronunciation beyond acceptable limits.

Being able to write metrical verse – which is not at all difficult to do, if you have a simple model like a nursery rhyme or a limerick running in your head – is therefore a matter of choosing words so that the sequences of beats and intervening syllables that naturally emerge when they are read aloud conform to one of the patterns with which readers are already familiar. (These patterns are very limited in number, and seem to derive from rhythmic principles observable in different languages all over the world, and in much of the world's music.) And recognizing the meter of a poem is a matter of reading it aloud in such a way that the sequence of beats and intervening syllables "hooks on to" one of those patterns, which may occasionally require us to try out different ways of reading until one of them works. Not all the meters of English poetry yield themselves so immediately to the reader as those of the nursery rhyme, but exactly the same process is involved in all metrical verse, and the habits learned in the first years of one's life remain the basis of all later responses to meter, however subtle or sophisticated.

EXERCISE

The familiarity of meter

(1) Mark the beats in the following nursery rhymes, by placing a B under them:

```
(a)   Georgie Porgie, pudding and pie,

      Kissed the girls and made them cry;

      When the boys came out to play,

      Georgie Porgie ran away.
```

```
(b)   To market, to market, a gallop, a trot;

      To buy some meat to put in the pot;

      Three pence a quarter, a groat a side,

      If it hadn't been killed it must have died.

(c)   The cock's in the woodpile a-blowing his horn,

      The bull's in the barn a-threshing of corn,

      The maids in the meadows are making of hay,

      The ducks in the river are swimming away.
```

How does language become metrical?

Meter – whether in music or poetry – is a way of *organizing* rhythm that gives it special *regularity* and *strength*. These three features are inseparable and mutually reinforcing: metered rhythm is strong because it is regular, and regular because it is strong, and it is both of these because of the way it falls into an organized pattern. Every rhythm involves a sequence of energy pulses, of peaks and falls, but as we have seen, when a certain level of regularity and patterning of movement is achieved, the strong pulses become *beats*. Beats in turn reinforce the regularity of the rhythm, marshaling the elements into clearly defined and measurable sequences. The first of the following examples when read aloud is rhythmic, like all English utterances, but not metrical, whereas the second is metrical as well as rhythmic:

```
(3)   The cold wind is howling, and the sand, over which I
      saw her depart on that day many years ago, is
      gleaming white.

(3a)  Cold is the wind, white is the sand; lost is my love
      in a distant land.
```

The difference between these two sentences is something all English speakers will perceive, even if they can't describe it.

As we saw in chapter 2, the basic elements that produce the rhythm of English speech are the *syllables*, each a small rhythmic pulse, and the *stresses* that increase the energy with which certain syllables are pronounced. Meter is therefore a way of organizing syllables and stresses (by organizing the words, phrases, and sentences which they make up) so that a repeating pattern emerges – a pattern in which some syllables are perceived as beats and others participate in the offbeats between the beats.

How is the continuous but only partially regular movement of language organized in order to create a meter and to turn rhythmic peaks into beats? There are a number of factors that can contribute to this transformation, some or all of which work in conjunction. Somewhat artificially, we can look at them one at a time.

(a) Placing of stressed and unstressed syllables

In the sequence of stressed and unstressed syllables that constitutes a metrical poem, the most likely place for the beats to fall is on the stressed syllables. There is an obvious reason for this: a stressed syllable is one which receives an extra discharge of energy, and a beat is also a burst of energy (one that is experienced as part of a larger pattern). And, as we saw in the previous chapter, stressed syllables have a tendency – other things being equal – to occur at regular intervals. This means that the arrangement of stressed and unstressed syllables is crucial in the establishment of regularity. Try reading these two sentences aloud with a regular emphasis on the stressed syllables (as always, it is easier to keep time if you tap as you read):

```
       /   x  /  x    x   x / x   x   /        /     /  x
(4)    Send a message to the office if John's cold worsens;

       x     /  x  /  -    /
       he'll need a week's rest.
```

```
       /   x  /   x   x / x   x   /   x     / x    x
(4a)   Send a note to the office if Johnny's fever gets

       /      x     / x  x  /    x  /
       worse; he'll probably need to rest.
```

It's likely that you found the second sentence slightly easier to read with a regular rhythm. This is because the number of unstressed syllables between stresses is consistently either one or two, allowing the stresses to fall at roughly equal intervals (thanks to the stress-timed nature of spoken English).

Various other arrangements of stressed and unstressed syllables establish regular rhythms, some more forceful than this, and we shall examine the most important ones in the following chapters. For the moment, we just need to note how simple it is to set up a regular rhythm, taking advantage of the language's own built-in movement of syllables and stresses.

(b) Regular syntactic divisions

A regular rhythm that consists merely of a repeated alternation between single stressed syllables and one or two unstressed syllables is only weakly felt, as the previous example shows, and is not yet what we mean by a meter. Another factor which helps to make language metrical is an arrangement of sentences that produces breaks at regular intervals. (This is one aspect of *phrasing*, which is the subject of chapter 8.) In the following example, the syntax divides the utterance into four parts, each of which contains three stressed syllables. If you attempt to read in such a way that these stresses fall at regular intervals, you will find your task is made a little easier by the repeated groups of three:

```
          /        /          /           /           /
(4b)   Send a note to the office, now Johnny's fever is

         /         /         /            /          /         /
       bad. I know the doctor would say, "He needs a week

          /
       of rest."
```

It's still not a very strong pattern, however, and if we encountered these sentences in a paragraph of prose, we probably wouldn't notice anything particularly regular about them. Other kinds of organization are necessary before a clear meter emerges.

(c) Fundamental metrical patterns and beats

We have seen how by controlling the arrangement of stressed and unstressed syllables, and by dividing them up into units of the same length, the experience of regularity is increased. But the *number* of stresses in these units is also an important factor in the establishing of a strong meter. Let us rewrite our example so that the stresses fall into *four groups of four*, and once more read it with the stressed syllables occurring at regular intervals. You will find now that there is a definite sense of a repeated pattern:

```
          /            /        /            /        /
(4c)   Send for the doctor, make him be quick; John has a

          /              /        /        /             /
       cold and he's feeling bad. "Away with the doctor,"

          /       /      /        /            /         /
       Johnny says, "All I need is a week of rest!"
```

Because of the strength of this regular rhythm, and the expectation it sets up for continued regularity, we are justified in saying that the language has become *metrical* and that the stressed syllables are functioning as *beats*. We can show this by means of a B below the appropriate syllables, and we can indicate the groups of four with the aid of a vertical apostrophe:

```
    /              /        /             /     ' /
Send for the doctor, make him be quick; John has a
    B              B        B             B       B

    /              /        / '   /               /
cold and he's feeling bad. "Away with the doctor,"
    B              B        B     B                B

    /       /    ' /       /            /          /
Johnny  says,  "All I need is a week of rest!"
    B       B      B       B            B          B
```

In the following section we shall ask why this particular structure of beats – four groups of four – gives rise to such a prominent rhythm; and in chapter 6 we shall examine groupings of beats that are less insistently regular than this one.

(d) Rhyme

The meter that has been established is still not a strong one, and most poems use other devices to make the meter prominent. Many use rhyme to signal the ends of the metrical segments, and we can easily rewrite our example to rhyme the end of the first group of four beats with the end of the second, and the third with the fourth:

(4d)   Send for the doctor, make him be quick; John has a
       cold and he's feeling sick. "Away with the doctor,"
       Johnny said, "All I need is a week in bed!"

If we encountered *these* sentences in a paragraph of prose, the chances are we would notice their distinctive regularity. The usually fluctuating rhythm of the language would fall into a more regular pattern, and we would find ourselves slightly altering our pronunciation of the words in order to bring out that pattern (or else we would have to make a conscious effort to avoid it). Try reading this example aloud:

(4e)   We were sitting on the verandah, enjoying the sunset,
        when Belinda came running out of the front door,
        closely followed by her son John. "Send for the
        doctor, make him come quick; John has a cold and he's
        feeling sick." "Away with the doctor," Johnny said,
        "All I need is a week in bed!" But at that point, he
        collapsed and had to be helped to a chair.

The transitions into meter and back again to irregular prose are immediately felt.

(e) Layout

There is now only one feature of a normal metrical poem lacking from our example: layout in lines. The syntactic breaks and the rhymes help to produce a metrical pattern of sixteen beats arranged in fours, but the full effect of the meter emerges only when the arrangement is given a visual representation. This is usually done by inserting line-breaks to divide the utterance into its four segments:

(4f)   Send for the doctor, make him come quick;
        John has a cold and he's feeling sick.
        "Away with the doctor," Johnny said,
        "All I need is a week in bed!"

We now have a four-line stanza, also known as a *quatrain*. What the layout does is to emphasize the division into four groups of four beats. We can now scan our little poem by showing both stresses and beats, four to a line:

```
         /              /          /                /
(4f)    Send for the doctor, make him come quick;
         B           B          B                B

         /           /               /        /
        John has a cold and he's feeling sick.
         B           B               B        B

          /              /          /         /
        "Away with the doctor," Johnny said,
          B              B          B        B

         /       /          /           /
        "All I need is a week in bed!"
         B       B          B           B
```

The metrical structure we have created here is the basis of a large part of the English poetic tradition, as we shall shortly see.

We have now looked at five of the most important ways in which the language of prose can be controlled and organized to make it metrical. There are additional factors that sometimes help to increase metrical regularity – syntactic parallelism and sound-patterns other than rhyme, for instance – but these five are the most common. In most metrical verse, all five are operative: the placing of stressed and unstressed syllables, regular syntactic divisions, the use of a simple metrical pattern, rhyme, and visual division into lines. Not all of them are essential, however, as we shall see when we turn to five-beat verse in chapter 6. In particular, some metrical forms can do without rhyme; and sometimes syntactic structures, instead of enhancing metrical regularity, play against it. It's also important to note that stresses and beats do not always coincide (an example of noncoincidence was the final line of example (2) above); we shall be discussing alternative possibilities in the following chapter. However, the principles we have found at work in the gradual shift from the more varied rhythm of prose to the patterned rhythm of metrical verse are fundamental to all poetry, whether it harnesses them or challenges them.

EXERCISE

Metrical language

(2) Find the four-line stanza embedded in this prose passage; write it out as a stanza, and mark the beats:

```
Here we are, after fifty years of marriage; hard to
believe that she and I have been together that long.
She is not without faults, of course: she does not
always see the point of little jests her husband
makes, and, when the world is out of joint, she makes
a hundred small mistakes – mistakes that have
oftentimes cost me dearly.
```

The four-beat rhythm

1. The four-by-four formation

The examples of English meter so far in this chapter have had four groups of four beats, producing a very familiar and insistently regular rhythm. This is the most common of all the possible rhythmic patterns, if every kind of verse is taken into account. It is the basis of most modern popular music, including rock and rap, of most folk, broadside, and industrial ballads from the Middle Ages to the twentieth century, of most hymns, of most nursery rhymes, and of a great deal of printed poetry. Its popularity is not limited to the English language, either; there is evidence of its use in a number of European and non-European languages, especially in children's verse. We shall refer to this pattern of sixteen beats arranged in four groups as the *four-by-four formation* (or, more conveniently, the *4x4 formation*), and more generally to the tendency to group beats in fours as the *four-beat rhythm*.

Here's a typical example of the 4x4 formation, a stanza of a popular folk-song on a perennial topic, with the stressed and unstressed syllables of a rhythmically regular reading marked above the line and the beats below it. (Notice that the number of unstressed syllables between the beats varies between one and two; this is the limited variation that, as we found earlier, encourages the emergence of beats and of metricality.)

```
        x   /   x   /   x   x   /   x   /
(5)     Oh love is teasing and love is pleasing,
          B       B           B       B

        x   /   x   /  x    x   /   x   /
        And love's a pleasure when first it's new.
            B           B           B           B

         x  /  x    x   /  x  x   / x   /  x
        But as it grows older it waxes colder,
          B           B          B     B

        x   /   x /   x    x   /  x   /
        And fades away like the morning dew.
          B       B           B       B
```

(A less rhythmic reading would give "grows" some degree of stress; but for our purposes we can treat it as an unstressed syllable.) The rhythm is strong but varied, accommodating easily the familiar phrases of the ballad tradition. As a shorthand for this particular realization of the 4x4 formation (and we shall see later that there are many others), we can indicate the beats per line: 4.4.4.4.

One feature that is noticeable in this example is the *hierarchy of syntactic breaks* that organizes the meter, a hierarchy which makes possible the *hierarchy of metrical divisions* characteristic of this form. The most complete syntactic and metrical division is at the end of the stanza, where it functions as a closure; the next strongest division occurs halfway through the stanza, with the period after "new" at the end of the second line; the two next strongest divisions are marked by the commas at the ends of the first and third lines;

and weaker divisions without punctuation can be felt halfway through each line, after two beats. The different divisions that correspond to the line-endings become obvious if we exaggerate the intonation as we read. At the end of the first line we sense a suspension, at the end of the second line a partial conclusion, at the end of the third line another suspension with a distinct I-am-coming-to-the-end intonation, and then a line of unmistakable finality. The feeling of finality arises because the conclusion is not just in meaning, but also in metrical movement. (Imagine the stanza ending after "away": even though the syntax would be complete, there would be a sense of inconclusiveness because this point is only a weak metrical division.) We might note that in this example, the metrical divisions that occur halfway through the line are emphasized by internal rhymes: "teasing – pleasing" and "older – colder."

In chapter 8 we shall examine more closely the different ways in which phrasing – here operating to produce a familiar meter – contributes to the movement of poetry. For the moment, we shall concentrate on the metrical organization, keeping in mind that it would not exist without a particular phrasal arrangement. Why is this particular pattern so widespread? And why is it the most strongly rhythmic? We need to look for a moment at this metrical pattern itself, as it exists independently of any particular medium such as the English language or tonal music, since what happens when we read regular four-beat verse is that the language *engages with* a metrical structure already deeply familiar to us.

The 4x4 formation arises from a very simple process of *doubling*: two single beats are heard as a pair of beats, two pairs of beats are heard as a four-beat unit (usually printed as a single line), two four-beat units are heard as an eight-beat unit, and two eight-beat units are heard as a sixteen-beat unit (the full 4x4 formation). Perceiving the beats in this rhythm is not a matter of counting to four several times, therefore, but of a continuous process of rhythmic accumulation. Sixteen beats is usually the limit of normal metrical perception, though strong rhythms can produce even longer units.

This means that a single four-beat unit seldom derives its rhythmic regularity and strength solely from its own contours; it is usually part of a larger movement which it helps to create and from which it derives some of its potency. When we represent such a line as a line of print on the page, we disguise the structure within it and beyond it. We can depict the 4x4 formation by means of a visual diagram, although we must not forget that what is being represented is actually a series of events in time:

```
————————————————————————————    ————————————————————————
————————————————————————————    ————————————————————————
————————————    ————————————    ————————————    ————————————
————    ————    ————    ————    ————    ————    ————    ————
B    B    B    B    B    B    B    B      B    B    B    B    B    B    B    B
1    2    3    4    5    6    7    8      9   10   11   12   13   14   15   16
```

This diagram shows sixteen single beats, grouped at the lowest level into twos, then above that into fours, then eights, then into the whole series of sixteen. The gaps between the units that occur at each level mark the metrical divisions we noted in example (5). If the reader chooses to pause at these places, the divisions are emphasized by the momentary suspension of the meter; but they are felt even if there are no pauses in the reading.

This is an ideal pattern which is never actualized in all its purity in language, but which underlies a large proportion of English poetry. If you look through the examples of four-beat verse in this book, you will find again and again that sense and syntax (together with layout on the page) produce this hierarchical structure. The first two lines are usually set against the second two in meaning, and are frequently divided by a syntactic break. Within this larger pattern, the individual lines often function as contrasting or complementary pairs in the same way; and the lines themselves often fall naturally into half-lines with two beats each.

When the phrasing of a 4x4 formation departs from this norm – by pitting the meaning of the last line against the first three, for instance, or by running two of the lines together – we register the departure, and this constant interplay between expectation and fulfillment or nonfulfillment is one of the creative resources available to the poet. It is evident that even in this simple form, meter is not just a matter of the sounds of the poetry, but of the organization of meanings. The sense of stronger and weaker beginnings and endings that gives the metrical formation its movement and its identity comes both from the arrangement of stressed and unstressed syllables and from the sense of the words and their grammatical arrangements. And the relationship works reciprocally: the meanings help to establish the regular meter while the metrical form provides a guide to the meanings.

As our discussion of the different levels of the 4x4 formation has shown, the *line* is a somewhat arbitrary feature in this very regular type of verse, since it is only one of a number of simultaneously effective levels. Line-junctures do correspond to important metrical divisions, but these are not the only metrical divisions. If we set out the stanza quoted earlier in eight lines instead of four, it retains the same basic meter, though the beginnings and endings of the *half-lines* now receive more emphasis, and reading it aloud with attention to these transitions will necessitate a slower and more deliberate pace:

(5a) Oh love is teasing
And love is pleasing,
And love's a pleasure
When first it's new.
But as it grows older
It waxes colder,
And fades away
Like the morning dew.

Or we can rewrite it as just two lines, which will encourage a rather more rapid reading that minimizes the lesser beginnings and endings but does not lose the powerful metrical drive:

(5b) Oh love is teasing and love is pleasing, and love's
a pleasure when first it's new.
But as it grows older it waxes colder, and fades
away like the morning dew.

These variations in layout retain the rhythmic pattern of the 4x4 formation, but give that movement a different dynamic. The examples demonstrate the important contribution made by the visual aspect of verse to our interpretation of its rhythms.

EXERCISE

The four-by-four formation

(3) The following is a nine-line poem by Langston Hughes. Turn it into a metrically regular four-line poem, and note how this changes its movement and therefore its meaning. Mark the beats with B under the appropriate syllables. In the rewritten poem, are there any lines in which the divisions of the syntax do not correspond to the divisions of the meter?

Motto

I play it cool

And dig all jive –

That's the reason

I stay alive.

My motto,

As I live and learn

Is

Dig and be dug

In return.

2. Actual and virtual beats

If you read the following stanza aloud, you will find that it has a catchy
rhythm that quickly establishes itself:

(6)   A man whose name was Johnny Sands
      Had married Betty Haig,
    And though she brought him gold and lands,
      She proved a terrible plague.

If you tap on the beats as you read, you will find that the lines have four
beats, three beats, four beats and three beats. Is this a different type of meter
from the 4x4 formation we have been examining?

Try reading the stanza as a very regular chant, and you will find that it
goes most naturally with an additional beat in the silence at the ends of the
second and fourth lines (once again, tapping will help):

(6)   A man whose name was Johnny Sands
      B   B   B   B

    Had married Betty Haig,
      B   B   B   [B]

    And though she brought him gold and lands,
      B   B   B   B

    She proved a terrible plague.
      B   B   B   [B]

The stanza is, after all, an example of the 4x4 formation. We call these
additional beats *virtual beats*, since they are not actually present in the words
of the verse even though they make themselves rhythmically felt, and we
use square brackets to show their special status. (By contrast, beats which are
present are called *actual beats*.) Virtual beats are sometimes known as "silent
beats," but this is a misleading name, because it is often by lengthening the
last syllable of the line that we extend it to four beats. Metrical regularity is
unaffected by the use of virtual beats, which are not pauses in the meter (the
equivalent in music would be a note extended over a second measure, or a
rest). Notice that the last virtual beat happens *after* the stanza has finished, as
the metrical rhythm prolongs itself of its own accord beyond the words of
the verse.

Virtual beats occur in only a few clearly defined places in the 4x4 formation, producing variants on the basic 4.4.4.4 stanza; the example I have just
given, known as the "ballad stanza" from its frequency in popular narrative

verse, is the most common of all. Using the same shorthand as before, we can refer to it as a 4.3.4.3 meter (the figures refer, of course, to actual beats only). In popular verse, the 4.3.4.3 stanza often appears with each pair of lines run into one, producing lines with seven actual beats and one virtual beat. This variant often comes in four-line stanzas, with the pattern 7.7.7.7. Here is an example, where it is easy to hear the articulation of the line into groups of four and three actual beats, and to feel an additional beat at the end of each line.

(7)   There's black-eyed Fan with the frying pan will cook
             B   B   B   B   B

        your eggs and bacon,
           B   B   [B]

    With beef and mutton, roast and boiled, if I am not
        B   B   B   B   B   B

        mistaken.
           B   [B]

    She'll make the puddings fat and good, all ready for
        B   B   B   B   B   B

        your dinner,
           B   [B]

    But if you grumble when she's done she'll cure you
       B   B   B   B   B

        with the skimmer.
          B   B   [B]

Although this passage is the equivalent of two 4.4.4.4 stanzas, the long lines and the rhyme scheme make the whole four-line stanza an expansive accumulation of lavishly descriptive detail in a single 32-beat sequence. Notice how the initial group of four actual beats in each line is divided syntactically in the middle ("There's black-eyed Fan ' with the frying pan"), while the groups of three beats form a single unit ("will cook your eggs and bacon"). The contrast between divided lines and continuous lines is part of the rhythmic flavor of 4.3.4.3 verse.

Another variant of the 4x4 formation is the 3.3.4.3 stanza, where only the third line has all four beats actualized. This is the line that has a coming-to-the-end feeling, and since all its beats are realized it can run straight on to the climactic line without a break. A familiar version of this is the limerick,

which divides the single four-beat line into two half-lines and rhymes them
to produce a jaunty rhythmic sequence:

(8)   There was an old person of Fratton
            B   B   B   [B]

         Who would go to church with his hat on.
            B   B   B   [B]

         "If I wake up," he said,
            B   B

         "With my hat on my head,
            B   B

         I shall know it hasn't been sat on."
            B   B   B   [B]

We also find some stress verse in 3.3.3.3 (or 6.6) meters; here the sense of a
fourth virtual beat is often weaker, since there are no four-beat lines to
remind us of the full length. It is more common in literary verse than in
popular verse; in this example, Thomas Hardy's speaker addresses a table that
is filled with personal significance:

(9)   Creak, little wood thing, creak,
            B   B   B   [B]

         When I touch you with elbow or knee;
            B   B   B [B]

         That is the way you speak
            B   B   B [B]

         Of one who gave you to me!
            B   B   B [B]

If we chant this stanza, and thus emphasize its rhythm, the virtual beats may
make themselves felt; but if we read it with more attention to the meaning,
we lose the sense of that emphatic meter and hear something closer to a
natural speaking voice. The liveliness of the rhythm springs from the relation between the simple regularities of the meter and the intimate voice that
moves against them.

The possibilities for replacing actual with virtual beats are strictly limited
by the inherent properties of the 4x4 formation. Even patterns that look
very similar to the acceptable ones can have an oddly awkward movement.

Try reading this 3.4.3.4. stanza aloud (it's an invented example, since such stanzas don't occur normally in the tradition):

(10)   The fleecy clouds are high,
      The breeze is blowing from the west;
       The branches shiver and sigh,
      The horses and cows now lie at rest.

The movement of the stanza is ungainly, and the reason is that the *weaker* metrical endings, after lines one and three, are marked by the absence of actual beats, whereas the *stronger* endings are not so marked. If we rearrange the lines, they take on the familiar lilt which tells us immediately that we're reading a deeply-ingrained rhythmic structure:

(10a)   The breeze is blowing from the west,
       The fleecy clouds are high;
      The horses and cows now lie at rest,
       The branches shiver and sigh.

EXERCISE

Actual and virtual beats

(4) Mark the actual and virtual beats in the following example. (It might be helpful to rewrite each line as two, in accordance with the rhythm.)

  But you whom love hath bound, by order of desire,

To love your lords, whose good deserts none other would

  require,

  Come you yet once again, and set your foot by mine,

Whose woeful plight, and sorrows great, no tongue may

  well define.

Summary

A. The familiarity of meter

The most fundamental metrical forms are deeply familiar to speakers of English. Readers readily agree on the performance of a simple stanza in such a way as to bring out the pattern of beats, and it is possible to predict where there is likely to be disagreement.

B. How does language become metrical?

The following factors are the most important in making a stretch of language *metrical* (i.e. perceived as a pattern of *beats*):

(a) The placing of stressed and unstressed syllables, so that the number of unstressed syllables between stresses is usually one or two;
(b) Syntactic structures that create units containing the same number of stressed syllables;
(c) Numbers of stressed syllables in these units that conform to fundamental metrical structures (e.g. four groups of four);
(d) Use of rhyme to mark the ends of metrical groups;
(e) Layout on the page that gives a visual indication of the metrical groups.

When a certain number of these factors are present, the language will be experienced as metrical, that is, as being organized in terms of regular beats.

C. The four-beat rhythm

The commonest meter in popular verse uses four-beat lines arranged in groups of four: the *4x4 formation*. The *hierarchical arrangement* of the beats in the 4x4 formation can be felt in a typical stanza. This derives from the process of *doubling* which produces the formation. Although the four-beat unit usually corresponds to the line on the page, this isn't necessarily the case.

   Virtual beats. In certain positions in the 4x4 formation, a beat may be experienced without being realized in language ; this occurs primarily as the fourth beat of a four-beat line, to produce the stanzas 4.3.4.3, 3.3.4.3, and 3.3.3.3.

Chapter 4

Stress verse and strong-stress verse: counting the beats

Stress meter

The following stanza by W. B. Yeats is, like all the examples of verse we considered in the previous chapter, in *stress meter.*

(1)   Out-worn heart, in a time out-worn,
         Come clear of the nets of wrong and right;
         Laugh, heart, again in the grey twilight,
         Sigh, heart, again in the dew of the morn.

The main feature of stress meter is that the *stress rhythm* of the language dominates the *syllabic rhythm,* allowing the number of syllables between the beats (and hence the total number of syllables per line) to vary within certain limits, while the number of beats remains constant. When used by a poet like Yeats, it deliberately echoes the tradition of popular verse, with strong beats and a constantly changing pattern of syllables producing a song-like quality that never becomes smoothly lyrical.

Verse in stress meter is *stress verse.* The rhythm of stress verse always derives ultimately from the doubling process we examined in chapter 3: pairs of beats themselves paired, and very often entering into further pairings. Although verse which uses the 4x4 formation is not always in stress meter, verse which uses stress meter, with very few exceptions, always falls into a four-beat rhythm.

The most popular kinds of verse in English tend to be in stress meter (and therefore in four-beat meter). Nursery rhymes, street games, popular ballads, advertising jingles, sports chants, rap lyrics, and a number of other kinds of widely familiar verse are versions of the same 4x4 formation with the same limited freedom in the syllable count. In all these forms, there is a greater tendency than there is in literary verse for the normal pronunciation of English to be adjusted in order to create a strong rhythm. These poems are often associated with tunes, which themselves determine a certain pronunciation, or with a chanted mode of delivery, which is simply a way of speaking verse with more attention to the meter than to the normal pronunciation of the words.

1. Beats and the scansion of stress verse

The most basic feature of metrical verse is the sequence of *beats*. We noted in chapter 3 some of the conditions that allow beats to emerge in a stretch of language. But beats are not simply "in" language; they are an aspect of the way we *experience* language. In reading metrical verse, it is crucial that we feel the beats as we read; if this happens there is no need to make a special effort to bring out the meter in our pronunciation.

So far, we have indicated beats by means of a B below the syllable, with stressed and unstressed syllables marked above the line by / and x. Here is another example of stress verse by a modern poet, the first stanza of Louis Untermeyer's "Song Tournament":

```
          /              /           /         /
(2)    Rain, said the first, as it falls in Venice
         B              B           B         B

         /        /          /        /
     Is like the dropping of golden pennies
         B        B          B        B

     /        /        /           /
     Into a sea as smooth and bright
     B        B        B           B

         /        /        /    /
     As a bowl of curdled malachite.
         B        B        B    B
```

The value of this notation, which we shall call *double-line scansion*, is that it makes crystal-clear the distinction between the stress pattern that arises from the norms of spoken English and the sequence of beats and offbeats that constitutes the meter. *It is extremely important to remember at all times that STRESSES are different from BEATS; they often coincide, but they are not the same thing.* In reading criticism of poetry you are likely to encounter many scansions and discussions of verse that run into trouble because they fail to keep this distinction clear. Double-line scansion is also useful for electronic transmission, as it uses keyboard symbols without any additional formatting (see Appendix 1, *Scansion*).

A more convenient method of scansion for handwritten work or regular word-processing is *single-line scansion*, in which all the information is contained above the line. Instead of a B beneath the line, we use an underlining of the stress mark to indicate a beat. Here's example (2) with single-line scansion:

(2)   Rain, said the first, as it falls in Venice

Is like the dropping of golden pennies

Into a sea as smooth and bright

As a bowl of curdled malachite.

In using single-line scansion it is crucial to remember that the underlining –
which indicates the beat – is distinct from the stress mark – which indicates
the stress on the syllable. As we shall shortly see, stress marks are not always
underlined, and underlines do not always accompany stress marks. Single-
line scansion can, of course, be converted to double-line scansion and vice
versa, since they convey exactly the same information.

Secondary stresses can function as beats in the same way as stresses, and
the final line of the previous example may be scanned as follows to show
this happening:

(3)   As a bowl of curdled malachite.

"Malachite" is a word that takes a main stress on its first syllable and a
secondary stress on its final syllable. In reading this line, there is no need to
give the final syllable of "malachite" an additional stress, since a secondary
stress sustains the meter just as well. It is therefore not essential to mark such
syllables as secondary in scansion, as the meter is not affected by their status.
We might want to do so, however, in order to show the variations in the
actual stress-pattern, in which case we underline the symbol for secondary
stress to show that it is functioning as a beat.

EXERCISE

Beats and scansion

(1) Scan the following lines by means of double-line scansion and then by means of single-line scansion. In each case, show stressed syllables and beats:

The steeds are all bridled, and snort to the rein;

Curved is each neck, and flowing each mane;

White is the foam of their champ on the bit;

The spears are uplifted; the matches are lit;   4

The cannon are pointed, and ready to roar,

And crush the wall they have crumbled before.

---

2. Offbeats

Here's another typical example of popular stress verse, with the stresses and beats marked in single–line scansion:

(4)   Had I the store in yonder mountain

Where gold and silver are had for counting,

I could not count for the thought of thee,

My eyes so full I could not see.

Look at the intervals between the beats in this example: they consist of either one or two unstressed syllables. Each of these intervals constitutes one *offbeat*. Those with one or two syllables are by far the most common, and are called *single* and *double* offbeats respectively. (Note the important distinction between beats and offbeats: the former always consist of one syllable, but the latter need not.) We indicate offbeats by marking the unstressed syllables in the usual way:

```
  x  ∠  x   ∠   x   ∠  x   ∠  x
Had I the store in yonder mountain

   x    ∠  x    ∠ x  x    ∠  x   ∠  x
Where gold and silver are had for counting,

 x ∠    x  ∠    x   x  ∠    x   ∠
I could not count for the thought of thee,

  x∠    x ∠  x ∠    x   ∠
My eyes so full I could not see.
```

Using the symbol x in this way (one for a single offbeat and two for a double beat) indicates *both* the occurrence of unstressed syllables *and* – since they are not underlined – their function as offbeats.

If you examine the earlier examples of stress verse in this chapter and the previous chapter, you will find that this variation between single and double offbeats is typical. Single offbeats are usually more frequent, but double offbeats can occur at any point in the line. It is very rare, however, to find more than two syllables between beats. In view of this limitation, what I am calling "stress meter" is sometimes called "regular stress meter" or "strict stress meter," to distinguish it from a looser variety discussed below under the name *strong-stress meter*.

The reason for the limitation of offbeats to one or two syllables is not difficult to deduce. If meter is produced by an alliance between the two rhythmic principles in spoken English, the stress rhythm and the syllable rhythm, too much variation in the number of unstressed syllables will start to put a strain on the alliance. Although the stress-timed nature of English means, as we saw in chapter 2, that we can squeeze unstressed syllables into a shorter time to keep stresses evenly spaced, it requires more and more effort from the reader as the number of unstressed syllables increases. Let us rewrite our example with additional unstressed syllables:

```
        x  ∠ xx    x  x ∠     x   ∠  x  ∠  x
(4a)    Had anyone the delights in yonder mountain

        x    ∠  x    ∠ x x  x    x ∠ x    x   ∠  x
        Where gold and platinum are delivered for counting,

        x   ∠ x  x    x   ∠    x   x ∠ x x x    ∠
        That person could not count for the memory of thee,

        x   x   x ∠    x    x  x ∠    x  ∠   x   ∠
        His or her eyes would be so full they could not see.
```

It is quite difficult to read this with rhythmic regularity, as the number of syllables between the beats varies from one to four.

In consistently separating the beats by only one or two syllables, stress verse engages with our normal reading habits to produce a metrical pattern of beats (in conjunction with the other features discussed in chapter 3). It's not as strictly regular a meter as is produced by the use of exactly the same number of unstressed syllables between every pair of beats, but it's regular enough to set up a definite swing which overcomes the slight variations. In fact, this actually brings it closer to song, because music usually provides some variety in the number of notes between the main beats, though their duration is controlled by the governing meter.

Occasionally in stress meter, beats occur in direct succession – that is, with no syllables between them. The first three beats of the following rhyme provide an illustration (with square brackets showing the missing offbeat):

    $\angle$ [x]$\angle$ [x] $\angle$ x $\angle$
(5)   Rain, rain, go away,

   $\angle$ x $\angle$ x $\angle$ x $\angle$
   Come again another day.

Usually the repetition of a beat without an intervening syllable would produce a moment of strain for the meter, since we expect beats to be separated by one or more syllables. However, used in certain places, and with a distinct gap between the stresses, it can actually produce a marked rhythm, as in this example. The three words that start the rhyme take an equal stress, and the reader naturally pauses between them. Since we experience a weaker pulse where there is no actual syllable, we call this kind of offbeat a *virtual offbeat*. As with virtual beats, the spoken utterance pauses but the meter does not – in fact, it is the pause in the utterance that make it possible for the meter to go on regularly as an alternation between beat and offbeat. (Recall that a pause can be either a silence or a prolonged word; in this example, it's most likely to be the latter.) *In stress verse, a beat is never followed immediately by another beat; an offbeat, actual or virtual, always intervenes.*

The most common position for a virtual offbeat within the line is in the middle, where it marks the metrical division of the line into two half-lines. Gerard Manley Hopkins uses a virtual offbeat in this way in "Inversnaid" to create a rocking, almost incantatory, rhythm:

(6)   What would the world be, once bereft

       Of wet and of wildness? Let them be left,

       x $\angle$ x x $\angle$ [x]$\angle$ x x $\angle$
       O let them be left, wildness and wet;

       Long live the weeds and the wilderness yet.

A virtual offbeat may also occur at the end of a line, usually in conjunction with a virtual beat, as in this example from a folk-song:

       x $\angle$ x x $\angle$ x x $\angle$ x $\angle$
(7)   When I was a bachelor young and gay

       x $\angle$ x   x $\angle$ x $\angle$ [x $\angle$]
       I followed the roving trade;

       x $\angle$ x $\angle$ x $\angle$ x x $\angle$
       And all the harm that ever I done,

       x $\angle$ x x $\angle$ x $\angle$ [x $\angle$]
       I courted a pretty maid.

When a stanza like this is sung, the melody has to allow for the missing offbeat as well as the missing beat (usually by increasing the length of the line's final syllable).

EXERCISE

Offbeats

(2) Mark the beats and offbeats (actual and virtual) in the following example:

   x x $\angle$ x x $\angle$ x $\angle$ x x
"Just the place for a Snark!" the Bellman cried,

   x x $\angle$ x $\angle$ x $\angle$ x $\angle$
As he landed his crew with care;

   x $\angle$ x x $\angle$ x x $\angle$ x x $\angle$
Supporting each man on the top of the tide

   x x $\angle$ x $\angle$ x x -
By a finger entwined in his hair.

(handwritten margin note: Supposed to have an off beat.)

3. Demotion

In all our examples so far, stressed syllables have been experienced as beats, and unstressed syllables have been experienced as offbeats, whether singly or in pairs. In other words, the stressed/unstressed opposition has coincided exactly with the beat/offbeat opposition. For many lines of verse this is true; such lines – we have considered several examples – are made up entirely of *stressed beats* and *unstressed offbeats* (/ and x or x x). However, under certain very specific conditions a stressed syllable can function as an offbeat, or part of an offbeat, and an unstressed syllable can take a beat. Since a stressed syllable is normally expected to function as a beat, it is said to be *demoted* when it occurs in an offbeat. Conversely, an unstressed syllable is said to be *promoted* when it functions as a beat. Only stressed syllables can be demoted (so "demoted syllable" means exactly the same as "demoted stress"); only unstressed syllables can be promoted. Fortunately, our familiarity with the rhythms of English and with basic metrical patterns enables us to read the lines where this happens without difficulty (often without our even noticing).

(a) Demotion in single offbeats

The first line of the following stanza reads easily with a four-beat rhythm:

(8)   Then out in the mead the poor girl ran
        To cull those flowers fast as they sprang.
        'Twas some she picked, some she pulled
        Till at length she gained her apron full.

Yet one of the stressed syllables – "girl" – occurs between the beats; that is, it functions as an offbeat:

```
     x  /  x   x  /   x   /    /    /
Then out in the mead the poor girl ran
```

In scanning the line, we show "girl" as stressed to reflect the fact that normally in prose this is how it is pronounced (it is a monosyllabic content word), but we do not underline it since it doesn't take a beat. It is a *demoted* syllable, doing a lower-grade job than it would usually be expected to do. (We can also refer to it as a *stressed offbeat*.)

There are three reasons why this apparently anomalous syllable poses no problem for the meter. First, it is *the middle stress in a sequence of three stresses*, a position in which it is especially easy for a stress to function as an offbeat since there is no neighboring syllable that is a more likely candidate for an offbeat. Second, thanks to the patterning of stresses in English phrases it is subordinated to the stressed syllable that immediately follows it (see the discussion of subordination in chapter 2). Third, the alternating tendency of the English language, also discussed in chapter 2, encourages this pattern of stronger–weaker–stronger.

Demotion produces a distinctive *rhythmic figure*; that is, a clearly defined rhythmic configuration that differs from the norm of alternating stressed beats and unstressed offbeats. (It is this rhythmic figure that is shaded in the example above.) As shorthand for this figure we can write / / /, indicating three stresses in succession, the first and third taking beats. Although demotion is often made smoother by the subordination of the demoted stress to a stress before or after it, we usually do not indicate this in the scansion, since it is perfectly possible to read a demoted stress with as much emphasis as those on either side of it. The smoothness of this example depends not on actually *pronouncing* "girl" with less emphasis, but in *feeling* it to be weaker than those on either side, for the three reasons just given. In other words, once a meter is established it will invest certain syllables with the special quality of beats and others with the special quality of offbeats, qualities which will register mentally without always having to be actualized in pronunciation. (Of course, if the arrangement of stressed and unstressed syllables begins to deviate too much from the expectation, the meter will cease to be perceived.)

It's perfectly possible to have a demoted stress that is not subordinated to either of the adjacent stresses – though the result is a marked slowing of the line and an increase of metrical tension. Here is an example in lines which have three actual beats (again, the entire rhythmic figure is shaded):

```
        x     /   x   x    /    x    /     [x /]
(9)    Your trade was with sticks and clay,


        x     /       /     /    x    / x      [x /]
       You  thumbed, thrust, patted, and polished...
```

The vigorous physical activity represented by the second line finds its embodiment in the succession of strong stresses, with the word "thrust" insisting on the same degree of emphasis as its neighbors. In a different metrical context these three stresses could function as beats separated by virtual offbeats (as in "Rain, rain, go away"); but this poem has set up an expectation for three beats a line, and the alternating rhythm allows us to experience "thrust" as an offbeat – even when we give it a full stress. *The term "demotion" does not refer to the way a syllable is pronounced, but to the way it relates to the meter.*

Secondary stresses are demoted very easily, since they are weaker than full stresses. A compound made up of a full stress and a secondary stress falls naturally into the pattern provided by demotion:

```
         x     Ʒ   \      Ʒ    x  /  x   /  x
(10)   "Yon screech-owl," says the Sailor, turning

       Back to his former cause of mourning...
```

The same is true of phrases that function as if they were compounds (see the discussion of secondary stress in chapter 2):

```
         x  /   x   Ʒ     \      Ʒ   x   x  /
(11)   She lived in Ross Street, close to the pub
```

A stress can also be demoted *at the beginning of a line before another stress* (/ Ʒ). In this example of four-beat verse I give two lines to establish the rhythm, followed by the line which begins with a stressed offbeat:

```
(12)   Have pity on my sore distress,

       I scarce can speak for weariness:

         /     Ʒ    x  Ʒ  x  Ʒ   x  Ʒ
       Stretch forth thy hand, and have no fear!
```

We can give both the words that start the last line equal stress, and the meter will not be disrupted.

(b) Demotion in double offbeats

Demotion can also occur in a double offbeat, when one of the two syllables is a stressed syllable functioning as if it were unstressed. There was an example in the lines by Hopkins quoted earlier (example [6]):

```
       O let them be left, wildness and wet;

         Ʒ    /    x  Ʒ   x    x  Ʒ x  x   Ʒ
       Long live the weeds and the wilderness yet.
```

Here the common phrase "Long live" takes its main stress on the first word, so it is the second stress that is slightly weaker. The rhythmic figure now consists of four syllables.

Either of the syllables in a double offbeat can be demoted. Here is a stanza of two-beat lines from a poem by Hardy entitled "Rain on a Grave" which uses both types of double offbeat demotion, giving some extra weight to the small-scale metrical units. (The demotions include examples of secondary stress.)

```
(13)    One who to shelter

        Her delicate head

        Would quicken and quicken

        Each tentative tread               4


        x    ⌟    /     x ⌟    x
        If drops chanced to pelt her


        x    ⌟ x  \    ⌟
        That summertime spills


        x    ⌟   \ x   ⌟
        In dust-paven rills


        x    ⌟ x   \     ⌟ x
        When thunder-clouds thicken        8


        x    ⌟    /     x   ⌟
        And birds close their bills.
```

There are three double offbeats with demotion of the first syllable, and two with demotion of the second syllable. The demoted secondary stresses cause less disruption to the meter: "summertime," "dust-paven," and "thunderclouds." The demoted verbs, "chanced" and "close," insist more on their own stress and thereby slow down the line. We shall discuss further examples of demotion in double offbeats in the section on "Triple verse" later in this chapter.

(c) Reading demoted stresses

Because it is in line with the ingrained rhythms of the language, demotion doesn't call for any special effort of pronunciation. However, in popular stress verse, such as ballads and nursery rhymes, we tend to emphasize the regularity of the rhythm more than we do in literary verse, and so the likelihood of actually reducing the stress on demoted syllables is higher. Sometimes we find ourselves treating demoted stresses as if they were unstressed syllables – especially in conventional epithets ("young man," "pretty maid") and in titles ("Lord Thomas," "Queen Jane"). However, for the purposes of scansion it is better to mark these syllables as stressed, thus indicating how they would be spoken in a careful prose pronunciation. In showing a syllable as demoted – that is, showing a stress without the underlining that marks a beat – we imply that the reader has the freedom to choose, according to the needs of the verse, whether to pronounce it as stressed, unstressed, or somewhere in between.

EXERCISE

Demotion

(3) Scan the following lines from Browning's "Meeting at Night." Show beats, offbeats (single, double, and virtual), and demoted stresses. How disruptive of the regular meter are the demoted stresses? Do they contribute to the emotional intensity of the stanza?

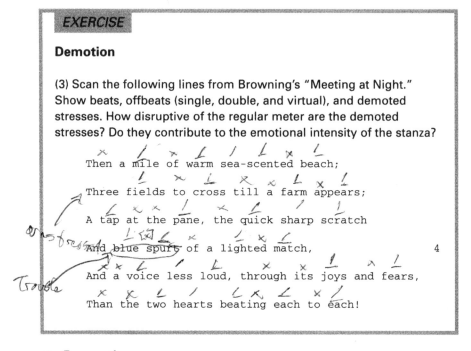

4. Promotion

Promotion is the reverse of demotion: under certain specific conditions an unstressed syllable functions not as an offbeat, which is what is normally expected, but as a beat. It is thus *promoted* to a role usually reserved for stressed syllables. In other words, a promoted syllable is an *unstressed beat*, a momentary contradiction of the general rule that beats are produced by stressed syllables. Promotion happens easily when the syllable in question is *the middle one of three successive unstressed syllables* (just as demotion occurs easily on the middle syllable of three stressed syllables). Here's a stanza which has examples of promotion in the first, third and fourth lines:

```
         x  /  x   x   x  /     x  /
(14)    You Englishmen of each degree,

         /   / x   / x / x  /
        One moment listen unto me;

         x    /   x  /  x  x x  /
        To please you all I do intend,

         x  /  x   x   x    /    x     /
        So listen to these lines I've penned.
```

As before, the underlining shows where the beats fall, but now in addition to / we have x, showing where an unstressed syllable takes a beat. When we scan a line to check whether it has the right number of beats we have to count the underlines, irrespective of the symbol above them. The rhythmic figure produced by promotion is x x x, again highlighted in our examples.

If we chant this stanza, we find ourselves stressing all the beats; and the style of the poem, like much of the popular verse we're considering in this chapter, does incline us away from the rhythms of speech towards a more chanted or song-like reading. But if we choose to read it with the natural stressing of the words, we will probably not stress the final syllable of "Englishmen" and the words "do" and "to." (We might also pronounce the first syllable of "unto" without a stress, since it is a function word, though I have chosen to show it as stressed.) This will not damage the meter, as the established rhythm (and the built-in alternating tendency of the language) will allow us to experience these syllables as beats. *The term "promotion" does not refer to the way a syllable is pronounced, but to the way it relates to the meter.* It is important, however, that we give these promoted syllables a distinct pronunciation that keeps the timing of the rhythm; we can't slur or hurry them.

Promotion can also happen on *the last syllable of a line when it's preceded by an unstressed syllable* (x x):

```
(15)    But the strangest thing: in the thick old thatch,

        Where summer birds had been given hatch,

        Had fed in chorus, and lived to fledge,

         x     /    x   / x   x   /  x x
        Some still were living in hermitage.
```

Normally, we would pronounce "hermitage" with only the first syllable stressed. Here we sense a beat on the third syllable as well, and if we were giving the verse a strongly rhythmical reading we might be tempted to give it a slight stress.

The other place where promotion occurs is *the beginning of the line, when it opens with two unstressed syllables* (x x). The second and third lines of the following stanza begin in this way:

```
        /  x   x   x   /   x   /   x
(16)    "Madam,  in  your  face  is  beauty,

        x   x   / x    / x      /    [x]
        In your bosom flowers grow,

        x   x   / x    x   x    /   x
        In your bedroom there is pleasure,

        /   x  /   x    /   x   /   [x]
        Shall I view it,  yes or no?"
```

Since this is a popular song, we are likely to give the word "In" some degree of stress, whereas in ordinary speech it would be unstressed. It doesn't *require* a stress in order to function as a beat, however. Since there is an expectation for four beats in the line, a distinct pronunciation of the syllable is all that is necessary. If we were expecting only *three* beats in the line, we would treat "In your" as a double offbeat – and we would speed up the pronunciation accordingly.

At both the beginning and the end of the line, the crucial condition that allows promotion to occur is that the syllable next to the one in question – just after it or just before it – should be unstressed as well. It is not possible for an unstressed syllable to carry a beat if it is next to a stress, except in verse where the natural rhythm of the language is dominated by a chant or a melody. In nursery rhymes, for instance, readers are sometimes induced to promote unstressed syllables next to stresses. The following lines are usually read with four actual beats:

```
        /   x  /  x   /[x]x
(17)    Little Tommy Tuck-er

        /  [x] /   x    /[x]x
        Sings for his sup-per...
```

This kind of promotion could only happen in literary verse if it was using the same kind of strong, chanted rhythm.

Promotion, like demotion, happens frequently in stress verse, and this makes it crucial not to confuse stresses and beats. What is sometimes misleadingly called "four-stress" verse may have more or fewer than four stresses, but it always has four beats.

EXERCISE

Promotion

(4) Scan these opening stanzas from Keats's "La Belle Dame sans Merci." Count the number of promoted syllables (i.e. unstressed beats). If you find the last line of each stanza difficult to scan, see if you can read them with the same rhythm as the following last lines from later stanzas: "And her eyes were wild," "A fairy's song," "I love thee true."

O what can ail thee, knight at arms,

Alone and palely loitering?

The sedge has wither'd from the lake,

And no birds sing. ← strug   4

O what can ail thee, knight at arms,

So haggard and so woe-begone? ← secondary stress

The squirrel's granary is full,

And the harvest's done.   8

---

5. Quadruple verse

In reading the 7.7.7.7 stanza quoted in the previous chapter, readers may find that they are inclined to give a somewhat stronger emphasis to the first, third, fifth, and seventh beats of each line, in contrast to the even-numbered beats (the last of which is only a virtual beat). The major beats are marked with double underlines, and the secondary beats with single underlines:

(18)   There's black-eyed Fan with the frying pan will cook

your eggs and bacon,

With beef and mutton, roast and boiled, if I am not

mistaken.

This alternation gives each line four strong beats, making it a kind of four-beat unit functioning over a longer span than usual. The duple movement of beat/offbeat alternation is itself organized in a duple alternation of stronger beat/weaker beat, giving rise to a *quadruple* rhythm. The use of virtual beats, together with a certain type of repetitive diction, can be a powerful way of harnessing the multi-leveled character of the four-beat meter to produce this rhythm. (The traditional term for it is "dipodic meter" – the Greek term means "two-footed.") We call the stronger and weaker beats *primary* and *secondary* beats.

Here's another example with a somewhat different and much quicker movement; if we read it rapidly the secondary beats are likely to lose their stress altogether.

(19)   Get a little table, then a little chair,

And then a little house in the corner of the

square;

Get a little teapot and save a little tin,

But don't forget the cradle for to rock the

baby in.

The quadruple movement gives the verse a jaunty, rapid motion that prevents us from taking the sentiments too seriously. Notice that when this strong rhythm is established in our minds, we can treat almost anything as a secondary beat, including the second syllable of "table" – which we have to chant as "ta-ble." (Compare the promotion of the second syllable of "Tucker" in example [17].)

Insistent quadruple verse also tends to produce strong–weak patterns over even longer stretches. It's easy when reading the previous example with a regular rhythm to find yourself giving the first and third primary beats of each line more weight than the second and fourth, producing for each two-line unit a four-beat movement. Perhaps even the whole stanza can be thought of as having four major beats, the first beat in each of the four lines, them-selves arranged stronger–weaker–stronger–weaker. Theoretically, there is no limit to this process of hierarchizing; but practically, at a certain point we cease to notice the distinctions – and the less insistent the rhythm and our style of reading, the sooner they become irrelevant.

The quadruple tendency is inherent in the 4x4 formation, arising as it does out of the doubling process that produces the formation. We can see now why the positioning of virtual beats is strongly constrained; they are most likely to occur where the beat is weak at higher as well as lower levels of the structure. How insistently the quadruple movement is felt in any given poem, however, depends on the way the verse is written: on whether the diction and content encourage a highly rhythmical reading, whether the use of virtual beats and offbeats places a particularly strong emphasis on beats in appropriate positions, and on whether the words and syntax bring out the hierarchical relations among beats of different strengths. A strong quadruple rhythm can be bombastic or trivializing, but it can also be flex-ibly and memorably rhythmic.

EXERCISE

Quadruple verse

(5) Mark the primary beats in this example with double underlines ($\underline{\underline{/}}$ and $\underline{\underline{x}}$) and the secondary beats with single underlines ($\underline{/}$ and $\underline{x}$), including all virtual beats. How would you describe the emotional effectiveness of the rhythm?

```
 ⤬     ⟋  ⤬ ⟋    ⟋  ⤬  ⤬    ⟋     ⟋   ⟋
If the home we never write to, and the oaths we never keep,

And all we know most distant and most dear,

Across the snoring barrack-room return to break our sleep,
```

```
Can you blame us if we soak ourselves in beer?            4

When the drunken comrade mutters and the great guard-lantern

  gutters

 And the horror of our fall is written plain,

Every secret, self-revealing on the aching whitewashed

  ceiling,

 Do you wonder that we drug ourselves from pain?          8
```

6. Duple and triple meters

If you read the following two stanzas as rhythmically as possible, you will notice that they are distinctively different from each other in their movement:

(20)   Where love is planted there it grows,
        It buds and blossoms like any rose,
        It has so sweet and a pleasant smell,
        No flowers on earth can it excel.

(21)   Says the master to me, "Is it true, I am told
        Your name on the books of the Union enrolled?
        I can never allow that a workman of mine
        With wicked disturbers of peace should combine."

Scanning these two stanzas, the explanation for this difference is immediately clear: in the first, almost all the offbeats are single, while in the second they are almost all double:

```
        x    ∠  x    ∠ x    ∠  x      ∠
(20)    Where love is planted there it grows,

        x  ∠  x    ∠ x    x  ∠ x  ∠
        It buds and blossoms like any rose,

        x  ∠  x  ∠  x   x  ∠  x     ∠
        It has so sweet and a pleasant smell,

         x   ∠ x   x  ∠     x  ∠  x  ∠
        No flowers on earth can it excel.
```

```
        x     x ∠ x   x ∠   x  x    ∠   x x   ∠
(21)    Says the master to me, "Is it true, I am told

        x   ∠ x   x ∠   x   x ∠ x    x ∠
        Your name on the books of the Union enrolled;

        x  x  ∠ x  x ∠   x  x ∠  x  x   ∠
        I can never allow that a workman of mine

        x   ∠ x   x ∠ x   x   ∠     x   x ∠
        With wicked disturbers of peace should combine."
```

Some stress meter varies freely between single and double offbeats (sometimes with occasional virtual offbeats), but most examples have a preponderance of one or the other. When this happens, the rhythm gains added regularity: it becomes basically duple or triple, and we can say that the verse is written in a *duple meter* or a *triple meter*.

Duple verse, like the first example above (and most of the examples we have considered so far in this chapter), takes advantage of the alternating rhythmic tendency of the language to establish a rocking, back-and-forth rhythm. Taking English verse altogether, duple verse is more common than triple verse, perhaps because it is closer to the movement of spoken English. When the occasional double offbeat occurs in such a meter, we automatically adjust our pronunciation to take care of it without endangering the duple movement.

Triple verse, like the second example above, is set in motion if there are enough double offbeats to overcome the built-in preference for a duple meter. A triple meter brings the verse closer to song, spacing the stresses out with a relatively high degree of evenness, and producing a distinctive 1–2–3 movement. The occasional single offbeat does not interfere with this rhythm, as we can hear if we rewrite a line of example (21):

```
        x     x ∠ x   x ∠   x ∠   x   x ∠
        Says the master to me, "A word or two more."
```

We usually handle this variation by lengthening the previous stressed syllable, though it's also possible to move into a duple rhythm for just a moment. In other words, the stress-timed nature of English allows us to compensate for the missing syllable, and we do not experience a virtual offbeat in its place.

We seldom read duple or triple stress verse with the aim of making the words conform exactly to the meter, but doing so is a useful exercise in establishing just what the meter is. First say:

```
two three ONE two three ONE two three ONE two three ONE...
```

Then in the same rhythm:

```
Says the MASter to ME, "Is it TRUE, I am TOLD...
```

Once this rhythm is running in the reader's head, the lines can vary quite considerably without disrupting it. In fact, the tendency of triple rhythm to dominate the language is what renders it inappropriate for most poetic purposes.

EXERCISE

Duple and triple meters

(6) Read the following stanzas from Blake's *Songs of Innocence and Experience* aloud. Decide whether each one is predominantly triple or duple. Scan the stanzas to check your response. Try to characterize the different emotional effect of the two rhythms.

```
(a)  When the voices of children are heard on the green,
     And laughing is heard on the hill,
     My heart is at rest within my breast,
     And everything else is still.

(b)  I wander through each chartered street,
     Near where the chartered Thames does flow,
     And mark in every face I meet
     Marks of weakness, marks of woe.
```

---

7. Demotion and promotion in triple verse

(a) Demotion

We noted earlier that one of the syllables in a double offbeat can be a demoted stress, and this possibility becomes particularly important in triple verse. As always, demotion occurs more smoothly if the demoted stress is felt to be subordinated to another stress. The words "wide" and "good" in the following extract function very easily as parts of double offbeats, since they are rather conventional adjectives, clearly subordinated to the following stresses:

```
       x  /   x  x /  x   x   /   x    x  /
(22)   O young Lochinvar is come out of the west,

       x   /    x  /    /  x  x   /   x   x  /
       Through all the wide Border his steed was the best;

       x   /   x  /   /    x   x / x   x  /
       And save his good broadsword he weapons had none,

       x  /  x  x /     x   x  /  x   x /
       He rode all unarm'd, and he rode all alone.
```

It's also quite common for the first of the two offbeat syllables to be a stressed syllable. Here is an example that has both kinds:

```
       x    x  /   /  x  /  x   x   /   x x   /
(23)   In the great town of London near Manchester Square,

       /   /   /   x /  x  x   /    \   x   /
       Jane Jones kept a mangle in South Street we hear;

       x /   x x    /   x  /   / x x   /
       A gentleman's coachman oft visiting came,

       x /    \  x   /  x   /  /   x  x   /
       A cold-blooded monster, Dan Good was his name.
```

In lines 1 and 2, "town" and "kept" are examples of the demotion of the first offbeat syllable; in lines 3 and 4, "oft" and "Dan" are examples of the demotion of the second offbeat syllable. The stanza also has two compounds with secondary stresses that are easily demoted, "South Street" and "cold-blooded." The rhythmic figures produced by these types of demotion are / x / / and / / x /.

In triple verse examples like these, it is tempting to show many of these demoted syllables as unstressed, since their weakness in comparison to the stresses that take beats means that we are hardly aware of their potential for stress. It is best to show them as stressed, however, since the absence of underlining is a clear enough indication that in a certain type of reading – where the regular rhythm dominates the normal speaking voice – they will lose their stress. It is up to the reader to decide what kind of delivery to use.

The occasional single offbeat in triple stress verse is usually realized by an unstressed syllable, but it can also be realized by a stressed syllable, producing the same type of demotion as duple verse ($\underline{/}$ / $\underline{/}$). The following lines have both types of single offbeat, the demoted stress ("fall," "last," "lone," "guest's") and the unstressed syllable ("and," "should," "be," "not"):

```
        x  L       /    L    x    x  L   x    L x
(24)   The fields fall southward, abrupt and broken,

        x   x  L    /   L    x    x  L    /    L
       To the low last edge of the long lone land.

        x   x  L    x    L   x   x  L    x    L x
       If a step should sound or a word be spoken,

        x    x  L    x    L   x    x  L      /       L
       Would a ghost not rise at the strange guest's hand?
```

As with all demotion, we don't have to give conscious attention to the fact that words like "fall" or "last" function as offbeats here. The alternating tendency of the language and the predominantly triple rhythm that has already been established in the poem induce us to place the beats on "fields" and "south," "low" and "edge." Demoted stresses work particularly well in this context, since their additional length – provided that we give them full stress – provides an equivalent for the two unstressed syllables they are replacing, and imparts a distinctive (though sometimes intrusive) bounce to the rhythm.

(b) Promotion

Promotion, by contrast, is not very common in triple verse – for obvious reasons. With an approximate ratio of two unstressed syllables to every stressed syllable, there is little call for yet more unstressed syllables. When normally unstressed syllables *do* occur as beats in this meter, the strong movement usually encourages some degree of stressing, however unnatural this would be in prose. The following opening stanza of a rhythmically rather rough traditional ballad – it has triple as well as double offbeats – demands beats on "of," "to," and "was," and although the scansion shows them as unstressed (indicating, as always, the normal prose pronunciation), these syllables are likely to receive additional emphasis when the verse is read:

```
        x   x  x  /   ∠  x     x  x  ∠  x   x  ∠
(25)    It's of a sea captain who was married of late

          x   x  x  /    ∠  x  x    x  ∠    x  x  ∠
        'Twas to a young lady and he gained her estate

          x  x  x  /  ∠  x   x   ∠    x    x  ∠
        He was a sea captain and bound for the sea

        x   x ∠   x  x  ∠  x   x  x  ∠    x ∠
        But before she was bedded he was called away.
```

EXERCISE

Demotion and promotion in triple verse

(7) Scan the following stanza, showing demotions and promotions.
Do any of them hinder the swing of the triple rhythm?

```
A sweet-scented Courtier did give me a Kiss,

And promis'd me Mountains if I would be his,

But I'll not believe him, for it is too true,

Some courtiers do promise much more than they do.   4

  My Thing is my own, and I'll keep it so still,

  Yet other young Lasses may do what they will.
```

---

8. Rising and falling rhythms

In chapter 2 we discussed the way in which unstressed syllables in English group themselves around stresses, producing *stress groups* that can be classified according to their type of rhythm. A *rising* rhythm is produced by a stress group that *ends* with a full stress, a *falling* rhythm by a stress group that *begins* with a full stress. Other groups have *mixed* rhythms or consist of *monosyllabic* words. Most often, rising and falling rhythms vary freely in poetry. Sometimes, however, a consistent pattern of one or the other can emerge, and this can be harnessed to produce a distinctive rhythmic quality.

We indicate groups by means of vertical lines, and sometimes it is useful to indicate the sequence of groups next to the line: R for rising groups, F for falling groups, and M for mixed or monosyllabic groups (neither of which contribute to either rising or falling rhythms). The following rhyme is largely in falling rhythm, as the position of the stress within each group makes clear:

```
      | ∠  x | ∠  x | ∠  x  | ∠  x  |          FFFF
(26)    Tinker, tailor, soldier, sailor,

      | ∠   \ | ∠   \ | ∠  x  \ |  ∠  |          FFFM
        Rich man, poor man, beggarman, thief.
```

(The two stresses on "man" are subordinated to the contrastive stress on "Rich" and "poor.") The following lines, on the other hand, are in rising rhythm:

```
      |  x    ∠ |x  ∠ |  x  ∠ |x    ∠  |          RRRR
(27)    There was a rat, for want of stairs

      | x    ∠  |x  ∠ | x  ∠ | x    ∠   |          RRRR
        Went down a rope to say his prayers.
```

Predominantly rising and predominantly falling rhythms have different qualities, as these examples begin to suggest. A falling rhythm has a tendency toward equalization of the syllables; that is to say, we tend to read "Tinker, tailor, soldier, sailor" in quite a rigid duple meter. A rising rhythm, on the other hand, tends to abbreviate and lighten the unstressed syllables as they move quickly into the stress; so that "There was a rat, for want of stairs" might be read with the stressed syllables given twice as much time as the unstressed syllables. (It could therefore easily be set to music in triple time, even though the verse is duple.)

The perception of a rising or a falling rhythm can also be influenced by the way lines of verse start – an initial falling group can predispose the reader to hear further falling groups, for instance – but this is of less importance in stress verse than in syllable-stress verse, which we shall consider in the following chapter.

EXERCISE

Rising and falling rhythms

(8) Mark the stresses and the stress groups in the following lines. Indicate the sequence of rising, falling, and mixed or monosyllabic groups next to the line, using the abbreviations suggested above. Is any rhythm dominant? How do the different types of stress group relate to the way the lines begin and end?

```
See the creature stalking

   While we speak!

Hush and hide the talking,

   Cheek on cheek!                    4


What so false as truth is,

   False to thee?

Where the serpent's tooth is

   Shun the tree —                    8


Where the apple reddens

   Never pry —

Lest we lose our Edens,

   Eve and I.                        12
```

Strong-stress meter

1. Old and Middle English

What happens if the four-beat line is allowed to take more than two un-stressed syllables between beats, or to use virtual offbeats freely? Or if additional stresses occur between the beats in positions that prevent them from being demoted? Or run-on lines and absence of rhyme inhibit the emergence of the four-line unit? The most likely result is verse with little feeling of being metrical at all; a kind of free verse, in other words.

However, there exists a tradition of stress verse with these characteristics that does produce a metrical pulse, at least if read in an appropriate manner. It is not quite as free as my description suggests, and it makes use of an important additional device – alliteration – to guide the reader. Here is an example:

(28)   Blind on the bride-bed, the bridegroom snores,
        Too aloof to love. Did you lose your nerve
        And cloud your conscience because I wasn't
        Your dish really? You danced so bravely   4
        Till I wished I were. Will you remain
        Such a pleasant prince? Probably not.

This is clearly very different from stress verse, as the term is being used in this book, and it is a useful negative demonstration of the importance of the various constraints that operate to keep the four-beat movement alive. There is little sense of an alternation between beats and offbeats, and without that no possibility for virtual beats, or promotion and demotion. In fact, there are few lines with beats. But most lines have four clearly marked stressed syllables, and many of these are further signaled by alliteration (that is, the stressed syllable – sometimes in the middle of a word – begins with the same consonant). Another obvious feature is the way the lines are divided by a strong syntactic break into two half-lines, each with two stresses. This division is so systematic that it is obviously an aspect of the metrical structure. (On the other hand, the divisions *between* the lines are sometimes only a matter of the layout on the page.)

We can scan this verse by showing the four main stresses, preceded by an "a" when they alliterate, as well as the division into half-lines (indicated by '):

```
        a/              a/        '    a/            /
        Blind on the bride-bed, the bridegroom snores,

          a /       a/   '          a/          /
        Too aloof to love. Did you lose your nerve

          a /        a/          '  a/          /
        And cloud your conscience because I wasn't

          a/    /    '    a/            /
        Your dish really? You danced so bravely        4
```

```
    a/        a/     'a/           /
Till I wished I were. Will you remain

    a /      a /    'a /           /
Such a pleasant prince? Probably not.
```

This type of stress meter is known as *strong-stress meter,* since it relies on the occurrence of a fixed number of strong stresses in the line (almost always four), which have to be clearly marked in pronunciation.

Modern literary strong-stress verse is not very common – this example is by W. H. Auden – and is usually written in imitation of Old English (also known as Anglo-Saxon) verse, dating from the seventh to the eleventh centuries. Old English meter is not fully understood; it appears to have been written according to complex rules, and was sung or intoned to musical accompaniment rather than recited. To modern ears, however, it sounds very like the Auden example. Here is a recent translation of part of an Old English poem, "The Seafarer," with the stresses marked (note that according to the conventions of this verse any vowel may alliterate with any other):

```
            a  /            a /      '   a/         /
(29)    The thriving of the treeland, the town's briskness,

         a/                a/   'a/    /
       a lightness over the leas, life gathering,

    a/            a/      '   a/          /
     everything urges the eagerly mooded

      /     a/      '          a/             /
     man to venture on the voyage he thinks of,      4

        a/            a /    '    a/   /
       the faring over flood, the far bourn.
```

No doubt the mode of performance, and the accompanying instrument, would have emphasized the rhythmic structure, probably timing the rhythm so that the four stresses functioned as beats.

In the late fourteenth century, contemporaneous with Chaucer's founding of syllable-stress meter in English (the meter which we shall examine in the next chapter), there occurred a revival of alliterative verse, again using four strong stresses per line, though with greater freedom in the number of syllables between them. Here is an example from the anonymous *Sir Gawain and the Green Knight*, in a modern translation that keeps the flavor of the rhythm:

```
              a  /         a  /  'a/                /
(30)    Then the grim man in green gathers his strength,

           a/        a/        '  a/              /
       Heaves high the heavy ax to hit him the blow.

              a/            a /  '   a/              /
       With all the force in his frame he fetches it aloft.

          a  /        a  / '              a  /          /
       With a grimace as grim as he would grind him to bits...
```

From having once been the dominant form in English poetry, strong-stress verse has become a rare visitor to the literary realm. However, it has continued to offer to many poets an alternative way of organizing the sounds and meanings of English, and its echoes can be heard in much of this century's free verse.

2. Rap

In recent years, a verse form which bears many resemblances to Old English strong-stress meter has gained immense popularity: rap. Before its emergence in the late 1970s no one could have predicted that a way of performing lyrics based on rhythm and not on melody would come to occupy the high ground of popular culture – not just the black American culture that is its home, but internationally. Rap's unlikely success is due, in part, to a widespread and continuing fascination with the rhythms of speech and their potential for artistic manipulation.

Like Old English verse, rap lyrics are written to be performed to an accompaniment that emphasizes the metrical structure of the verse. The two forms have essentially the same metrical structure: lines with four stressed beats (falling naturally into two half-lines of two beats each), separated by other syllables that may vary in number and may include other stressed syllables. The strong beat of the accompaniment coincides with the stressed beats of the verse, and the rapper organizes the rhythms of the intervening syllables to provide variety and surprise. A major difference between the two traditions is that Old English verse uses alliteration and allows frequent run-on lines, while rap uses rhyme and prefers end-stopping (bringing it closer to the tradition of four-beat stress verse, to which it is also linked by its tendency to fall into quadruple rhythms).

On the page, rap lyrics often disguise their potential for powerful rhythms. Here are some lines from EPMD's "It's My Thing":

(31)   They mean business, no time for play
           If you bite a line, they blow you away
           The more you bite, your body gets hot
           Don't get too cold because you might get shot   4
           Knowin' that my rhyme's like a poisonous rat
           Don't play dumb boy, you're smarter than that
           It's my thing.

Reading this as if it were a poem, it's not difficult to discern a somewhat irregular four-beat rhythm, with the usual tendency for lines to divide into two two-beat halves, plus a short refrain. Listening to it performed, however, the beats take on a precise regularity (though they do not always fall on the syllables where we might expect them), and the rhythm gains life through the varying patterns that separate the beats.

We can use the conventions of scansion to give some idea of the rhythm of the recorded performance, as long as we remember that here those conventions are being used to represent a rhythm that may be imposed on the language, rather than – as is usually the case with scansion – indicating the inherent movement of the words and sentences. As in all scansion of quadruple verse, double underlining indicates primary beats; single underlining indicates secondary beats.

```
        B  B  B  x     b  B   x   B   [B]
(31)    They mean business, no time for play

        B  x  B  x  B [B] x   B  x  x B  [B]
        If you bite a line, they blow you away

          x  B   x   B [B] x    B x  B    B
        The more you bite, your body gets hot

        B   B  B  B   x x   x   B   B    B  [B]
        Don't get too cold because you might get shot    4

         B x   x  x  B    x  x B   x   B  [B]
        Knowin' that my rhyme's like a poisonous rat

        B   B  B  B   x      B  x   x   B
        Don't play dumb boy, you're smarter than that

        x   B  B
        It's my thing.
```

Four strong beats punctuate each line in the performance, and the rhyme at the end of the line is crucial in providing a climactic articulation on the fourth beat.

Between the main beats there is a wide variety of rhythmic patterning. Basically, the main beats are separated by secondary beats, but these can be manifested in many ways. A secondary beat may occur as a single stress between beats:

```
  ∠    ∠    ∠               ∠    ∠   ∠     ∠     ∠   ∠
They mean business   Don't get too cold   Don't play dumb
```

It may occur as a stress occurring with an unstressed syllable either before or after it:

```
  ∠ x   ∠    ∠     ∠    ∠   x        ∠
body gets hot    dumb boy, you're smarter
```

It may occur as a stress between two unstressed syllables:

```
 ∠   x   ∠   x   ∠
If you bite a line
```

On the other hand, it may occur as an unstressed syllable in any of the same situations:

```
  ∠    x    ∠    ∠   x    ∠
time for play    more you bite
```

```
   ∠      x   x  ∠          ∠  x    x    ∠
rhyme's like a poisonous   smarter than that
```

```
  ∠    x x    x   ∠        ∠ x    x   x   ∠
cold because you might   Knowin' that my rhyme's
```

And it may occur as a virtual beat, when the syllable on which the previous beat fell is extended until it encompasses the secondary beat as well:

```
 ∠ [∠]  x    ∠      ∠ [∠] x    ∠ x
line, they blow    bite, your body
```

Virtual beats in the rap lyric are, of course, heard as actual beats in the accompaniment.

This representation of the rhythmic details of EPMD's performance still leaves out many subtleties, like pronounced stresses that fall just before or just after the beat of the accompaniment. The catchy quality of the rhythm of rap is in part due to the way the performance to some degree reflects, to some degree deforms, both the natural rhythms of the language and the metronomic beat of the accompaniment, playing between them with a virtuosic freedom that is inherited from a black musical tradition with a long history. As in many examples of rap, the lyrics of "It's My Thing" are self-reflexive: they boast about the rhythmic power which they simultaneously demonstrate.

"It's My Thing" is a relatively simple example of the rhythm of rap. Tone Lōc's "Wild Thing" is performed with a more complex rhythm, using a marked alternation between primary and secondary beats in long lines, and much variation between these beats. It would be hard to read the following lines as four-beat verse unless one already had a rap rhythm running in one's head (and even then they could be made to fit it in a number of ways):

(32)   Workin' all week nine to five for my money
        So when the weekend comes I can go get live with
          the honey
        Rollin' down the street I saw this girl and she was
          pumpin'
        I winked my eye and she got into the ride, went
          to a club, it was jumpin'   4
        Introduced myself as Lōc, she said, "You're a
          liar"
        I said, "I got it goin' on baby doll, and I'm on
          fire."

Here are the main and secondary beats that emerge in the recorded performance of the lines:

    _∠_   ∠   ∠ [∠]   ∠   ∠   ∠   [∠]
    Workin' all week nine to five for my money

[∠]   ∠   ∠   ∠   ∠   ∠
    So when the weekend comes I can go get live with

       ∠   [∠]
    the honey

     _∠_   ∠   ∠ [∠]   _∠_   ∠
    Rollin' down the street I saw this girl and she

       ∠   [∠]
    was pumpin'

```
    /́          /́                /́            /́
I winked my eye and she got into the ride, went

    /́   /́            /́       [/́]
to a club, it was jumpin'                                    4

  /́   /́      /́        /́         /́       /́
Introduced myself as Lōc, she said, "You're a

    /́    [/]
liar"

            /́     /́   /́          /́  [/́]  /́
I said, "I got it goin' on baby doll, and I'm on

    /́      [/]
fire."
```

These markings will be of little use to readers who don't know the record-
ing: the variety in the rhythmic patterns between beats is even greater than
in the previous example, and the meter is even less deducible from the
natural spoken rhythm of the words. The lines are rapped against the usual
steady duple rhythm (with eight beats to the line), using frequent slight
syncopations. There are even more complex examples of rap rhythm than
this, in which different possibilities of verbal rhythm are played against one
another as well as against the steady accompaniment. Comparing rap lyrics
on the page with actual performances leads to the realization that Old English verse, for which we only have the words on the page, may never yield
up its secrets.

EXERCISE

Strong-stress meter

(9) Imagine the following rap lyrics as they might be performed, and mark the beats in each line:

A child is born with no state of mind

Blind to the ways of mankind

God is smiling on you but he's frowning too

Because only God knows what you go through   4

You grow in the ghetto, living second rate

And your eyes will sing a song of deep hate

The place that you play and where you stay

Looks like one great big alleyway.   8

Summary

A. Stress meter

Much popular verse is in stress meter (which is invariably based on a four-beat rhythm). The main components of stress verse are as follows:

(a) *Stressed beats* ($\angle$). Except as noted in (d) below, all stressed syllables are experienced as beats. Syllables with secondary stress may also be experienced as beats.

(b) *Unstressed offbeats* (x). Except as noted in (e) below, all unstressed syllables are experienced as offbeats, either *single offbeats* (one unstressed syllable, x) or *double offbeats* (two unstressed syllables, x x). Syllables with secondary stress may also be experienced as offbeats. Consistent use of single offbeats produces *duple rhythm*; consistent use of double offbeats produces *triple rhythm*.

(c) *Virtual offbeats* ([x]). Occasionally, an offbeat may be experienced between two successive stressed beats ($\angle$ [x] $\angle$), especially when the stresses are equally strong and separated by a pause, and at major divisions in the metrical pattern. A virtual offbeat can also occur before a virtual beat in the positions specified in chapter 3 ([x $\angle$]).

(d) *Demotion* (/). A stressed syllable can function as (1) a single offbeat, when it occurs between stressed beats (/̠ / /̠) or at the beginning of a line before a stressed beat (/ /̠), or (2) part of a double offbeat between stressed beats, when it occurs before or after an unstressed syllable (/̠ x / /̠; /̠ / x /̠). Demotion occurs most easily when the stress in question is subordinated to the stress before or after it in the line.

(e) *Promotion* (x̠). An unstressed syllable can be promoted, i.e. experienced as a beat, when it occurs between two unstressed syllables (x x̠ x), at the beginning of the line before an unstressed syllable (x̠ x), or at the end of the line after an unstressed syllable (x x̠).

Other features of stress verse are its *quadruple* tendency (when the beats themselves alternate between stronger and weaker), and the existence of *rising, falling, mixed,* and *monosyllabic stress groups. Virtual beats* were discussed in chapter 3.

Stress verse may be scanned by *double-line scansion* or *single-line scansion;* these convey the same information, and each can be converted to the other. In both kinds of scansion a clear distinction is made between *stresses* and *beats.*

B. *Strong-stress meter*

Strong-stress meter is a form based on four strong stresses per line, divided by the phrasing into half-lines of two stresses each. It usually requires a special mode of performance, and in two major forms, Old English verse and twentieth-century rap, it is characterized by a strongly rhythmic accompaniment. Old English verse also uses extensive alliteration on the strong stresses, and does not settle into an insistent pattern of four beats, nor does it align itself with the 4 x 4 formation.

Chapter 5

Syllable-stress verse: versatility and variation

Stress meter and syllable-stress meter

Consider the differences in the rhythmic movement of the following two stanzas:

(1)   I never thought that my love would leave me
           Until one evening when he came in.
           He sat him down and I sat beside him
           And then our troubles did begin.

(2)   A hot wind presses at my lips.
           I peel. Am totally undressed.
           Pinkish, as though a part-eclipse,
           Heat licks upon my naked breast.

The first stanza is from a traditional ballad, the second is by the modern poet Karl Shapiro; both are 4.4.4.4 duple meter stanzas. In spite of the use of the same basic meter, however, they vary strikingly in their movement (and this difference is one aspect of their different style, tone, and meaning). The first quickly sets up a jaunty rhythm, which encourages us to exaggerate the beats, even when they're on syllables that might not be stressed in prose. There's a tendency, which is easy to emphasize, to make the first and third beats of each line a somewhat stronger beat than the second and fourth, and this helps to bring out the division of each line into two roughly equal parts. The syntax and sense follow closely the hierarchical structure of the 4x4 formation, and the rhyming of the second and fourth lines brings the stanza to a pleasant chiming close. The stanza feels quite close to song, and it's not difficult to imagine a tune for it. In all these respects, it is quite typical of regular stress meter, as discussed in the previous chapter. It is also typical in its presentation of a stock theme – the faithless lover – and its use of common phraseology.

The second example is less easily heard as a metrical form. The beats are not strongly pronounced, and although we can bring out the meter by artificially stressing every second syllable (except the second syllable of "pink-ish"), this does great violence to the language and is far from an acceptable way of performing the stanza. Reading it sensitively means reading it almost as prose, though with more deliberation and with full articulation of all the syllables. There is no temptation to read with a quadruple rhythm emphasizing the first and third beats, and the lines don't divide into equal halves. Although the lines are end-stopped, their relation to one another is not that of the four-line hierarchy, and although every line is rhymed, the rhymes seem less clinching than in the first example. It's difficult to imagine a tune that might turn it into a song. In all these respects, it takes advantage of the particular characteristics of *syllable-stress meter*. In so doing, it is able to present a much more idiosyncratic subject and viewpoint, to draw more fully on the resources of English speech, and to exploit a wider range of vocabulary.

Stress meter, as we saw in chapter 4, is based on the stress-timed rhythm of spoken English – that is, the tendency of stressed syllables to fall at rhythmically equivalent intervals, even when they are separated by differing numbers of syllables. Such verse tends to override the other basis of English rhythm, the procession of *syllables*. Syllables, irrespective of whether they are stressed or unstressed, also have a tendency – though a much weaker one – to take a rhythmic pulse. (In certain other languages, such as the Romance languages, the syllabic rhythm is more pronounced, and enters more fully into poetic meter.) In chapter 2 we used the simple device of emphasizing the syllables in speaking a sentence, as if counting them, in order to bring out the syllabic rhythm that is usually subordinated to the stress rhythm.

The weakness of the syllabic rhythm can be judged from the infrequency of pure syllabic verse in English – verse, that is, which is measured according to the *number of syllables per line*, with no attention being given to the number or placing of stresses. Here's an example from a poem by Thom Gunn about a tattooist; it is written in seven-syllable lines, without any other metrical principle (except for rhymes or half-rhymes that signal the line-ends):

```
(3)     We watch through the shop front while
        Blackie draws stars – an equal

        Concentration on his and
        the youngster's faces. The hand            4

        is steady and accurate;
        but the boy does not see it...
```

Most readers would probably not notice if one of the lines had a syllable more or a syllable less (though the counting of syllables may have been important in the creative process). This fact makes the poem seem a type of free verse, in which the careful deliberateness of the tattooist's work finds expression in the short lines and the tense pauses at the end of many lines.

Yet even though the syllabic rhythm of spoken English is much weaker than the stress rhythm, it does have a distinctive contribution to make. As we have seen, stress verse, in its tendency to override the syllabic rhythm, often requires an emphatically regular reading in order to sustain the meter, pushing it toward chant or song. The beats are very clearly marked, and the distinction between syllables functioning as beats and syllables functioning as offbeats is strongly felt. On the other hand, poetry which allows the syllabic rhythm to emerge, while still controlling the placing of stress, has a markedly different movement. Beats are no longer so central to the experience of rhythm: they are less strongly felt and less clearly contrasted with offbeats. The rhythms of ordinary spoken English are less likely to be altered to produce a chant-like recitation.

Because both syllables and stresses are controlled, this type of meter – which makes up the bulk of the literary tradition of English metrical verse – is called *syllable-stress meter* (or, for the same reason, "accentual-syllabic" meter), and verse which employs it is *syllable-stress verse*. Here's a regular example by John Betjeman, without any departures from the simplest realization of the meter, which we can scan using the conventions already established:

```
      x   /   x   /  x  /  x   /
(4)   In country churches old and pale

      x  /   x  / x   /  x  /
      I hear the changes smoothly rung

      x   /    x / x    / x    /
      And watch the coloured sallies fly

      x  /  x  /   x  / x  /
      From rugged hands to rafters high          4

      x  /  x   /   x  / x   /
      As round and back the bells are swung.
```

Each line has eight syllables, and every second one is stressed, producing a highly regular alternation of offbeats and beats. Though the result is, in one sense, even more regular than stress verse, it is less *powerfully* rhythmic. The beats are not as insistent, since they don't have to dominate the intervening syllables to produce regularity – regularity is already present in the exact alternations between single offbeats and beats. The reader is not induced to mold the pronunciation of the sentence to conform to the meter, since the meter emerges in a normal reading.

Because of its extreme regularity, we might say that the appeal of the verse lies more in its mimetic appropriateness to the"smoothly rung"changes of the bells than to any emotional subtlety. Such exactness of alternation is highly unusual, and the other examples of syllable–stress verse we shall examine in this chapter make use of a number of variations to introduce the tones and timbres of the speaking voice.

One major difference between stress verse and syllable–stress verse is that the latter is not bound to the 4x4 formation to the degree that the former is. Syllable–stress verse is found in a much wider variety of line-lengths and stanza forms; most importantly, a great deal of syllable–stress verse is written in five-beat lines, which are rare in stress verse. We shall discuss the crucial difference between four-beat and five-beat (or more strictly, non-four-beat) lines in the following chapter. In the remainder of this chapter, which is devoted to the characteristics of syllable–stress verse in all its forms, we shall consider examples of both. We shall devote most of our attention to duple verse, which is considerably more common than triple verse, and makes possible the fullest exploitation of the distinctive potential of syllable–stress verse.

Duple syllable-stress meter

1. Beginnings and endings of lines

(a) Heptasyllabic verse

Once the number of syllables in the line is controlled, the beginnings and endings of lines become a significant part of the meter. The freedom that lines of stress verse have to start and end on either a beat or an offbeat, single or double, is absent in syllable–stress verse. In four-beat duple syllable–stress verse, for instance, the core of the line is a sequence of four beats separated by single offbeats. This core can itself be a regular meter, every line of which has seven actual syllables:

```
        /   x   /  x      / x    /    [x]
(5)     Beauty, midnight, vision dies:

        /   x  /   x   /    x    /  [x]
        Let the winds of dawn that blow

        /  x  /    x    / x    /   [x]
        Softly round your sleeping head
```

```
  /  x  /  x   /  x     /   [x]
Such a day of welcome show              4


  /  x    /  x    /    x    /  [x]
Eye and knocking heart may bless...
```

This makes for a very simple, secure meter, with clearly marked line-ends, highly appropriate for the comforting tones of a lullaby. (The extremely regular alternation between stressed and unstressed syllables in this example by W. H. Auden contributes to the song-like effect.) Such verse, which is fairly uncommon, is sometimes called *heptasyllabic verse* (from the Greek prefix hepta-, seven), since it has seven syllables a line. (Rarer still are the equivalent five-beat lines with nine syllables.)

(b) Iambic verse

As the virtual offbeats in the above scansion suggest, heptasyllabic verse is not entirely smooth: line-ends are marked by a pause in the movement of the language (though it is not a pause that introduces any sense of irregularity or tension into the poem). To produce a more smoothly continuous rhythm, an unstressed syllable is needed at this point – either at the end or at the beginning of the lines. It is most often placed at the beginning, to provide an introductory upbeat for the line. The result is the most common arrangement of line-beginnings and endings in syllable-stress meter, in both four-beat and five-beat verse:

```
        x   /    x /    x   /    x  /
(6)     This day, whate'er the fates decree,


        x     /   x /   x    /  x  /
        Shall still be kept with joy by me:


        x   /   x    /  x   x   x  /
        This day then, let us not be told,


        x   /  x    /   x   /   /   /
        That you are sick, and I grown old...



        x  /x    /     x     /    x   x   x /
(7)     In pious times, ere priestcraft did begin,


        x /    x /x x   x    /   x   /
        Before polygamy was made a sin;
```

```
 x   ⌐ x   ⌐ x  ⌐ x  x    x   ⌐
When man on many multiplied his kind,
```

```
 x   ⌐   x ⌐   x   ⌐ x  x   x  ⌐
Ere one to one was cursedly confined...
```

This meter – duple stress meter beginning normally with an offbeat and ending normally with a beat – is known as *iambic meter*, from the Greek word for a unit consisting of a short syllable followed by a long syllable (according to the rules of syllabic length in that language). Hence the type of line in example (6) is known as *iambic tetrameter* and the type of line in example (7) is known as *iambic pentameter*. (Recall that "tetrameter" means a four-beat line or four-beat verse, and "pentameter" means a five-beat line or five-beat verse.)

These are the most flexible and richly exploitable meters in the language. The above examples are unusually regular, the only variations being stressed offbeats (demotion) and unstressed beats (promotion), with which we are already familiar (and which we scan in exactly the same way as in stress verse). They use this regularity for different purposes, however. The first conveys a defiance of the effects of time that is also at the same time a wistful acknowledgment of them, the second strikes an epic pose whose satiric purpose is immediately evident. The shorter lines, drawing on the four-beat tradition, have a gentle lyric quality about them; the longer lines are more expansive, though kept in bounds by the strictness of the meter and the rhyme-scheme.

It is important to specify that this meter "normally" begins on an offbeat and ends on a beat, because other possibilities exist: individual lines may begin on a beat or end on an offbeat. However, these alternative beginnings and endings are sensed as variations from the norm. Beginning on a beat is something that can happen only under certain conditions, which we shall discuss shortly. Lines ending on an offbeat can occur more freely – especially in five-beat verse, in which individual lines have more integrity as independent units than is the case in four-beat verse. Here is an example of iambic pentameter with final offbeats:

```
                                              ⌐  x
(8)     Thus have I had thee as a dream doth flatter:
```

```
                                          ⌐ x
        In sleep a king, but waking no such matter.
```

This type of ending is known as a *duple ending* (and, when it rhymes as it does here, a *duple rhyme*), since it prolongs the duple meter beyond the final beat. It contrasts with the more common *single ending* on a beat. A duple ending produces a weaker finish to the line, in this case appropriate to an expression of disappointment.

It's even possible for an iambic line to end with a beat followed by *two* unstressed syllables, producing a *triple ending*, which momentarily suggests a triple rhythm. This ending – usually in the form of a *triple rhyme* – is very rare and is most often done for comic effect. Here is Byron's response, in his long comic poem *Don Juan*, to the rumor that John Keats's death was brought about by a bad review of his poetry:

(9)   'Tis strange the mind, that very fiery particle,

       Should let itself be snuffed out by an article.

(c) *Trochaic verse*

Much less common than iambic meter, and virtually non-existent in five-beat verse, is a meter that begins normally on a beat and ends normally on an offbeat. The following example also uses promotion and demotion:

(10)   Cruel children, crying babies,

        All grow up as geese and gabies,

        Hated, as their age increases,

        By their nephews and their nieces.

This is called *trochaic meter*, from the Greek name for a unit of long plus short; this example, like almost all trochaic verse, is trochaic tetrameter. It is a very insistent rhythm, encouraging a chanted reading, and hence is not very suitable for most poetry – though as this example shows it's suitable for light verse.

The insistence of trochaic meter can be moderated somewhat by varying between trochaic and heptasyllabic lines:

```
    L   x  L  x   L  x   L  x
(11) Airly Beacon, Airly Beacon;

       L   x   L  x   L     x  L  [x]
       O the pleasant sight to see

       L    x    L     x  L  x  L  x
     Shires and towns from Airly Beacon,

        x    x  L    /    L  x  L  [x]
      While my love climbed up to me!
```

The virtual offbeats help to promote the 4x4 formation, as does most of the stanza's phrasing – except for the run-on from the second to the third line, which pushes the reader past the virtual offbeat marking the end of the major division of the stanza. The effect is to give "see" a feeling of strong anticipation.

(d) Eights and sevens

Four-beat syllable-stress verse is sometimes written in lines that vary in their use of different openings and endings. Milton uses this variable meter to create a light, shifting, somewhat child-like movement:

```
      L  x   x   x  L x   L x
(12)  Zephyr with Aurora playing,

      x   x  L   x  L    x  L x
      As he met her once a-Maying,

       L   x  L  x   L  x    L
      There on beds of violets blue,

      x    L    \   L x  L    x   L
      And fresh-blown roses washed in dew...
```

Here Milton uses two trochaic lines, followed by a heptasyllabic line and an iambic line. Unlike stress verse, however, this meter – sometimes called *eights and sevens*, because of the numbers of syllables – does not use double offbeats (except under strict conditions to be discussed below). Milton thus preserves the syllabic rhythm intact, and keeps at bay the heavier jog of a stress-dominated movement. Notice, however, that the meter is strong enough to encourage the reader to give unstressed beats some additional stress: we are quite likely to read "As he met her once a-Maying" with more emphasis on the first word than would be normal outside verse.

EXERCISE

Beginnings and endings of lines

(1) Scan the following extracts, using the symbols introduced in chapters 3 and 4 for stressed and unstressed syllables, beats, unstressed beats, and virtual beats and offbeats. Name the meter in which each is written, and consider its appropriateness:

(a) Lying, robed in snowy white

     That loosely flew to left and right —

     The leaves upon her falling light —

     Through the noises of the night   4

        She floated down to Camelot.

(b) Oh, Thou, who didst with Pitfall and with Gin

     Beset the Road I was to wander in,

      Thou wilt not with Predestination round

     Enmesh me, and impute my Fall to Sin?   4

     Oh, Thou, who Man of baser Earth didst make,

     And who with Eden didst devise the Snake;

      For all the Sin wherewith the Face of Man

     Is blacken'd, Man's forgiveness give — and take! 8

(c) In the nightmare of the dark

     All the dogs of Europe bark,

     And the living nations wait,

     Each sequestered in its hate;   4

```
Intellectual disgrace

Stares from every human face,

And the seas of pity lie

Locked and frozen in each eye.          8
```

2. Rising and falling rhythms

We noticed in chapter 4 that stress verse is sometimes perceived as having a *rising* or a *falling* rhythm; that is, stressed syllables feel as if they *culminate* (in a rising rhythm) or *initiate* (in a falling rhythm) groups of syllables (each of which is a *stress group*). (See pp. 85–6.) Most syllable-stress verse, like most stress verse, is in a mixture of rising and falling rhythms, and you may not be aware of this feature of rhythm when you read it. However, a meter that begins consistently on an offbeat and ends consistently on a beat – iambic meter – will, all other things being equal, tend to promote a rising rhythm (in which stresses feel as if they culminate groups of syllables); whereas one that begins on a beat and ends on an offbeat – trochaic meter – will tend to promote a falling rhythm (in which stresses feel as if they initiate groups of syllables). For this reason iambic meter is sometimes known as *duple rising meter*, and trochaic meter as *duple falling meter*. The line-ends are more likely to have this effect in shorter lines. We will look at some four-beat examples.

Here is a stanza of iambic tetrameter which begins by strongly support-ing the rising tendency of the meter but, after some varied lines, ends by opposing it. Stress groups are marked, and the sequences of rising (R), falling (F), and mixed or monosyllabic (M) groups are indicated after the line.

```
         |x  ∠ | x  ∠ |x   ∠  |x    ∠ |        RRRR
(13)     I hid my love in field and town

         | x   ∠  | x   ∠  | x      ∠ | x  ∠ |   RRRR
         Till e'en the breeze would knock me down;

         |  x  ∠ | \    ∠ x | ∠ x |∠  |        RMFM
         The bees seemed singing ballads o'er,

         |  x   ∠ | / | ∠   |x ∠x  | ∠ |        RMMMM
         The fly's buzz turned a lion's roar;          4
```

```
|x   ∠ x | / x  | ∠  |x  ∠   |        MFMR
And even silence found a tongue,

| x  ∠    x|∠ |  x  ∠ x | ∠ |        MMMM
To haunt me all the summer long:

| x  ∠  x| ∠ x  | ∠    x | ∠ |       MFFM
The riddle nature could not prove

| x   ∠ x |∠  | x   ∠ x |∠ |         MMMM
Was nothing else but secret love.          8
```

It's clear that in iambic verse a falling rhythm is harder to establish than a rising rhythm, given the fact that lines usually begin with an offbeat and end on a beat. This doesn't mean that a falling rhythm is strained or awkward in iambic verse; all the lines in this extract read smoothly, though with differing qualities of rhythm.

Trochaic meter acts more powerfully to encourage expectations of a falling rhythm, which contradicts the more prevalent rising movement of the English language and, as we noted in chapter 4, has a more rigidly duple character. Here is an example by Edward Lear in which those expectations are largely met:

```
      | ∠ |x  ∠ x | ∠ x  | ∠ x  |      MMFF
(14)    There on golden sunsets blazing,

      |∠  x|∠  x  | ∠    x | ∠ x  |    FFFF
       Every evening found him gazing...
```

But such lines are rare (and a bit mechanical); usually the rhythm modulates to the more common rising rhythm during the line, before it reverts to falling or mixed at the end. Lear's poem again provides an example:

```
      | ∠ |x ∠ |x  ∠    | x  ∠  x   |
(14)    Long ago, in youth, he squandered    MRRM

      |∠ | x  ∠ |x ∠ | x   ∠ x  |        MRRM
       All his goods away, and wandered...
```

Although the effect of the metrical scheme on the rising or falling quality of the line is not very great, it does in part account for the different rhythmic effect of iambic and trochaic verse, and – given the more varied and flexible movement of rising rhythm as well as its conformity to the norms of spoken English – for the widespread preference for iambic meter. It is also part of the reason why these meters are sometimes discussed in terms of *feet*, a topic to which we shall turn later in this chapter.

EXERCISE

Rising and falling rhythms

(2) Scan the following stanzas by Sir Thomas Wyatt, then indicate the stress groups. Count the number of rising (R), falling (F), and mixed or monosyllabic (M) groups in each line. Is the predominant movement rising or falling? What is the effect of any exceptions to the movement?

```
    All heavy minds
    Do seek to ease their charge,
    And that that most them binds
      To let at large.              4

    Then why should I
    Hold pain within my heart
    And may my tune apply
      To ease my smart?             8

    My faithful lute
    Alone shall hear me plain,
    For else all other suit
      Is clean in vain.             12
```

---

3. Beats and offbeats; demotion and promotion

The operation of beats and offbeats in syllable-stress meter, and their rela-tion to the stressed and unstressed syllables of the language, is fundamentally the same as in stress verse. As always, it is crucial to keep the distinction between *beats* and *stresses* clear. Stressed syllables are normally experienced as beats ($\angle$), and unstressed syllables – in duple verse – as single offbeats (x):

```
        x  /   x  /   x  /   x   /
(15)    Disturb no more my settled heart

        x  /x /   x   /    x  /  x  /
(16)    A very little thing, a little worm
```

Secondary stresses functioning as beats may be shown in the scansion if desired ($\searcharrow$):

```
      x    ∠  x  ∖ x ∠  x     ∠ x   ∠
(17)  Most like a monumental statue set

      x ∖ x ∠ x     ∠   x    ∠  x    ∠
      In everlasting watch and moveless woe...
```

Once again, to count the number of beats in a line, we look just at the number of underlinings, irrespective of the symbol which is underlined.

These examples represent a norm from which most lines of syllable-stress poetry diverge. This divergence is achieved by a number of rhythmic variations, some of which we have already examined in discussing stress verse. Demotion and promotion are common in syllable-stress verse, and since there is less pressure from a strong rhythm, *demoted and promoted syllables are usually pronounced as they are in prose.* All that is necessary is a *distinct* pronunciation, allowing each syllable its own rhythmic space. (In stress verse, as we saw, the insistence of the meter often induces us to give demoted syllables less stress and promoted syllables more.) Let us recall that the terms "promotion" and "demotion" refer not to the way we pronounce a syllable, but to the way it relates to the expectations generated by the meter.

Because demoted syllables in syllable-stress verse usually retain their full stress, and promoted syllables remain light, these variations tend to have more effect on the movement of the actual language as we read the lines than they do in stress verse. The stressed offbeats produced by demotion make the line move more slowly and heavily, since the successive stresses require extra energy and take up extra time. In Keats's "Ode to a Nightingale," slow-moving demoted stresses cause the verse to dwell on the dismal picture of the world the poet longs to leave:

```
      x    ∠  x   ∠   x  ∠    /   ∠   /  ∠
(18)  Where palsy shakes a few, sad, last gray hairs,

      x    ∠    /  ∠    x    ∠ x   ∠  x    ∠
      Where youth grows pale, and spectre-thin, and dies.
```

The effect of the stressed offbeats here can be tested by rewriting them as unstressed syllables:

```
       x    ∠  x    ∠   x  ∠   x ∠  x     ∠
(18a)  Where palsy shakes a few remaining hairs
```

The line now moves rapidly to its close, and there is none of Keats's drawn-out pathos.

Promotion, on the other hand, makes the line feel faster and lighter. Whereas in stress verse unstressed beats are often given more emphasis than they would receive in prose, in syllable-stress verse they can be as light as the reader wishes. One of the commonest faults in reading syllable-stress verse is giving too many beats a stress, and thus losing some of the variety and expressiveness of which the meter is capable. If we remember that the stress-pattern is quite distinct from the pattern of beats, we shouldn't make this mistake.

Byron uses promotion extensively in *Don Juan* to lighten and quicken the verse. The tone of the somewhat garrulous narrator encourages the reader to maximize the possibilities of unstressed beats, so that the speaking voice can be heard chattering unstoppably on:

```
          x  x  x  / x    /     x  /   x  /
(19)    'Twas on a summer's day — the sixth of June —

        x  /  x  x  x  / x x  x   /
        I like to be particular in dates,

        x  / x x   x /   x  /    x  /
        Not only of the age, and year, but moon;

        x  x  x  /  x  /   x     x    x  /
        They are a sort of post-house, where the Fates    4

          /    / x   / x   /   x  /   x  /
        Change horses, making history change its tune.
```

Note that we're encouraged to read "post-house" without a secondary stress on the second syllable, thus allowing the following syllable — "where" — to be promoted.

The conditions under which demotion (/) occurs are the same as those which operate in stress verse. The most usual context is *between two stressed beats* (/ / /). These lines from Shakespeare's Sonnet 2 contain three examples, "deep," "proud," and "worth":

```
          x   / x / x    x    x /    x   /
(20)    When forty winters shall besiege thy brow,

        x   /   /    /   x  x   x  /  x   /
        And dig deep trenches in thy beauty's field,

        x   /         /     / x x   x  /   x   /
        Thy youth's proud livery, so gazed on now,
```

```
  x    x x  ⌣  x     ⌣   x   ⌣    /     ⌣
Will be a tottered weed of small worth held.
```

The second common situation is *the beginning of a line before a stressed beat*:

(21)   What wondrous life in this I lead!

```
 /   ⌣   x   ⌣  x ⌣   x  ⌣
Ripe apples drop about my head...
```

The third common situation for demotion that we found in stress verse – in a double offbeat, next to an unstressed syllable – will be discussed separately later, since double offbeats do not occur freely in duple syllable-stress verse. (They occur all the time in *triple* syllable-stress verse, of course, and we shall see that this type of demotion is common there.)

As in stress verse, the stressed offbeat is most often one which is felt to be syntactically subordinated to the one before or the one after. We can show this in the scansion if we wish:

```
       x   ⌣   \    ⌣  x  x   x  ⌣  x   ⌣
(20)  And dig deep trenches in thy beauty's field
```

```
       x   ⌣   \    ⌣    x   ⌣ x   /
(22)  And oak leaves tipped with honey dew
```

In (20), "deep" as an adjective is subordinated to the noun "trenches," and in (22), "leaves" is part of a compound phrase, "oak leaves," which is pronounced like "Main Street" (or as if it were the word "oakleaves"). Even if we pronounce these words with a full stress, the syntax and our metrical expectation make us experience them as weaker. Usually, however, there's no need to show subordination in scansion.

When there is little or no possibility of subordination, the rhythm slows considerably, as the stressed offbeat is experienced with its full weight, and creates pauses before and after it. This effect is less noticeable at the beginning of the line, before the rhythm is underway, but still produces a moment of deceleration and emphasis, as in this frantic appeal by Marlowe's Faustus as he faces damnation:

(23)   Then will I headlong run into the earth:

```
 /       ⌣   x  ⌣ x   x   x  ⌣ x   ⌣
Earth, gape! O no, it will not harbour me!
```

In midline, the effect is more marked, as on "sons" in this characteristic example from one of Browning's dramatic monologues:

(24)   Man goeth to the grave, and where is he?

        x ∠ / ∠ x   x x ∠ / ∠
        Did I say basalt for my slab, sons? Black —

        'Twas ever antique-black I meant! How else

        Shall ye contrast my frieze to come beneath?

The strong demotion helps – with another earlier demotion and a promo-tion – to create for the line the tones of a vigorous speaking voice, shifting in a second from platitudinous moralizing to sharp self-aggrandizement, and only just held within the constraints of the meter.

Here is an example by another metrical extremist – Shelley – where there is both initial demotion and demotion of the second offbeat – and in both cases, the stressed offbeat is not subordinated:

(25)   If it be He, who, gentlest of the wise,

        /   ∠   /   ∠ x   x x / x ∠
        Taught, soothed, loved, honoured the departed one...

The first four words of this line demand very slow phrasing, each taking the same degree of stress. The alternating movement is temporarily suspended, until the second part of the line picks up speed with a promotion before reverting to the norm. In an example as extreme as this, it is something of a fiction to show the beats in the scansion, though probably at some level the mind registers that these are the places where they should fall.

The circumstances under which promotion (x̲) occurs are also similar to those we observed in stress meter. Most commonly, it occurs *between two unstressed syllables* (x x̲ x). Here are four-beat and five-beat examples:

(26)   So runs my dream: but what am I?

        x ∠ x   /x x̲   x ∠
        An infant crying in the night:

        x ∠ x   /x x̲   x ∠
        An infant crying for the light...

(27)   A living man is blind and drinks his drop.

```
     x   /  x  x    x  /   x  x   x  /
```
What matter if the ditches are impure?

Promotion also occurs *at the end of the line after an unstressed syllable*; again, here are four-beat and five-beat examples:

(28)   We passed before a House that seemed

A Swelling of the Ground –

```
     x  /   x    /    x  / x  x
```
The Roof was scarcely visible –

The Cornice – in the Ground –

(29)   And folly, doctor-like, controlling skill,

```
     x   /  x  /   x  /     x  / x x
```
And simple truth miscalled simplicity...

The third situation in which promotion occurs is *at the beginning of the line before an unstressed syllable*. This is a very rare type, since it can only happen in heptasyllabic or trochaic verse, where there is an expectation for an initial beat:

(30)   Phoenix and the turtle fled

```
  x  x  / x   /    x   /
```
In a mutual flame from hence...

In order to preserve the meter, promoted syllables in this position – unusually for syllable-stress verse – may require more stress than they would in prose.

Demotion and promotion allow the poet to achieve a continual variation in the rhythm of syllable-stress verse without disrupting the flow of the alternating meter. Other devices, which we turn to next, are more transgressive of the metrical norm.

EXERCISE

Beats and offbeats; demotion and promotion

(3) Scan the following extract, showing beats (stressed or unstressed) and offbeats (unstressed or stressed). How do the demotions and promotions contribute to the effectiveness of the poetry?

> Come, friendly bombs, and fall on Slough
>
> It isn't fit for humans now,
>
> There isn't grass to graze a cow
>
> > Swarm over, Death!   4
>
>
> Come, bombs, and blow to smithereens
>
> Those air-conditioned, bright canteens,
>
> Tinned fruit, tinned meat, tinned milk, tinned beans
>
> > Tinned minds, tinned breath.   8

(4) Scan this passage from *Romeo and Juliet*. In your scansion, try to reflect the fact that a good actor would probably maximize the use of unstressed beats (i.e., promotions).

But soft, what light through yonder window breaks?

It is the east and Juliet is the sun.

Arise, fair sun, and kill the envious moon,

Who is already sick and pale with grief   4

That thou, her maid, art far more fair than she.

Be not her maid, since she is envious;

Her vestal livery is but sick and green,

And none but fools do wear it; cast it off.   8

It is my lady, O, it is my love!

4. Inversion

Syllable-stress verse makes use of another type of metrical variation, which introduces flexibility into the rhythm and allows poets to use the full range of English words and phrases without adding syllables to the line. It goes by various names in traditional prosody, one of which we shall employ, as it captures an important aspect of its operation: *inversion*.

The following discussion will concentrate on the workings of inversion in iambic verse, by far the most common form of duple syllable-stress verse. (Inversion does occur in trochaic verse, but it is much rarer there – and, as we have noted, trochaic verse itself is much rarer than iambic verse.)

(a) Initial inversion

The least disruptive modification we can make to an iambic line is to drop the first syllable; it is unstressed, and it is outside the main metrical pattern of the line. To do so, however, would be to reduce the number of syllables of the line to reach what I called earlier the "core" of the meter (a possibility in some looser forms of syllable-stress meter, such as Chaucer's, but one that is usually avoided.) But if the missing unstressed syllable is compensated for by an additional unstressed syllable immediately *after* the first beat, the stress pattern x / x / becomes / x x /, and a satisfyingly rhythmic alternative line-opening is created:

(31)   If I have freedom in my love

     And in my soul am free,

     / x   x /   x   /   x /
     Angels alone, that soar above,

     Enjoy such liberty.

The line begins with a stressed beat followed by a double offbeat, and then reverts to the normal alternation of beat and single offbeat. One way of looking at this variation is as a reversal of the usual stressing of the first two syllables, x /, putting the stressed syllable first and the unstressed syllable second, / x. This is why it is called an *inversion*, and since it happens at the beginning of the line, it is an *initial inversion*. It is sometimes useful in scansion to highlight the rhythmic figures produced by inversions (by underlining the appropriate syllables, for instance), since the symbols themselves are no different from the usual ones – it is their combination that matters. In this book, rhythmic figures will continue to be shaded when it is desirable to do so.

Initial inversion is an extremely common variation in iambic verse, even of the strictest kind, and does not significantly increase the complexity of the rhythm. Though its function is often simply to contribute variety to the line-opening, this variation always has a potentially emphatic effect – as in the above example, where it helps to make "Angels" the most prominent word in the stanza, underlining the extravagance of the poet's comparison.

Here is a group of lines with several initial inversions (the stanza is 4.4.4.4.4.4 – that is, the normal 4x4 formation without virtual beats, plus an additional four-beat couplet):

```
         /     x    x  /    /   /    x    /
(32)     But, where the road runs near the stream,

         /     x    x  /    x  /  x   /
         Oft through the trees they catch a glance

         Of passing troops in the sun's beam –

         /  x  x   /    x   /  x   /
         Pennon, and plume, and flashing lance!        4

         /    x   x  /    x   /  x   /
         Forth to the world those soldiers fare,

         To life, to cities, and to war!
```

Here it is in lines 4 and 5 that we feel most strongly the expressive potential of initial inversion: line 4 assertively announces the colorful military spectacle, and line 5 begins with an inversion that increases the emphasis on the adverb "Forth," separated by the entire line from its verb, "fare." There is a slight, but significant, difference between these two inversions: the first involves a single word, "Pennon," whereas the second involves two words, "Forth to." In the first case, there is no way in which the sequence "fully stressed syllable – unstressed syllable" could be moderated; the inversion is consequently strongly felt. In the second case, there exists the possibility of *blurring* the rhythm, that is, of adjusting the stress on the two syllables (making "Forth" quite weak, for instance), and bringing the opening closer to the normal one. Blurring the sharp contours of the alternating rhythm is an important resource in syllable-stress verse, allowing it to tap the movements of speech more fully than stress verse, in which rhythmic blurring is very rare.

If we look at the first four syllables of a line with initial inversion, we see a very clear stress pattern: / x x /. It is this group of four syllables that constitutes the rhythmic figure associated with initial inversion: it stands out from the alternating norm with its own distinctiveness and integrity.

(b) Falling inversion

(i) With virtual offbeat

If an unstressed syllable is omitted after the beginning of a line of syllable-stress verse, the rhythmic alternation is disrupted much more severely. We saw that in stress verse, the absence of an unstressed syllable leads to a pause between the successive stresses which is felt as a virtual offbeat ("Rain, rain, go away"). This is also what usually happens in syllable-stress verse, the pause coinciding with a syntactic break. After the two stressed beats, the loss of a syllable then has to be compensated for by means of a double offbeat. Here are examples in four-beat and five-beat verse:

```
        x  ∠    /    ∠ [x]∠  x  x  ∠
(33)    My horse moved on; hoof after hoof

        He raised and never stopped...
```

```
(34)    The sea lay laughing at a distance; near,

        x ∠ x ∠  x      ∠ [x] ∠   x    x  ∠
        The solid mountains shone, bright as the clouds...
```

Once again, the variation in the regular alternation of stressed and unstressed syllables can be seen as an *inversion*, / x / x becoming / / x x when the middle two syllables are switched. Since the result is one in which two stressed syllables are followed by two unstressed syllables, we term the variation a *falling inversion* on the analogy of falling rhythm in stress groups (though the actual stress groups can vary greatly). But it is not this group of four that is felt as a unit; after the virtual offbeat there is a clearly marked rhythmic figure, beginning and ending with a stressed beat – the same figure produced at the start of the line by initial inversion: ∠ x x ∠. In the examples above, it is realized in the distinct, and distinctive, phrases "hoof after hoof" and "bright as the clouds." (Compare these with the initial inversions "Pennon and plume" and "Forth to the world.")

The only place where a falling inversion is very rare is the *end of the line*. The following rewritten example is not experienced as a full five-beat line, even though the scansion makes it look acceptable.

```
       x   /   x / x   /   x       /  [x] /   x  x
(34a)  The grand, majestic mountains shone, cheerfully
```

The rhythmic figure that begins after the break does not arrive at its final stressed beat, and the line lurches to an unsatisfactory close.

(ii) Without virtual offbeat
Sometimes a falling inversion occurs without a syntactic break between the successive stressed beats, and the result is a different rhythm and a different figure:

```
(35)   That light we see is burning in my hall.

       How far that little candle throws his beams!

       x   /   x  /   /   x  x  /   x  /
       So shines a good deed in a naughty world.

       x  /   /     x  x   / x  /   x   /
(36)   My heart aches, and a drowsy numbness pains

       My sense, as though of hemlock I had drunk...
```

Although the same inversion of a sequence of stressed and unstressed syllables occurs, the rhythmic movement of these lines is quite distinct from that of examples (33) and (34). We can highlight this difference by rewriting one of these lines to create a virtual offbeat:

```
       x   /    x   /  [x]/   x   x    /   x  /
(35a)  So shines the deed, goodness in spite of all
```

When the two stresses are syntactically linked (as in [35] and [36]), there is no strong sense of a virtual offbeat, and the second beat does not fall so unmistakably on the second stress. Once again, we can say that the alternating rhythm is momentarily *blurred*, and the clear-cut distinction between beats and offbeats loses its edge. However, the syllabic rhythm is maintained, and with it the sense of metrical order. (Poets usually do not allow a single word to occupy the middle two syllables of the / / x x figure without a virtual offbeat, as this would prohibit any blurring.)

When a falling inversion without a virtual offbeat is used, there is a distinct increase in *tension*, as the rhythm of the words pulls away from the expected metrical pattern. The stressed words usually gain in emphasis, while their emotional or mimetic force is often enhanced. The closer the syntactic link between the stressed syllables, the greater the tension; and if there is any tendency for the first to be subordinated to the second, it is necessary to read with particular care to ensure that they both receive a full stress. If this is not done, the line will slip into a four-beat meter with a triple swing, as indicated in the following scansion:

```
         x   /   x  \   /   x  x  /   x  /
(35)     So shines a good deed in a naughty world
```

Falling inversion is fairly uncommon in pentameter verse, except in the form of initial inversion (which is simply a falling inversion that occurs at the beginning of the line). Apart from initial inversion, it occurs most frequently with a syntactic break between the stresses to produce a virtual offbeat. It is even less common in tetrameter verse, where it is a highly disruptive presence. But for all its infrequency, it has remained for centuries an indispensable part of the rhythmic repertoire of the poet writing in syllable-stress verse, providing unexpected shifts of movement with expressive and emphatic potential.

EXERCISE

Falling inversion

(5) Scan the following lines from Milton's *Paradise Lost*, which describe the Archangel Gabriel's search for Satan in the Garden of Eden. Mark the instances of falling inversion. How do they contribute to the forcefulness of the account?

```
So saying, on he led his radiant files,

Dazzling the moon; these to the bower direct

In search of whom they sought: him there they found

Squat like a toad, close at the ear of Eve;              4

Assaying by his devilish art to reach

The organs of her fancy, and with them forge

Illusions as he list, phantasms and dreams...
```

(c) Rising inversion

We have seen how a falling inversion functions by the omission of an unstressed syllable between stresses which is later compensated for by the addition of an unstressed syllable. The reverse sequence is also possible: an additional unstressed syllable is followed later by the loss of an unstressed syllable.
(In stress meter, of course, adding an unstressed syllable merely produces a
double offbeat, and has no further repercussions.) This means that a double
offbeat in syllable-stress verse is always followed by two successive stressed
beats. The normal stress pattern x / x / becomes x x / /; that is to say, a
stressed and a following unstressed syllable change places to produce a *rising
inversion*.

This is a very common variation in iambic verse in any part of the line,
and you will meet it much more frequently than falling inversion (discount-
ing initial inversion). In this type of inversion, there is usually no syntactic
break and no virtual offbeat between the stresses. Example (37), in four-
beat meter, has two rising inversions; example (38), in five-beat meter, has
one rising inversion, at the end of the line; and example (39), also in five-
beat meter, has three rising inversions.

(37)   Annihilating all that's made

        x x /̣   /̣   x x /̣   /̣
        To a green thought in a green shade.

(38)   Thou still unravish'd bride of quietness,

            x /̣ x /̣   x /̣ x   x   /̣ /̣
            Thou foster-child of silence and slow time...

        x   /̣   x   /̣   x x   /̣ ·/̣   x /̣ x
(39)   And there, that day when the great light of heaven

        Burned at his lowest in the rolling year,

        x   x /̣   /̣   x x /̣   /̣   x   /̣
        On the waste sand by the waste sea they closed.

Although rising inversion is the mirror-image of falling inversion, it provides a very different rhythmic experience. Two unstressed syllables (usually

of equal lightness) lead into a stressed beat and then another, equally strong
or even stronger, stressed beat. The alternating rhythm is challenged and
then restored, the movement is speeded up and then slowed down. The
words containing the stressed beats usually stand out as emphatic. The rhythmic figure produced is x x ⁄ ⁄, with the second stress functioning as the
climax of the group. Marvell's famous line from "The Garden" – example
(37) above – is simply two of these figures in succession.

Whereas in the first type of inversion we discussed the poet has to avoid
the subordination of the first stress to the second, here it is just this subordination that helps to keep the rhythm smooth by blurring the distinction
between beat and offbeat. We therefore seldom find this figure with a syntactic break between the stresses, which would usually mean a weaker second stress (subordinated to a later stress). Pope manages to get away with it
in the following example by ensuring that both the stressed syllables carry
the same weight (they are adjectives qualifying the same noun). The syntactic break allows for a virtual offbeat, unusually for rising inversion, and
produces a distinctive rhythmic figure:

(40)   Then mount the clerks, and in one lazy tone

    x   x ⁄ [x] ⁄ x ⁄ x ⁄ / ⁄
Through the long, heavy, painful page drawl on...

The purpose of Pope's metrical feat is clear: the rhythm gives us a taste of
the clerks' excruciating drone.

As is the case with falling inversion without a virtual offbeat, many poets
avoid the use of disyllabic words in the middle of a rising inversion. Those
who do not avoid them produce lines that have a high degree of rhythmic
tension, and the words in question are strongly emphasized:

(41)   All whom war, dearth, age, agues, tyrannies,

Despair, law, chance hath slain, and you whose eyes

    x   x ⁄   ⁄   x   ⁄ x ⁄   /   ⁄
Shall behold God, and never taste death's woe.

(42)   As clear as elemental diamond,

x x ⁄   ⁄ x   ⁄   x   ⁄ x ⁄
Or serene morning air; and far beyond,

The mossy tracks made by the goats and deer...

There is no way in which these examples of rising inversion can be read with the first of the two stresses weakened in a blurring of the beat–offbeat alternation; the disruption to the meter is unavoidable. Notice, however, that these strong disruptions *suspend* the meter for a short period rather than creating a different meter. Many poets writing in five-beat duple meter allow such suspensions but avoid variations that threaten to turn the line into four-beat stress verse.

EXERCISE

Rising inversion

(6) Scan the following stanza of Arnold's "The Scholar-Gipsy," and mark the rising inversions. What is their function in the verse?

```
Screen'd is this nook o'er the high, half-reaped field,

  And here till sundown, shepherd! will I be.

    Through the thick corn the scarlet poppies peep,

And round green roots and yellowing stalks I see        4

    Pale pink convolvulus in tendrils creep;

      And air-swept lindens yield

Their scent, and rustle down their perfumed showers

  Of bloom on the bent grass where I am laid,           8

    And bower me from the August sun with shade;

And the eye travels down to Oxford's towers.
```

(d) Demotion in double offbeats

In stress verse, as we saw in chapter 4, one of the commonest positions for the demotion of stressed syllables is in *double offbeats*, with one stressed and one unstressed syllable instead of two unstressed syllables, producing the rhythmic figures ∠ x / ∠ and ∠ / x ∠. An example is the word "caught" in this line of stress verse:

```
        x   x   ∠     x  ∠    /     x ∠     x   ∠
(43)    From their sighs the wind caught a mournful tone
```

Here "caught" is a demoted stress (assuming a certain degree of emphasis on "wind"). Is demotion possible in the occasional double offbeats allowed in duple syllable-stress verse?

The answer is yes, though much more frequently in falling inversion than in rising inversion. Demotion of the second syllable of the offbeat in initial inversion is very common, even in the strictest meter, giving a rhythmic figure already familiar from triple verse, ∠ x / ∠ (which is just a variant of the common figure ∠ x x ∠). In the following examples, "quick" and "strong" are demoted – which, of course, doesn't mean that they need be weakened in pronunciation but that we *feel* them as less prominent than the stress that follows:

```
(44)    How woulds't thou shake at Britain's modish tribe,

        ∠    x   /     ∠       x   ∠     x  ∠     x   ∠
        Dart the quick taunt, and edge the piercing gibe?
```

```
        ∠    x   /      ∠   x ∠    x  ∠  x   ∠
(45)    Form a strong line about the silver bound,

        And guard the wide circumference around.
```

There is not a great deal of tension here, but the variation does contribute a liveliness to the opening of the line. Of course, the more the demoted stress is felt to be syntactically subordinated to the following stress, the smoother this variation is. It most frequently occurs in the form found in these two examples, that is, a monosyllabic adjective followed by a noun, in which the subordination is clearly felt.

Less common is demotion on the *first* syllable of the offbeat, producing the rhythmic figure ∠ / x ∠ (also familiar from triple verse, and also a variant of / x x /). Here is an example in four-beat verse:

```
          ∠     / x      ∠      x  ∠   x    ∠
(46)    - Pass, banners, pass, and bugles, cease;

        And leave our desert to its peace!
```

The rarity of this type of demotion is easy to explain: it relies on the subordination of a stress to a *preceding* stress, and this doesn't happen very often in English. In the above line it is the strong repeated stress on "pass" that potentially weakens the stress on "banners."

These figures also occur on rare occasions within the line; as we would expect, they are most likely to happen when a syntactic break replicates the conditions at the beginning of the line. In the following examples, "dark" and "soft" are demoted stresses, which gain emphasis as a result of the momentary tension they produce:

(47)   See there that boy, that murthring boy I say,

```
    x    x    x    ∠  [x] ∠   x    /    ∠    x    ∠
    Who  like a    thief,  hid  in  dark bush doth lie...
```

(48)   ...the pregnant earth

```
    x    ∠    x    ∠    x    ∠  [x] ∠    x    /    ∠
    And  all  her  tribes rejoice.  Now  the  soft hour
```

    Of walking comes...

Demotion in rising inversion (/ x ∠ ∠) is much less frequent, though it can happen at the start of a line:

(49)   Light quirks of music, broken and uneven,

```
    /         x    ∠    ∠    x ∠ x ∠  x ∠ x
    Make the  soul dance  upon a jig to heaven...
```

Here it is only the relative weakness of the first stress compared with the third that yields this rhythm. If it seemed appropriate to stress "Make" strongly, we would have the more usual initial inversion with demotion:

```
    ∠         x    /    ∠    x ∠ x ∠  x ∠ x
    Make the  soul dance  upon a jig to heaven
```

Fortunately for readers, the tricky task of interpreting these complex figures does not have to be performed consciously – though to become conscious of them is to enhance one's appreciation of the contribution made by rhythm to the immense variety of English poetry.

EXERCISE

Demotion in double offbeats

(7) Scan the following stanza from Shelley's "Adonais." Which lines require demotion in a double offbeat in order to sustain the iambic meter? To what extent do syntax and meaning co-operate with this need?

> Out of her secret Paradise she sped,
>
> Through camps and cities rough with stone, and steel,
>
> And human hearts, which to her aery tread
>
> Yielding not, wounded the invisible   4
>
> Palms of her tender feet where'er they fell:
>
> And barbèd tongues, and thoughts more sharp than they,
>
> Rent the soft Form they never could repel,
>
> Whose sacred blood, like the young tears of May,   8
>
> Paved with eternal flowers that undeserving way.

5. Free double offbeats

Syllable-stress meter can be used with varying degrees of strictness. Not only may a particular line be regular or irregular, depending on the variations it employs, but a particular poem, poet, or age will often have a characteristic kind and degree of strictness. The strictest syllable-stress verse adheres rigidly to the fixed number of syllables per line, even avoiding duple endings, and makes use only of the least disruptive variations. Some verse allows occasional duple endings and the more disruptive variations, while still observing the syllable count. And some verse takes liberties with the syllable count, while freely using variations as well. Of course, to loosen up syllable-stress verse beyond a certain point turns it into something else: either stress verse (if it is four-beat, and conforms to the conditions for strict stress verse) or a kind of free verse.

Because of the power of the stress rhythm in English, the adding of a single unstressed syllable to a line of syllable-stress verse does not unduly disturb the duple meter. It is least noticeable when the double offbeat is divided by a syntactic break, as in this example:

```
         x   /   x   /  x   x   /   x /   x   /
(50)    What youthful mother, a shape upon her lap

        Honey of generation had betrayed...
```

The added syllable does cause a momentary ripple in the steady rhythm, as we realize if we rewrite the line without it and listen to its more regular movement:

```
         x   /   x   /  x      /   x /   x   /
(50a)   What youthful mother, child upon her lap
```

We call double offbeats of this kind *free double offbeats*, since they are not bound by the conditions that are observed by the strictest syllable-stress meter; that is to say, they don't occur in conjunction with two successive stresses in an inversion.

6. Elision

When, in syllable-stress verse, we encounter what appears to be a free double offbeat that is *not* divided by a syntactic break, it is important that we take account of the possibility that one of the syllables can be *elided*. In chapter 2, we noted that some syllables in English are optional, depending on pronunciation. Words such as "previous," "flowering," "traveler," and "battery," for instance, can have two or three syllables. In most cases, the elisions encountered in poetry are no different from the elisions we tend to make in our own speech, though occasionally they reflect older pronunciations. One important fact to note about elision is that, unlike demotion and promotion, it requires a specific pronunciation in reading verse. It is, however, almost always a pronunciation that comes naturally.

Sometimes elision is marked in poetry by means of an apostrophe, in which case the reader's task is easy: "wand'ring," "vet'ran," "Heav'n." The apostrophe may represent an older pronunciation – often a pronunciation which died out in normal speech but survived much longer in poetry, such as "o'er" with one syllable in place of "over," or "'tis" for "it is." Some poets and editors use an apostrophe even for syllables that we would not consider elided, such as "liv'd" or "detain'd." What this usually means is that if such words are printed *without* an apostrophe they are to be given the older pronunciation with an additional syllable: "lived" as two syllables, "detained" as three. Others show this distinction by adding an accent mark when the syllable is to be pronounced: "livèd," "detainèd."

Most often, elision is not marked on the page. Being able to read verse with the appropriate elisions is a valuable skill, and it is partly just a matter of practice. Most elisions happen very easily when the verse is read with the right rhythm, and most of the time readers aren't even aware what they are doing when they elide a syllable. (Since elided syllables are always unstressed, they are prone to being squeezed by the stress-timed rhythm of English anyway.) It should be noted, too, that there is no absolute dividing line between a full syllable and an elided syllable: often all that is required is that a syllable lose a certain proportion of its duration and energy. The result is close to a double offbeat, and it imparts a momentary quickening to the rhythm. You can try reading the elided syllables in the following examples with different degrees of fullness to test the effect.

Most of these examples of the three different types of elision are taken from one poem, Pope's "Epistle to Bathurst," written in iambic pentameter with strict observation of the syllable count. The lines are given here without apostrophes marking elisions. In scansion, we show elision by a hyphen or short dash (–) above the syllable that is most likely to lose its syllabic status. (Sometimes both syllables lose part of their weight, in which case the symbol should go above the first.) In these examples, the five beats of the line are shown, together with the elided syllable and the adjacent offbeat.

(a) Two vowels in succession (whether in one word or two) slurred together:

(51)   Builds life on death, on change duration founds,

    ∠   – x ∠   ∠   ∠   ∠
And gives the eternal wheels to know their rounds.

The scansion indicates a pronunciation something like "th'eternal." Another example:

(52)   Who suffer thus, mere charity should own,

    ∠   ∠   ∠ – x   ∠   ∠
Must act on motives powerful, though unknown...

If "powerful" is to be pronounced with three syllables, as it sometimes is, the "w" has to be present; if it disappears, the two vowels can be slurred together and the word becomes disyllabic. Other examples of the slurring of vowels in this poem are "the Elect" ("th'Elect"), "the unwilling" ("th'unwilling"), "to enjoy" ("t'enjoy"), "towers," "bower" (both of which lose the "w" and slur the two vowels), and "diamond" ("di'mond"). In all these examples, the elided vowel need not completely disappear for the rhythmic effect of elision to be felt.

(b) An "i" pronounced as a "y," or a "u" pronounced as a "w." Here is an example of the first:

```
       ∠        ∠         ∠ -x   ∠       ∠
(53)   What Nature wants, commodious gold bestows,

       'Tis thus we eat the bread another sows.
```

In this line, the vowel "i" in "commodious" can be read as the semivowel "y," giving it two instead of three syllables, "commod-yus." We put − over the "i" to show that it is not functioning as a syllable in the meter. Other examples in the "Epistle to Bathurst" are: "happier" ("happ-yer"), "congenial" ("congen-yal"), "valiant" ("val-yant"), "Indian" ("Ind-yan").

The same kind of elision can happen *between* words:

```
       ∠         ∠      ∠ - x  ∠     ∠
(54)   The world had wanted many an idle song
```

Treating the phrase "many a" or "many an" as two rather than three syllables is very common in English poetry; again it involves converting the "i" sound with which the word "many" ends into a "y," by running it into the next word: "men-ya."

The pronunciation of "u" as "w" is rarer; the following example comes from a different poem:

```
        ∠   ∠  -x    ∠      ∠       ∠       ∠
(55)   And in huge confluent join at Snow Hill Ridge,

       ∠          ∠ -x   ∠    ∠      ∠
       Fall from the conduit prone to Holborn Bridge.
```

Here "confluent" and "conduit" are pronounced something like "conflwent" and "condwit."

(c) A vowel dropped before a consonant (usually within the same word):

(56)   No, 'twas thy righteous end, ashamed to see

 $\angle$ $\angle$ - x $\angle$ $\angle$ $\angle$
Senates degenerate, Patriots disagree...

Many words have an optional syllable like the third one of "degenerate." Other examples in this poem are "embroidery" ("embroid'ry"), "general" ("gen'ral"), "scrivener" ("scriv'ner"), "Heaven" ("Heav'n") – this was a normal pronunciation for a long period), "Devil" ("Dev'l" – also a common pronunciation), "different" ("diff'rent"), "unopening" ("unop'ning").

It's important to realize that what we're dealing with here are *elidable* syllables: whether or not they're actually elided in any particular example depends on what the meter requires. All the examples above could appear in contexts in which elision is not appropriate. The word "avarice" appears in both contexts in Pope's poem:

         $\angle$ x $\searcharrow$ $\angle$ $\angle$ $\angle$
(57)   Poor avarice one torment more would find;

Nor could profusion squander all in kind...

         $\angle$ $\angle$ $\angle$ $\angle$ - x $\angle$
(58)   Congenial souls! Whose life one avarice joins,

And one fate buries in the Asturian mines.

Pope writes the strictest type of syllable-stress verse, so that if there is an additional unstressed syllable in the line we *have* to take advantage of the opportunity offered by elision to reduce two syllables to one, or else we will distort the meter. In looser styles of syllable-stress meter, however, the reader often has a choice. Consider the following line by Wordsworth:

(59)   And chattering monkeys dangling from their poles

If this had been in a poem by Pope, we would have no choice but to elide the middle syllable of "chattering":

         x $\angle$ - x $\angle$ x $\angle$ x   x   x $\angle$
(59)   And chattering monkeys dangling from their poles

But since Wordsworth is a poet who occasionally allows free double offbeats (where elision is impossible), we could, if we preferred, keep the syllable in our pronunciation:

```
      x     /  x x    / x    /  x     x    x    /
(59)  And chattering monkeys dangling from their poles
```

We might feel that the sound being referred to is caught more fully in the version that has a double offbeat.

How do we know if the verse is strictly syllabic, calling for elision in order to avoid free double offbeats? We may already have a good idea of whether the poem is likely to be one or the other; the poetry of the Augustan period, for instance, is usually strict, whereas much Romantic and modern syllable-stress meter is not. But when in doubt, it is only by reading a long-ish stretch of verse that you can tell: if *all* the apparent free double offbeats can be elided by one of the normal procedures, then it's very likely that the poet expected them to be. If some of them are unelidable, then it is clear that the poet is allowing lines with extra syllables, and that elision is optional.

EXERCISE

Free double offbeats and elision

(8) These lines are by Yeats, whose verse does not always observe a strict syllable count. Scan them without any elisions, putting in parentheses any of the syllables in free double offbeats that lend themselves to elision. How would you choose to read this verse?

```
Mere dreams, mere dreams! Yet Homer had not sung

Had he not found it certain beyond dreams

That out of life's own self-delight had sprung

The abounding glittering jet; though now it seems    4

As if some marvellous empty sea-shell flung

Out of the obscure dark of the rich streams,

And not a fountain, were the symbol which

Shadows the inherited glory of the rich.             8
```

(9) These stanzas are by Samuel Johnson, written in a period when we would expect a strict observance of the syllable count. Scan them, showing all the elisions.

```
When fainting Nature called for aid,

  And hovering Death prepared the blow,

His vigorous remedy displayed

  The power of art without the show.          4


        . . .


His virtues walked their narrow round,

  Nor made a pause, nor left a void;

And sure the Eternal Master found

  The single talent well employed.            8
```

7. Emphatic stress

We saw in chapter 2 how the neutral stress pattern of a spoken sentence is often varied by the use of emphatic phrasing, either to make a particular word the focus of the sentence or to bring out a contrast. To read a poem well is, among other things, to be sensitive to the placing of possible emphases. Emphatic stress usually falls on syllables that would be stressed in any case, making no difference to the actual metrical organization of the line and not requiring any indication in the scansion. However, there are two circumstances in which emphatic stress can be important: (a) when it falls on a function word that would normally not be stressed, and (b) when it causes a *neighboring* stress to be subordinated.

Such a change in stress-pattern can have a number of possible effects. It can turn a line that would otherwise be *unmetrical* into a *metrical* line; it can turn a relatively *complex* line into a *simple* one, metrically speaking; or it can turn a *simple* line into a more *complex* one. Very occasionally, poets write lines in which emphatic stress turns a *metrical* line into an *unmetrical* one – in which case the reader has to make some kind of compromise in performing the line. Let us look at some examples.

(a) Unmetrical to metrical

The following line from Shakespeare's Sonnet 42, if read in isolation, appears to be metrically irregular, given our tendency to stress the verb ("hast") rather than the pronouns ("thou," "her"):

(60)   That thou hast her, it is not all my grief

In its context, however, it invites contrastive stress on both pronouns; the speaker is regretting that the man he loves – who is being addressed – and the woman he loves have become sexually involved. Here is the opening quatrain, with italics added to show the contrasts:

```
            x    ∠   x    ∠   x   x̱   x   ∠    x   ∠
(60)    That thou hast her, it is not all my grief

        And yet it may be said I loved her dearly;

            x    ∠  x    ∠  x   x̱   x   ∠  x      ∠
        That she hath thee is of my wailing chief,

        A loss in love that touches me more nearly.
```

The third line of the quatrain has an identical pattern of stresses, contrasting "thou" and "her" in the first line with "she" and "thee."

(b) Complex to simple

The third line in the following example, also from a sonnet by Shakespeare, may at first seem a complex variant of the iambic pentameter. But if we give contrastive stresses to "this" and "that" and to "art" and "scope," as the sense requires, it becomes a quite simple metrical sequence (again, italics have been added):

(61)   Wishing me like to one more rich in hope,

        Featured like him, like him with friends possessed,

            x ∠ x   ∠ \   ∠ x   ∠ \   ∠
        Desiring this man's art and that man's scope...

What happens is that the unemphatic, repeated word "man's" is subordinated, and is easily felt as demoted. Rewriting the line so that the contrasts occur differently, we produce a more complex line with two rising inversions:

```
          x ∕ x      x    ∕  ∕  x     x     ∕  ∕
(61a)   Desiring this high art and these low jokes
```

(c) Simple to complex

In the next example, the poet himself has indicated an emphatic stress on the first "both"; this subordinates the following stress and produces a *more* complex line than would otherwise have been the case:

```
          x   x̲  x    x   ∕   ∕      x  ∕  x   ∕ x
(62)    Now was it that both found, the meek and lofty

        Did both find helpers to their hearts' desire...
```

Without the italicization, we would probably read the line with two promotions:

```
          x   x̲  x   x̲   x    ∕       x  ∕  x   ∕ x
        Now was it that both found, the meek and lofty
```

(d) Metrical to unmetrical

There are rare occasions when an emphatic stress has even more disruptive consequences for the meter. Thus the contrast between the audience and the speaker in Prospero's epilogue at the end of *The Tempest* threatens, by subordinating the stresses on either side of "me," to produce a highly disruptive falling inversion at the end of the line (italics have been added):

```
(63)    As you from crimes would pardoned be,

          x   ∕  x ∕ x     ⟍  ∕  ⟍
        Let your indulgence set me free...
```

But fortunately it is possible to emphasize a syllable like this by means of pitch alone, so that all three words can be given the same degree of energy and a normal demotion can occur:

```
                         ∕  /  ∕
        Let your indulgence set me free
```

As all these examples show, emphatic stress is one of the places where the reader's responses to the meter and to the meaning of a poetic line are inseparable.

EXERCISE

Emphatic stress

(10) Scan the following lines, which open Donne's poem "The Flea,"
paying particular attention to emphatic stress:

Mark but this flea, and mark in this,

How little that which thou deniest me is;

Me it sucked first, and now sucks thee,

And in this flea our two bloods mingled be.

---

8. Reading and scanning duple syllable-stress verse

We have now discussed all the ways in which lines in the main body of
English literary verse may deviate from the regular alternation of unstressed
single offbeats and stressed beats: demotion, promotion, inversion (falling
and rising), and the use of free double offbeats and elision. Different peri-
ods, different poets, different poems use different combinations of these to
produce the extraordinary array of styles, moods, and patterns to be found
in this metrical tradition. And the reader who has grasped these few variations is in a position to analyze the possibilities of rhythmic movement
inherent in any line.

What are the conditions that have to be met for a line to be experienced
as duple syllable-stress meter, to conform, in other words, to the metrical
norm of the most common type of metrical verse? There are only three:
(1) All the beats must be either *stressed syllables* or *unstressed syllables occurring
in one of the contexts that allow promotion*, and all the offbeats must be either
unstressed syllables or *stressed syllables occurring in one of the contexts that allow
demotion*. (See section 3, "Beats and offbeats; demotion and promotion,"
above.)
(2) Every *double offbeat* must be either (a) preceded by *a stressed beat that opens
the line* or (b) preceded by or followed by *two successive stressed beats*. (See
section 4, "Inversion," above.)
(3) Every occurrence of *two successive stressed beats* must be preceded or followed by *a double offbeat that is not at the end of the line*. (See section 4,
"Inversion," above.)

These conditions recapitulate the relevant parts of the discussion above, and they can easily be reworded to apply to other meters, or to more narrowly defined meters. Freer iambic meter also allows a few double offbeats that do not meet condition (2) (sometimes only at a syntactic break). Trochaic meter does not observe condition (2a), which allows for initial inversion, though it may have its own equivalent condition. The number of beats in the line and the way lines open and end may also be controlled.

It is true that there are, in the large body of English duple verse, a number of lines that do not conform to this model. But the significant point is that we *experience* such lines as deviant, as pulling away from the expected movement or as difficult to perform. And it is by examining the ways in which they depart from the expectations built into the tradition that we can come to understand their particular qualities. Scansion is a technique whereby we heighten our awareness of the distinctive rhythm of a poem; it shows either that a given line conforms to a metrical norm, with a greater or lesser degree of complexity in realizing it, or that it departs from metricality at certain points. Every sensitive reading of verse implies a certain scansion; and becoming skilled at scansion increases one's ability to read the diverse body of English poetry with understanding and pleasure.

EXERCISE

Duple syllable-stress verse

(11) Examine the following scansion of a passage of iambic pentameter verse by Shelley that has been rewritten in places. As a result of the rewriting, some lines are highly irregular. Identify the irregular lines, and say in what ways metrical expectations are not met. Then say whether the scansion correctly shows this irregularity, or whether it misleadingly suggests that the line is regular. (The exercise requires that you examine apparent instances of demotion, promotion, and inversion to check whether the conditions for these variations have been met, that you count the beats in the line, and that you test whether any alternative meter is more insistent than the iambic pentameter.)

```
 /   x   x  / x   /    x  /   x  /
Nor where the tropics bound the realms of day

 x  x  /   /  x  /  x   /   x    /
With a broad belt of mingling cloud and flame,

  x   /  /     x   x  x  / x   x  /
Where blue mists through atmospheric displays
```

```
    ∠ x     x  ∠   x   ∠  x x    x   ∠
Scattered the seeds of pestilence, and fed          4

x  ∠ x    ∠ x ∠ x      ∠    x ∠ x    ∠
Unwholesome vegetation, where the aching land

  ∠    x    /    ∠   x     ∠ x   x   x ∠
Teemed with storms, earthquake, tempest and disease,

  x  ∠ x  ∠  x  /x      ∠ x x
Was Man a nobler being; slavery

  x   ∠    x  ∠ x  x  ∠   x   ∠
Had crushed him into his country's dust;            8

x  ∠ x   ∠ x    x  ∠  x   x  ∠
Or he was bartered for fame and for power,

  x   ∠  x ∠ x ∠ x  x   x  ∠ x
Which all internal impulses destroying,

  x     ∠    ∠  x  /   ∠ x x   ∠   ∠
Makes man's will a prized item of free trade;

x  x  x   ∠    x    ∠ x   x   x   ∠
Or he was changed with Christians for their gold,  12

x   ∠ x   x  ∠ x   x ∠ [x] ∠   x  x  ∠
And carried to distant domains, where to the sound

x   x   ∠  ∠  x   ∠    x ∠   x ∠
Of the flesh-mangling scourge, he does the work

x  ∠   x  ∠ x   / x x x    ∠
Of all-polluting luxury and wealth.
```

(12) Scan the following lines from Book 1 of *The Ring and the Book*, Browning's long novel in verse. Next to the lines, note all occurrences of demotion, promotion, inversions (initial, falling, rising), and free double offbeats. Mark elision with – and virtual offbeats with [x]. Where appropriate, take account of additional emphasis demanded by the sense and of subordinated and secondary stresses. Comment on any lines that seem to be at the limits of metricality. How does Browning's use of a constantly varying meter contribute to the sense of an animated speaking voice? Are there any mimetic or expressive effects in the rhythm?

The speaker has just bought an old book at a market stall in Florence.

That memorable day,

(June was the month, Lorenzo named the Square)

I leaned a little and overlooked my prize

By the low railing round the fountain-source   4

Close to the statue, where a step descends:

While clinked the cans of copper, as stooped and rose

Thick-ankled girls who brimmed them, and made place

For marketmen glad to pitch basket down,   8

Dip a broad melon-leaf that holds the wet,

And whisk their faded fresh. And on I read

Presently, though my path grew perilous

Between the outspread straw-work, piles of plait   12

Soon to be flapping, each o'er two black eyes

And swathe of Tuscan hair, on festas fine:*

Through fire-irons, tribes of tongs, shovels in
  sheaves,

Skeleton bedsteads, wardrobe-drawers agape,   16

Rows of tall slim brass lamps with dangling gear, -

And worse, cast clothes a-sweetening in the sun:

None of them took my eye from off my prize.

*festas: feast-days

Triple syllable-stress meter

In syllable-stress verse the poet has to choose, as the basis of the meter, between separating the beats of the line by one syllable or separating them by two syllables; that is, between duple meter and triple meter. There is no possibility of moving between these options in the same line, as there is in stress verse (except in so far as syllable-stress verse allows double offbeats in inversions and the occasional free double offbeat). The vast majority of syllable-stress poems are in duple meter, but a number of poets have chosen to write in triple meter, with its very noticeable rhythmic lilt.

In this century, triple meter has become associated with light verse, though it did not always have these connotations. Triple syllable-stress meter is scarcely distinguishable from triple stress meter, since in both forms the triple meter establishes a powerful rhythm that tends to fall into the four-beat formation and to override the normal pronunciation of the words. Because the number of syllables is controlled in syllable-stress verse, however, all the lines in a poem will begin and end in the same way. Usually the lines end on a beat, but they may begin on a single offbeat, a double offbeat, or a beat. In example (64) the lines start on a double offbeat and end on a beat; in example (65) they start on a single offbeat and end on a single offbeat:

```
        x    x ∠ x  x   ∠    /      x  ∠ x   x ∠
(64)    At the corner of Wood Street, when daylight appears,

        /   x   ∠   x  /   ∠  x  x  ∠   x
        Hangs a thrush that sings loud, it has sung for

            /  ∠
            three years...


        x   ∠  x  x ∠ x  x ∠   /   x   ∠ x
(65)    Oh, talk not to me of a name great in story;

          x ∠ x  x   ∠  x   x ∠  x  x   ∠ x
          The days of our youth are the days of our glory...
```

As these examples indicate, demotion in the double offbeats of triple verse is very common and, provided that the stress in question is subordinated to a stress on one side of it, does not perturb the regular rhythm. We're tempted, as in stress verse, to pronounce the demoted syllables as if they were actually unstressed:

```
        x    x    /    x    x    /    x    x    /    x
(64)    Hangs a thrush that sings loud, it has sung for

        x    /
        three years
```

This is one of the problems of triple meter: a poet trying to draw on the expressiveness of the spoken language finds that the powerful metrical movement tends to override the rhythms of natural speech. We could certainly mark the stress as secondary, though it's important to remember that the stress marks in scansion indicate the *prose* stressing of the sentences (or one possible prose stressing); they do not reflect what may happen when the sentences are chanted.

Sometimes the stress in question is a little more resistant to being demoted, causing the regular meter to undergo a moment's strain:

```
(66)    Or is it only the breeze, in its listlessness

        ∠ - x    x  ∠    x  /  ∠    x  x  ∠
        Travelling across the wet mead to me here...
```

In this line, "wet," although it is syntactically subordinated to the following noun, demands some attention from the reader because of its meaning, and we therefore do not mark it as secondary. If we allow it this attention, the rocking rhythm set up by the poem steadies for a moment, making the word stand out all the more effectively.

EXERCISE

Triple syllable-stress verse

(13) Scan the following stanza by Thomas Moore. To what extent do you find the natural stressing of the words going against the rhythm of the meter?

```
Dear Harp of my Country! in darkness I found thee,

The cold chain of silence had hung o'er thee long,

When proudly, my own Island Harp, I unbound thee,

And gave all thy chords to light, freedom, and song!
```

Foot-scansion

Syllable-stress meter, as the main type of meter used in English literary verse, is the basis for a method of scansion that differs from the one we are using in this book. It is a method with a long history, deriving from the scansion of Latin verse (itself derived from the scansion of Greek verse) as it was taught in the schools of Great Britain for centuries. We have been using names for different meters (iambic pentameter, trochaic tetrameter, etc.) drawn from this tradition. In initially getting to grips with the working of rhythm and meter in English it is probably best not to be concerned with foot-prosody, but since this system of scansion is widely used in criticism of poetry and offers a set of agreed terms for the analysis of the main tradition of syllable-stress verse, there is much to be gained from understanding its terms.

When verse is written in strict iambic or trochaic meter, it is possible to divide each line into two-syllable units which for the most part have the same stress pattern. In the following iambic pentameter lines, the majority of the units have the pattern x /:

```
         |x   /      |x  /  |  x    / |x    x |  x   /|
(67)     Announced by all the trumpets of the sky,

         |x  /  |  x    /  |x       /|x   /  |  x  /    |
         Arrives the snow, and, driving o'er the fields,

         |  x     /|  x    x|x  /   |  x   /|x  /  |
         Seems nowhere to alight: the whited air

         | /    /  |x    /    |  x  /|x    x  |  x  / |x
         Hides hills and woods, the river, and the heaven,4

         |x    /  |  x  /  |  x    x |  x  / |x     /  |
         And veils the farm-house at the garden's end.
```

These repeated units are called *feet*, a term taken, like most of the terms used in this approach, from classical prosody. (Feet should not be confused with stress groups; the former are an indication of the *meter* while the latter are an indication of the speech rhythm.)

Stress verse, with its variations in numbers of syllables between beats, does not lend itself easily to foot-prosody, and nor do some of the types of syllable-stress meter that we have looked at – heptasyllabic verse, eights and sevens, and many kinds of triple verse. It is what we might think of as the major tradition of literary syllable-stress verse that is most amenable to foot-analysis (though not without problems that have produced lengthy debates).

Among its advantages are the provision of a number of technical terms that
can be used economically to describe the stress-pattern of lines of syllable-
stress verse and the rising or falling tendency of certain meters. Among its
disadvantages are the failure to indicate clearly the position of beats, the
introduction of metrical divisions which may play no part in our experience of the verse, the driving of a wedge between stress meter and syllable-
stress meter, the tendency to obscure the role of rhythmic figures larger than
the foot, and the tendency to overvalue the distinction between rising and
falling rhythm. Foot-prosody brings with it the danger – not avoided by
some eminent commentators on verse – of developing elaborate accounts
of poetic lines, or finding tricky problems in metrical analysis, on the basis
of units that are more of a theoretical convenience than an experiential
reality.

   The principles of foot-scansion are simple. An iambic pentameter without any variations is made up of five *iambs*, or *iambic feet*:

| x / | x / | x / | x / | x / |

Here is a scanned line:

```
|x     /   |  x   / |x     /  | x     /|x   / |
```
(68)   And touch the stubble-plains with rosy hue

An unvaried trochaic tetrameter is made up of four *trochees*, or *trochaic feet*:

| / x | / x | / x | / x |

This is an example:

```
|  / x | /    x  | /    x|/  x |
```
(69)   She is gone, and loves another

   Variations are handled by means of *substitution*: the expected foot is
replaced by a different foot. We shall confine ourselves to iambic verse in
the following examples, in which the substitute feet are in bold type. Promotion is registered as the substitution of a *pyrrhic* foot – two unstressed
syllables (x x) – for the normal iamb (x /):

```
|  x   /  |x     / |x    x| x   / | x   / |
```
(70)   When faith is kneel**ing by** his bed of death

```
|x  / |x    /   | x     /|x    / | x  x |
```
(71)   Of beechen green, and shadows numb**erless**

Demotion, similarly, is treated as the substitution of a *spondee* – two stressed syllables (/ /) – for the basic iamb (x /):

```
      |  x  /|x    /  | /    / |x /   |  x  / |
(72)    The lowing herd wind slowly o'er the lea
```

```
      |/     /   |x / |x    x |  x   /  |
(73)    Eight times emerging from the flood
```

Inversion is handled in different ways, according to whether the inversion crosses the foot-boundary or not. Falling inversion is regarded as the substitution of a trochee (/ x) for an iamb (x /), whether within the line or at its start:

```
      |  /    /  |x    /  | /  x  | x  / | x x
(74)    Things base and vile, holding no quantity,
```

```
      | /   x  | x   /  | x  / |x    / |x x|
        Love can transpose to form and dignity...
```

Showing rising inversion – the more common type of inversion in English poetry – involves substitutions in two feet, a pyrrhic (x x) and a spondee (/ /). The foot-divisions obscure the fact that this variation (like falling inversion) is also produced by reversing the expected position of a stressed and an unstressed syllable.

```
      | /      /|x    /  |x  x | /     / |x    /  |
(75)    Love's stories written in Love's richest book
```

Again, when demotion occurs in the double offbeat of an inversion, the appropriate foot is shown. Here is the most common type:

```
      | /   x| /    /  | x   x| /     /|x    /  |
(76)    Pluck the keen teeth from the fierce tiger's jaws
```

As these examples suggest, foot-scansion does not accurately reflect the degree of metrical tension or disruption in a line.

Triple verse in syllable-stress meter can be divided up into feet as well; it does this most easily when line openings and endings allow the same feet to be shown throughout the line. The following is a line divided into *anapests*, or *anapestic feet* (x x /):

```
      |x      x   /  | x   x    / |x        x / | x   x /   |
(77)    And the tents were all silent, the banners alone
```

The following lines are made up of *dactyls*, or *dactylic feet* (/ x x):

```
      |  /    x  x| / x x|
(78)    Cold inhumanity,
```

```
      |  /   x    x  |/ x x|
        Burning insanity...
```

But other common triple meters are not so easily reduced to feet. The
following line could be scanned as dactylic or anapestic, in both cases with
an extra stressed syllable:

```
      |/   x    x|  /  x    x  | /     x    x| /
        /  |x    x  /| x    x   /   |x    x /    |
(79)    Under the blossom that hangs on the bough
```

And the following could be anapestic with a missing first syllable, or dactylic
with an initial extra offbeat and an extra stressed syllable at the end, or even
amphibrachic (feet of x / x), with a missing last syllable:

```
        x    /    x   x   / x   x    / x   x     /
(80)    I sprang to the stirrup, and Joris, and he
```

The common demotions in triple verse also pose problems for foot-
scansion. To take an example quoted earlier, the second line here has substitute feet in three places, thanks to demotions:

```
(64)    At the corner of Wood Street, when daylight
          appears,
```

```
      |  /    x    /  | x   /     /   |x   x   /  | x
        Hangs a thrush that sings loud, it has sung for
```

```
          /   /   |
        three years...
```

The basic anapest (x x /) is replaced once by / x / and twice by x / /. We
would have to ransack the Greek dictionary to find names for these feet –
though the rhythm of the line is simple and strong. Notice, too, that scansion in terms of feet does not indicate the most significant feature of the
metrical line: where the beats fall. (This may occasionally be useful in syllable-stress verse, when the meter is blurred to the extent that the reader does

not perceive sharply defined beats.)

Foot-scansion is not really suited to syllable-stress triple verse, which, as we've seen, is never very far from stress verse. It is most appropriate for five-beat verse, and those forms of four-beat verse that avoid strong rhythms: in other words, it reflects the syllabic rhythm that tends to be overridden in strongly regular meters but that is of crucial importance in the bulk of English literary verse. But it does so at the cost of masking the fundamental operations of English rhythm.

EXERCISE

Foot-scansion

(14) Scan the following passage by showing feet, as in the examples above. Name the normal foot, and the substitute feet that replace it:

```
Fly, fly, my friends! I have my death wound - fly!

See there that boy, that murthring boy I say,

Who like a thief, hid in dark bush doth lie,

Till bloody bullet get him wrongful prey.          4

So tyrant he no fitter place could spy,

Nor so fair level in so secret stay,

As that sweet black which veils the heavenly eye:

There himself with his shot he close doth lay.     8
```

Summary

This chapter surveys the major types and features of syllable-stress verse. The main points can be summarized as follows:

A. Duple verse

Beginnings and endings

These are significant in syllable-stress verse, as they determine the type of meter. The most important duple meters are as follows:

Heptasyllabic meter is a four-beat meter that regularly begins and ends on a beat.

Iambic meter is a meter that normally begins on an offbeat and ends on a beat (with exceptions noted below). It promotes a *rising rhythm* in the line. *Iambic tetrameter* is four-beat iambic meter; *iambic pentameter* is five-beat iambic meter (see chapter 6 on these meters). A *single ending* is an ending on the beat; a *duple ending* is an ending with a beat plus a single unstressed syllable; a *triple ending* is an ending with a beat plus two unstressed syllables.

Trochaic meter is a meter that normally begins on a beat and ends on an offbeat. It almost always occurs in four-beat meter. It promotes a *falling rhythm* in the line.

Variations and rhythmic figures

The following variations of the basic alternation of stressed beats and single unstressed offbeats are possible:

Demotion and promotion function as in stress verse (/ / /, and / / at the beginning of the line in iambic verse; x x x, x x at the end of the line in iambic verse, and x x at the beginning of the line in trochaic verse).

Inversion occurs when the stressing of a pair of syllables is reversed (/ x becomes x / or x / becomes / x). In *falling inversion* (/ / x x), two stressed beats are followed by a double offbeat. When the stressed beats are separated by a syntactic break, which is usual, the rhythmic figure / x x / follows a virtual offbeat. When they are not, the rhythmic figure produced is / / x x. Falling inversion is especially common at the beginning of the line, where it is called *initial inversion* and always produces the rhythmic figure / x x /. In *rising inversion* (x x / /), a double offbeat is followed by two stressed beats, usually not separated by a virtual offbeat. It is least disruptive when the first beat is weaker than the second.

Demotion in the double offbeats produced by inversion occurs most commonly on the second offbeat syllable of a falling inversion with a virtual offbeat, producing the rhythmic figure / x / /. It sometimes occurs on the first offbeat syllable of the same type of inversion, / / x /. In rising inversion, demotion is very rare (/ x / / or x / / /).

Free double offbeats, which add a syllable to the line, occur in looser styles of syllable-stress meter, often at a break within the line.

Elision is often used to avoid a double offbeat, by (1) slurring two vowels together; (2) pronouncing a vowel ("i," "u") as a semivowel ("y," "w"); or (3) dropping a vowel before a consonant. The stricter the metrical style, the more appropriate it is to elide what would otherwise be free double offbeats.

B. *Triple verse*

Triple verse in syllable-stress meter is not clearly distinguishable from triple verse in stress meter; it is almost always in four-beat verse, and may begin and end on a beat, a single offbeat, or a double offbeat.

Chapter 6
Major types of syllable-stress verse

The immense metrical richness of the English poetic tradition has in part been made possible by the variations which occur within lines of syllable-stress verse: demotion, promotion, inversion, free double offbeats and elision. We examined these in the previous chapter, together with the variety introduced by rising and falling rhythms and the distinctive qualities of duple and triple verse. But we have not yet considered the contribution made by the different line-lengths and groupings of lines that can be used in syllable-stress verse. We shall consider some of the most important of these in this chapter.

Four-beat verse

Four-beat syllable-stress meter is most often divided into stanzas, although it can be used in continuous forms as well (couplets or, rarely, unrhymed lines). The stanza forms are for the most part the same as those used in stress verse, based on the doubling architecture of the 4x4 formation. These stanzas usually employ syntactic structure to assist in producing metrical structure, thus bringing out the hierarchical quality of the rhythm and sometimes giving it a quadruple movement (see the discussion of quadruple verse in chapter 4).

When the line-divisions coincide with the four-beat units, the result is tetrameter verse. The commonest form of tetrameter is, as we have seen, *iambic tetrameter*: duple four-beat lines that normally begin on an offbeat and end on a beat. The word "tetrameter" can refer either to the meter ("This poem is in iambic tetrameter") or to a line of that meter ("The poem begins with an iambic tetrameter"). Here is an example of a regular iambic tetrameter quatrain (known in the classification of hymns as "long measure"), rhyming *aabb* and syntactically organized to bring out the hierarchical arrangement of the 4x4 formation:

```
          x  ⌐    \      ⌐   x   ⌐  x   ⌐
(1)    The mill-stream, now that noises cease,
```

```
x  /    x   x   x   /   x    /
Is all that does not hold its peace;

/  x    x   /   x   /  x    /
Under the bridge it murmurs by,

x    /   x    /   x    /   x    /
And here are night and hell and I.
```

Notice that the first and third lines are internally divided by syntax at the expected midpoint, but the second and fourth are more continuous. In the last line this continuity contributes to the shock effect of the word "hell," slipped in without any disruption in the rhythm to call attention to it, and so imbued with an ironic potency.

Virtual beats occur as frequently in four-beat syllable-stress verse as they do in stress verse, and in the same places. (However, since syllable-stress verse is rhythmically less insistent than stress verse, virtual beats are usually not as strongly felt.) The commonest form with virtual beats, as in stress verse, is the 4.3.4.3 stanza (known as "common measure" in the classification of hymns, and "fourteeners" when occurring in the form of seven-beat couplets):

```
       x   x   x   /    x   x   x    /
(2)    It was not Death, for I stood up,

       x   /   x  /   /   /    [x /]
       And all the Dead, lie down –

       x   x   x   /    x   /   x  /
       It was not Night, for all the Bells

        x  /    x    /      x   /  [x /]
       Put out their Tongues, for Noon.
```

As usual, the syntax helps to confirm the 4x4 movement: the major break of the stanza occurs at the end of the second line; there are somewhat weaker breaks at the ends of the first and third lines; and there are distinct syntactic breaks halfway through the first and third lines. In the 4x4 formation, the first and third lines are more likely to be run-on, since they have a weaker metrical closure and no virtual beat at the end; line 3 is a good example. Although virtual beats at the ends of lines two and four are so common that they seldom have any special poetic effect beyond their contribution to the strong and simple rhythm, Emily Dickinson here makes skillful use of the momentary pauses to let the surprising information resound.

Other common forms of the 4x4 formation include the 3.3.4.3 stanza, which has the same pattern of beats as the limerick. It is known as "poulter's measure" when set out as six-beat and seven-beat couplets and as "short measure" in the classification of hymns. Another variant is the 3.3.3.3 stanza; in addition, three-beat lines can be used continuously. There are also many stanza forms which extend the four-line unit, or which use half-lines to vary the meter. One common variant is the Burns stanza, which splices two half-lines into the quatrain:

```
       /      L  x    L  x     L  x     L  x
(3)    Wee, sleekit, cow'rin', tim'rous beastie,

       L    x  x  L x    x    x    L  x
       O, what a panic's in thy breastie!

         x   L   x   L   x L  x   L  x
       Thou need na start awa sae hasty,

                 x   L  - x     L  x
                 Wi' bickering brattle!                4

       x  x   x   L    x  L x     L     x
       I wad be laith to rin an' chase thee

                 x   L  x    L  x
                 Wi' murd'ring pattle!
```

The rather domineering rhythm of the 4x4 formation is interrupted by the half-lines, which prevent the hierarchical doubling from taking place across the whole stanza and inject the qualities of a speaking voice into the verse.

Strict trochaic verse is much rarer than iambic verse. Somewhat more common is heptasyllabic verse, and the two are often mixed in 4.3.4.3 stanzas:

```
       L  x L  x   L  x    L   [x]
(4)    Out upon it, I have loved           (heptasyllabic)

          L   /   L   x L  x   [L x]
       Three whole days together;          (trochaic)

       x   x   L   x   L    /   L  [x]
       And am like to love three more,     (heptasyllabic)

       x  x   L   /    L  x  [L x]
       If it prove fair weather.           (trochaic)
```

The lines are all clearly demarcated by virtual beats and offbeats; and the rhythm has a springiness especially suited to ironic and light-hearted topics.

As we've seen with stress verse, four-beat lines can be combined to make longer lines, or divided into shorter lines. The meter of the following example, from Poe's "The Raven," has eight beats per line, but it's easy to feel the division after four beats. (In the first, third and fourth lines, in fact, it is emphasized by a syntactic break and internal rhyme.)

```
       /    x /  x  / x        / x    x   x / x        /
(5)    Once upon a midnight dreary, while I pondered, weak

       x    /  x
       and weary,

       / x    / - x   /    x      / -x    / x   x   x / x
       Over many a quaint and curious volume of forgotten

        /
       lore -

       /   x / x    /   x / x      /  x  x   x    /
       While I nodded, nearly napping, suddenly there came

       x  /  x
       a tapping,

       / x   /   x    /  x / x      / x   x   x   / x
       As of some one gently rapping, rapping at my chamber

        /   [x]
       door...
```

One effect of this eight-beat line is that we are encouraged to emphasize the second level of the hierarchy of beats – that is, to give additional stress to the first, third, fifth, and seventh beats. This brings out the quadruple tendency of the four-beat movement discussed in chapter 4. We thus make of the four lines a kind of 4.4.4.4 stanza. The result is a highly rhythmic movement, which tends to force out of the poem the inflections of speech or the subtleties of thought, and replace them with a mesmeric metrical drive. Lines that slightly resist this movement (like line two in this extract) draw attention to themselves.

It's possible to bring out the quadruple rhythm even more noticeably than this. Here's an example by Browning in which the stronger beats are the second, fourth, sixth, and eighth of each line. (The scansion shows the primary and secondary beats by double and single underlining, and the stronger and weaker stresses by slash and backslash. Promotion is shown in the usual way.)

```
         \       /       \       /     x       /
(6)     Here you come with your old music, and here's all

            /       /
        the good it brings.


           /         /       \       /       x
        What, they lived once thus at Venice where the

           /       x       /
        merchants were the kings,


           x         /         x       /   \       /
        Where Saint Mark's is, where the Doges used to wed

              /       /
        the sea with rings?
```

Notice that the weaker beats sometimes have no stress, sometimes second-ary stress, and sometimes full stress, whereas the stronger beats all have full stress. Browning does not sustain this clear distinction in every line of the poem, because the rhythm is very insistent once it has been initiated, and he can play speech-rhythms against it in a bravura manner (not inappropriate to the poem's subject, the eighteenth-century Venetian composer Baldassare Galuppi).

Instead of combining four-beat lines into longer lines, poets sometimes divide them into half-lines:

```
        x   /  x   /
(7)     With serving still

        [x] /   x   x  /
          This have I won:

        x   x  x   /
        For my good will

           x   x x  /
           To be undone.     4


        x   x   x  /
        And for redress

        x   /   x  /
           Of all my pain,
```

```
    x  /  x  x
    Disdainfulness

    x  /  x /
    I have again.    8
```

In this expression of the spurned lover's anguish, the fragmented rhythm is able to hint at the comforting contours of the familiar 4x4 pattern while at the same time registering a distance from them. Although we usually don't show a virtual offbeat before an initial inversion, it seems appropriate in line two of this poem, since the first two lines are so closely connected.

When tetrameter verse is written in continuous couplets (*aabbccdd...*), it often gravitates toward four-line units which echo the 4x4 formation we are so familiar with. The poet can, however, use syntax and sense to produce a more flexible meter. Tetrameter couplets are often used for comic verse, in which the slight doggerel effect of the short line and the rhymes is all to the purpose:

```
          /     /  x   /  x   /  x   /
(8)       Now, this is Stella's case in fact;

      x  /  x    /   x /  x   /
      An angel's face, a little cracked

        x     /x  x  x    /  x    /
      (Could poets or could painters fix

      x  /  x   /  x    /  x /
      How angels look at thirty-six);      4

         /    /  x / x   /     x /
      This drew us in at first, to find

      x   /  x  /  x  / x    /
      In such a form an angel's mind.
```

The more strongly the poet opposes the 4x4 hierarchy by means of run-on lines and semantic groupings that counter its preferences, the more the movement of the verse takes on the qualities we associate with the iambic pentameter. This is the topic we shall turn to next.

EXERCISE

Four-beat verse

(1) How does the following stanza – from Herrick's "To Music, to Becalm His Fever" – exploit the 4x4 formation? Mark the beats (actual and virtual), and arrange the poem into four-beat lines. What is the effect of the run-on lines produced by the printed layout of the poem?

```
    Charm me asleep, and melt me so

       With thy delicious numbers;

    That being ravished, hence I go

       Away in easy slumbers.            4

         Ease my sick head,

         And make my bed,

    Thou power that canst sever

       From me this ill:                  8

       And quickly still

       Though thou not kill

          My fever.
```

Resisting the four-by-four formation

One way of classifying English metrical verse is into verse that falls into the 4x4 formation and verse that doesn't. Although the second category is only negatively defined, the distinction is a valid one because of the peculiar force and constant temptation of the four-beat movement. As we saw in chapter 3, this metrical form derives its strength from a multi-leveled architecture, with beats receiving varied degrees of reinforcement from their participation in rhythmic sequences of different lengths. It is a powerful rhythm quite apart from its embodiment in language, and as readers of verse we find ourselves falling into it whenever the words allow us to do so. Poets – known and anonymous – have used it for a variety of effects in a vast array of verse across the centuries.

Verse which does not fall into the 4x4 formation, therefore, can be thought
of as resisting it by some means or other. Such verse, because of its avoid-
ance of the infectious swing of doubled beats, has a less insistent rhythm and
is more open to the tones and movements of the spoken voice. It progresses
in a more line-by-line fashion, since its metrical units are not so completely
part of larger units. We have already noted that syllable-stress verse – especially in iambic meter – is further from the strong rhythms of song and
closer to the rhythms of speech than stress meter, and is therefore less fully
susceptible to the 4x4 movement. A way of further reducing the four-beat
swing is to counter the hierarchic structure by means of sense and syntax.
The first stanza of the following poem by W. H. Auden uses grammar and
meaning to reinforce the 4x4 formation as it presents the ugly logic of early
lessons in mistrust, while the second stanza deviates from the expected structure as it represents the nightmare of the adult's life:

```
          /    x   /  x  /    x    / x
(9)       Once for candy Cook had stolen

          /  x   / x      x   x /
          X was punished by Papa;

          /   x /      x    / x    /      x
          When he asked where babies came from,

          /  x   /    x  x   x /
          He was lied to by Mama.                          4


          /    x  / x    /    x    /  x
          Now the city streets are waiting

          x  x  /   x   x    x  /
          To mislead him, and he must

          /  x /   x  / x      /  x
          Keep an eye on ageing beggars

          /     x    /    x  x   x  /
          Lest they strike him in disgust.                8
```

The insistence of the 4x4 formation can also be reduced by the use of
metrical variations, as in this stanza by W. B. Yeats:

```
        ∠   x   x   ∠   x  ∠ x        ∠
(10)    She that but little patience knew,

        x    ∠  x   ∠   x   ∠   x   ∠
        From childhood on, had now so much

        x  ∠  /   ∠  x   ∠   x      ∠
        A gray gull lost its fear and flew

        ∠   x  x   ∠   x      ∠   x ∠
        Down to her cell and there alit,          4

        x     ∠  x  ∠    x   ∠   x      ∠
        And there endured her fingers' touch

        x    x̲   x   ∠  x   ∠   x     ∠
        And from her fingers ate its bit.
```

Here, Yeats chooses a four-beat iambic meter (with some of the common variations), and uses run-on lines (especially the strong run-on of "flew/ Down") and a six-line stanza rhyming *abacbc* that works against the usual *aabb* or *abab* schemes of the 4.4.4.4 stanza. The result still has something of a lilt to it, but it doesn't encourage any kind of chanted reading. (See also example 2 in chapter 5 [p.97], which, in addition, breaks the line internally at irregular places.)

Another way of resisting the 4x4 formation is to use line-lengths that don't allow the insistent rhythm to impose itself. This can involve using a variety of lines in a single stanza (or in a more random arrangement), provided that the result is not one of the variants of four-beat verse with virtual beats — such as 4.3.4.3 or 3.3.4.3 — or a variant that combines or divides these lines — such as 7.7, 6.7, 2.2.3.2.2.3, or 3.3.2.2.3. (The tradition of the *ode* is one in which varied line-lengths are often used.) Many poets over the centuries have devised stanza forms with varied line-lengths, and these often exploit the familiar rhythm of the four-beat unit without being caught up by the simple movement of the 4x4 formation. Here is a stanza by Henry Vaughan that includes four-beat lines, but in which the variety in line-lengths works against the inclination of those lines to form a hierarchical rhythm.

```
        ∠          ∠      ∠         ∠
(11)    A ward, and still in bonds, one day

               ∠    ∠
        I stole abroad;
```

     /   /   /   /
It was high spring, and all the way

    /   /   /
Primrosed and hung with shade;   4

    /   /   /
Yet it was frost within,

       /   /
And surly winds

   /   /   /   /
Blasted my infant buds, and sin

      /   /   /
Like clouds eclipsed my mind.   8

Although this example is made up of the types of line that are commonly found in four-beat stanzas (two-beat, three-beat, and four-beat lines), they don't form a structure which can be read with a 4x4 rhythm – in other words, we're not encouraged to experience virtual beats filling out the meter to produce a sense of four-beat units. At most, we get intimations of that pattern, which is never fully present. The feeling is of expressive flexibility, as we are never quite sure how long the next line is going to be, which suits the open-ended narrative of the poem. Poets have invented thousands of different stanza forms like this, often shifting toward and away from the 4x4 formation.

If, on the other hand, the poet wishes to use the same line-length consistently and keep from slipping into the 4x4 formation, the choices are rather few. Two-beat lines (*dimeters*) will tend to form into pairs to produce a four-beat rhythm; four-beat lines themselves are ruled out; seven-beat lines tend to fall into a 4.3.4.3 pattern and eight-beat lines into a 4.4.4.4 pattern. (Of course, in all these cases the four-beat rhythm can be resisted by the use of run-on lines, internal line-breaks in unexpected places, and stanza forms that counter the expected hierarchy.) Three-beat lines (*trimeters*) are more promising: although they sometimes imply a fourth virtual beat, they can be used with run-on syntax and varied rhyme-schemes to keep the insistent rhythm at bay. Here is Auden in light-hearted mood:

         /   /   /
(12)   Be patient, solemn nose,

       /   /   /
Serve in a world of prose

      /   /   /
The present moment well,

       /   x   /
Nor surlily contrast   4

     /   /   /
Its brash ill-mannered smell

      /   /   /
With grand scents of the past.

To indicate that these lines do not have the rhythm of the 4x4 formation, we show no virtual beats.

Six-beat lines (*hexameters* or *alexandrines*) also have some of the self-sufficiency of five-beat lines, and have been used from time to time in English verse.

      /   /   /   /   /
(13)   I sought fit words to paint the blackest face of

   /
woe,

  /   /   /   /   \   /
Studying inventions fine, her wits to entertain:

   /   /   /   /   /
Oft turning others' leaves, to see if thence would

  /
flow

   /   /   /   /   /
Some fresh and fruitful showers upon my sun-burned

  /
brain.

These lines tend, however, to break into two halves, partly because of the lurking inclination to slip into a four-beat rhythm by introducing virtual beats. This encourages a slightly sing-song movement. The six-beat line is more often used as a variant in continuous five-beat verse, where it doesn't slide toward the four-beat rhythm and can be useful for variety or closure.

The line which most successfully resists, by its very structure, being assimilated to the 4x4 formation, and therefore into the hierarchical layering, is the five-beat line, the pentameter. Although some of the effects associated with the pentameter are also possible in verse using other line-lengths, or a variety of line-lengths, it is so central a meter in the English tradition that it requires special attention in any account of English poetic rhythm.

EXERCISE

Resisting the 4x4 formation

Six-beat Iambic.

(2) Scan the two following extracts. How do they avoid falling into a 4x4 formation?

← elision

(a) Our brains ache, in the merciless iced East winds that

knive us...

Wearied we keep awake because the night is silent...

Low, drooping flares confuse our memory of the salient...

Worried by silence, sentries whisper, curious,

nervous,   4

But nothing happens.

(b) The forest ended. Glad I was   *Consistent*

To feel the light, and hear the hum   *tetrameter,*

Of bees, and smell the drying grass   *rhythm,*

And the sweet mint, because I had come   *But each*

But each line division,

To an end of forest, and because   4

Here was both road and inn, the sum

Of what's not forest. But 'twas here

They asked me if I did not pass   8

Yesterday this way. "Not you? Queer."

"Who then? and slept here?" I felt fear.

Iambic pentameter

1. Constraints on five-beat verse

Resistance to the simplest and strongest rhythmic pattern, and consequent openness to more speech-like rhythms, lies at the heart of the five-beat line's special character, and helps to explain its widespread use in literary verse (and its virtual absence in popular verse, which tends to prefer more salient rhythms). The five-beat line does not occur with all the variety that the four-beat line does, and we shall begin by examining some of the constraints upon its use.

(a) Five-beat lines are almost always written in *syllable-stress meter*. Since they do not participate by virtue of their structure in the hierarchy of pairs that gives four-beat verse such force and firmness, they need the continuous stabilization provided by a metrical form that controls every syllable; without this control, they easily begin to sound formless. Here is an example of four-beat stress verse discussed in chapter 4 (example [4]), first in its original form and then rewritten with an additional beat per line to produce five-beat stress verse. Compare the way the two stanzas move:

(14)   Had I the store in yonder mountain
         Where gold and silver are had for counting,
         I could not count for the thought of thee,
         My eyes so full I could not see.

(14a)   Had I the store in the cave of yonder mountain
         Where precious gold and silver are had for counting,
         I would not be able to count for the thought of thee,
         My eyes so full I would scarcely be able to see.

The swing of the four-beat rhythm is gone, but the shifts between single and double offbeats prevent the meter from settling into a clear alternative pattern:

```
    x  /  x  /  x   x  /  x  /  x  /  x
    Had I the store in the cave of yonder mountain

    x    /  x   /  x   /  x  x   /   x  /  x
    Where precious gold and silver are had for counting,

    x  /   x   x /  x  x  /    x   x  /    x   /
    I would not be able to count for the thought of thee,

    x /   x  /  x  x     /   x  x / x  x  /
    My eyes so full I would scarcely be able to see.
```

This is certainly a possible meter, and it has been used by poets in the twentieth century, but it lacks many of the special qualities of the long tradition of five-beat verse in English, notably its combination of tight syllabic control with a free-ranging employment of the tones and movements of English speech.

(b) Five-beat meter is also almost entirely restricted to *duple meter.* Triple verse, like stress verse, encourages insistent emphasis on the beats, and falls naturally into the 4x4 formation; it is not suited to five-beat lines. Notice how the lines in this example of five-beat triple verse (example [21] of chapter 4 rewritten with an additional beat per line) seem to go on too long:

(15)
```
Says the master one morning to me, "Is it true, I am
 told
That your name on the membership books of the Union
 enrolled;
I can never allow that a regular workman of mine
With those wicked disturbers of peace should so
 quickly combine."
```

(c) Not only is five-beat verse almost always in duple syllable-stress meter, it is almost always in *iambic meter*, starting regularly on an offbeat and ending on a beat (with the usual allowable variations). This means that there is essentially one type of five-beat verse, the iambic pentameter. This was the most widely used meter in English poetry from the late sixteenth century to the early twentieth century – the meter which Chaucer chose for most of *The Canterbury Tales*, Spenser for *The Faerie Queene*, Shakespeare for his plays, Milton for his epics, Pope for virtually all his verse, Wordsworth for *The Prelude*, Browning for *The Ring and the Book*, and Yeats, Frost, and Stevens for many of their most substantial poems.

Here is an example of iambic pentameter:

(16)
```
x   ∠  x ∠     x  ∠   x   x̲   x  ∠
Of little use the man you may suppose,

  x  ∠   x   ∠     x  ∠ x   ∠  x   ∠
Who says in verse what others say in prose;

 x  ∠   x   ∠   x ∠x    x̲   x    ∠
Yet let me show, a poet's of some weight,

x      ∠   x  ∠ x    ∠  x  x̲   x  ∠
And (though no soldier) useful to the State.
```

Duple syllable-stress meter and the five-beat line are perfectly matched here; the language is quite definitely metrical, yet the intonations and rhythms of speech are strongly present. The lines can be read with just sufficient rhythmic heightening to bring out the organization of the meter, but without giving any additional stress to the unstressed syllables functioning as beats ("may," "of," "to"). This is not to say that the iambic pentameter is in some absolute sense "better" than other meters, just that for certain poetic purposes (for instance, drama in verse that aims for a certain expressive naturalism) it is more suitable. Once it became established as the pre-eminent meter for large-scale literary verse, of course, it acquired a set of associations which later poets were able to exploit, or work against.

(d) All the beats in five-beat meter have to be *actual* beats. Since there is no strong larger pattern into which the lines fit there is no encouragement to perceive virtual beats. We need to feel the five beats passing in rhythmic sequence before we sense the completion of the line (though this is less a matter of counting than of processing a familiar rhythmic structure). An iambic tetrameter in iambic pentameter verse will thus be heard merely as a shorter line rather than one with a virtual beat filling in the missing slot. Verse which alternates five-beat and four-beat lines (not a very common form) sustains the flexible movement of the pentameter in spite of a slightly more springy rhythm, and there is no sense of a fifth virtual beat in alternate lines:

```
        x / -x    /    x   /   x   /   x  /
(17)    Luxurious Man, to bring his vice in use,

        x  /  x   /    x  /     x /
        Did after him the world seduce;

        x    x   x  /     x   / -  x    /    x  /
        And from the field the flowers and plants allure,

        x   /x    x   x    /   x    /
        Where Nature was most plain and pure.
```

The shorter line closes down on the rhyme sooner than we expect, giving it a slightly epigrammatic quality, but in general the movement retains the characteristic qualities of five-beat verse, as do a number of other mixtures of five-beat verse with shorter or longer lines.

2. The movement of five-beat verse

A crucial feature of five-beat verse is the absence of any strong rhythmic hierarchy. There is no obvious way lines of five beats could divide into half-lines, and since no doubling movement is set up within the line, there is no encouragement to group the lines into pairs and larger units. Five-beat lines are consequently more self-sufficient than four-beat lines; unlike the latter, they arouse no strong expectation for further lines to continue an unfolding pattern, but at the same time they do not provide the strong sense of finality brought about by the completion of one part of a larger pattern. As a result they accept pauses in reading, both within the lines and between them, more easily than four-beat lines. This is one reason why they are much more suitable for drama, where the pause can be part of the actor's delivery of the line, or can mark a shift to a different speaker. (The creation of pauses by means of syntax is one aspect of *phrasing*, to be discussed in chapter 8.)

One way of highlighting the distinctiveness of the five-beat movement is by rewriting pentameter verse as tetrameter verse. Here is the opening of a Shakespeare sonnet followed by such a rewriting:

(18)   That time of year thou mayst in me behold
        When yellow leaves, or none, or few, do hang
        Upon those boughs which shake against the cold,
        Bare, ruined choirs where late the sweet birds sang.

(18a)   That time of year thou mayst behold
        When yellow leaves, or none, do hang
        On boughs which shake against the cold,
        Like choirs where late the sweet birds sang.

In spite of the run-on lines, the four-beat version takes on the slight jauntiness and the predetermined intonation-pattern of the 4x4 formation, and the lines have less opportunity to develop their own rhythmic and emotional qualities.

Because of the absence from five-beat verse of strong patterns longer than the line, it works very well without rhyme. Instead of implying a larger structure with points of culmination that call out for rhyme, five-beat verse proceeds in a line-by-line fashion, so that the poet can choose whether to organize the verse into groups by rhyme (couplets, as in example [16] above, or stanzas), or whether to write a continuous poem without rhymes, perhaps organized into verse paragraphs.

Unrhymed iambic pentameter is known as *blank verse*. Compare the following examples of iambic pentameter, the first – by Katherine Philips – in

the form of an *abab* stanza (echoing the 4x4 formation's main divisions) and
the second – by John Milton – in the form of a blank verse paragraph:

```
        /     ∠ x  ∠    x   ∠ x   ∠ x    ∠
(19)   Twice forty months of wedlock I did stay,
```

```
       x   ∠  x  ∠    ∠      x   x  ∠  x  ∠
       Then had my vows crowned with a lovely boy;
```

```
       x   ∠ x   ∠ x ∠   x   ∠    x ∠
       And yet in forty days he dropped away,
```

```
       x    ∠   x ∠ x ∖   x   ∠ x   ∠
       Oh swift vicissitude of human joy.
```

```
        x   ∠   x   x x ∠   x  ∠     x   ∠
(20)   He spake: and, to confirm his words, outflew
```

```
       ∠  -x  x   ∠ x    ∠ [x] ∠    x    x  ∠
       Millions of flaming swords, drawn from the thighs
```

```
       x  ∠  x   ∠ x x    x ∠ x    ∠
       Of mighty Cherubim; the sudden blaze
```

```
        /   ∠   x  ∠ x    ∠ [x]∠  x   x   ∠
       Far round illumined Hell. Highly they raged        4
```

```
       x ∠     x  ∠ -   x   ∠-   x    ∠ x ∠
       Against the Highest, and fierce with graspèd arms
```

```
       ∠   x    x   ∠ x   ∠    x ∠ x  ∠
       Clashed on their sounding shields the din of war,
```

```
       ∠ x   x ∠x    - x    x ∠   x  ∠ -
       Hurling defiance toward the vault of Heaven.
```

The quatrain by Philips moves in a pattern of accumulations – one line
answered by a second, after which we expect another pair. These duly follow: a line of further statement, and a final line of sorrowful comment. The
stanza traces a narrative of joy and loss, not from inside the powerful emotions themselves, but from a distance that allows them to be contained within
a reflection on the general condition of humanity. The distance is achieved
in part by the use of a regular and highly familiar stanza form. Milton's blank
verse, on the other hand, catches us up into a tempestuous scene; we never
know from line to line where the verse is taking us and how long the
description will last. Initial inversions give maximum impetus to the words

"Millions," "Clashed," "Hurling"; the verse surges past the line-ends in frequent run-ons; and the lines break at every possible point – after the first, second, third, or fourth beat – or run continuously from start to finish. Only a full phrasal analysis (the topic of chapter 8) could do justice to the movement of this passage. Read in context, in fact, these lines become something of a parody of the pentameter's epic power, since this vaunting of the fallen angels is empty – as is suggested by the ironic repetition in "Highly they raged against the Highest."

When neither rhyme nor consistent end-stopping is used, five-beat verse is at its greatest distance from the song-like qualities of stress verse. Here is an example from Shakespeare's *King Lear*. It is not difficult to sense the freedom an actor feels in working with such verse – freedom to invest the language with emotional power without being inhibited by the demands of the meter (which, nevertheless, is consistently observed). A possible scansion is given, showing demotion, promotion, rising and falling inversions (which are shaded), elision, and free double offbeats.

```
             /   ∠ x    x    x  ∠ x      x  ∠ ∠
(21)    Thou, nature, art my goddess; to thy law

        x  ∠ x x   x    ∠ [x]  ∠  x     x   ∠
        My services are bound. Wherefore should I

        ∠   x    x   ∠    x  ∠ x   x    x ∠
        Stand in the plague of custom, and permit

        x  ∖ x∠ - x x    ∠ x      x  x  ∠   x
        The curiosity of nations to deprive me,            4

        x    x  x x   x     ∠   x  ∠ x   ∠   x
        For that I am some twelve or fourteen moonshines

        ∠ x  x  ∠  x    ∖  ∠ x      ∠  x  ∠
        Lag of a brother? Why bastard? Wherefore base?
```

It would be possible to read these lines with a more regular rhythm than this scansion shows, but the value of the iambic pentameter for drama is precisely the way it allows varied speech rhythms to remain within the ambit of the metrical scheme. It makes sense, therefore, to scan the lines with the variations that an actor might want to exploit in order to bring out the explosive emotional force of this speech.

EXERCISE

Syllable-stress verse

(3) Scan the following stanza. What meters does it use? How does it exploit the characteristics of these meters?

```
Come let us go, while we are in our prime,
And take the harmless folly of the time.
We shall grow old apace and die
Before we know our liberty.                        4
Our life is short, and our days run
As fast away as does the sun;
And, as a vapour, or a drop of rain,
Once lost, can ne'er be found again:               8
So when or you or I are made
A fable, song, or fleeting shade,
All love, all liking, all delight
Lies drowned with us in endless night.             12
Then while time serves, and we are but decaying,
Come, my Corinna, come, let's go a-maying.
```

Summary

This chapter considers the distinction between *four-beat* and *five-beat verse* in syllable-stress meter, and the various line-lengths and stanza forms in which they are used.

A. Four-beat verse

Much syllable-stress four-beat verse has the same characteristics as four-beat verse in stress meter, including virtual beats and the use of stanza forms that divide and combine the four-beat units.

B. Resisting the 4x4 formation

Verse which does not fall into the 4x4 formation comes closer to the rhythms of speech; this includes five-beat verse and verse with varied line-lengths that cannot be read as a variant of the 4x4 formation. Four-beat verse can also be written in a way that counters the 4x4 formation by syntax and choice of stanza form.

C. Iambic pentameter

Five-beat verse is almost always iambic: it is very rare to find examples in trochaic or triple verse (or stress verse). It has a relatively weak rhythmic architecture, neither dividing into half-lines nor forming larger units. It can be rhymed or unrhymed (*blank verse*), stanzaic or continuous. It makes no use of virtual beats. These characteristics make it particularly suited to the evocation of speech and thought, to drama and to long narrative or meditative poems.

Chapter 7

Free verse: metrical and rhythmic analysis

Free verse and metrical verse

The history of English metrical practice is often thought of as a series of waves in a rising tide: accepted norms of regular verse being repeatedly swept away by currents of freer writing that increasingly approximate the speaking English voice, followed by returns to new kinds of strictness. In the fifteenth century, Chaucer's regular meters gave way to verse that, by contrast, seems highly irregular (this shift being partly caused by changes in the English language). In the mid sixteenth century, the Earl of Surrey and the editor Richard Tottel helped to usher in a new period of strict regularity which gave way later in the century to the inventive freedoms of Spenser, Sidney, and Shakespeare, and the even greater liberties of Donne, the Jacobean dramatists, and, in a different style, Milton. By the end of the seventeenth century, however, regularity was back in fashion, and was exploited with unparalleled subtlety by Dryden and Pope. The next wave of metrical freedom was that of late-eighteenth and early-nineteenth-century Romanticism, when an emphasis on individual expressiveness produced both a loosening of traditional meters and a search for new metrical forms. This last wave has never fully receded: later in the nineteenth century Browning and Hopkins molded traditional forms into new contours, and Whitman broke with metrical form altogether – a revolutionary step which in the twentieth century Pound, Eliot, Williams, and others confirmed and developed. Metrical verse has now ceased to be the staple form for English poetry, though no one is in a position to predict if this will remain true for the twenty-first century.

This view of verse history, although it is useful as a sketch, obscures the fact that regular metrical poetry continued to be written during all these shifts, often with great success, and that it remains an essential and in no way outdated part of current poetic practice. But what has been demonstrated by the successive waves of metrical loosening, and the move away from meter in the twentieth century, is that poetry does not *depend* on metrical patterning: although verse always implies some principle of regularity or equivalence, it need not be based on the production of controlled numbers of beats by the disposition of stressed and unstressed syllables in certain syntactic and linear arrangements.

167

The usual name for verse that does not fall into a metrical pattern is *free verse,* a name which derives in large part from the propaganda of poets staking a claim for the merits of their own new practice, and one which should not be taken to imply that metrical verse is, by contrast, limited or restricted. A more accurate name would be *nonmetrical verse,* which, as a negative definition, has the advantage of implying that this kind of verse does not have a fixed identity of its own, whereas "free verse" misleadingly suggests a single type of poetry. But a negative name might seem to suggest the superiority of what is named positively, and that would also be a mistake. Free verse, of which there are many different kinds, is, in general terms, neither better nor worse, neither harder to write nor easier to write, than metrical verse. There is probably much more bad free verse in print now than bad metrical verse, but that is a product of cultural history rather than any inherent properties of the two forms.

In pentameter verse that has many strong run-ons and many strong breaks within the line, we sometimes have to rely on what we *see* on the page to tell us where the line-endings fall. The examples we considered from Shakespeare's *King Lear* and Milton's *Paradise Lost* in the previous chapter are of this kind. Free verse takes us even further in this direction: it follows no system that determines the length of its units, and therefore relies entirely on the visual layout to provide the reader with a linear structure. (Some free verse relies on alternative prosodic systems – one sentence per line, for instance, or the signaling of line-ends by rhymes – but it is to this extent not "free.") Free verse often exploits the possibilities of spatial organization, in a way that is impossible to reproduce in a performance of the poem.

Here are some short examples to illustrate the variety of rhythmic types covered by the label "free verse," with very brief comments after each one.

```
(1)     These fibres of thine eyes that used to beam in
          distant heavens
        Away from me, I have bound down with a hot iron;
        These nostrils, that expanded with delight in
          morning skies,
        I have bent downward with lead melted in my
          roaring furnaces                                    4
        Of affliction, of love, of sweet despair, of
          torment unendurable.
```

At the beginning of the nineteenth century, William Blake, experiencing the urgency of great prophetic truths he felt he was compelled to communicate, expanded and loosened the normal metrical form of his time until it became a kind of oracular long-lined free verse. One important precedent for Blake was Biblical verse, which relies on syntactic and semantic parallelism – that is to say, the lines are determined by their internal structure as meaningful units, not by a metrical scheme. Blake, however, frequently used run-on lines to counter the somewhat static and cumulative effects of a meter based on parallelism.

(2)　　How to kéep - is there ány any, is there none such,
　　　　nowhere known some, bow or brooch or braid or
　　　　　brace, láce, latch or catch or key to keep
　　　　Back beauty, keep it, beauty, beauty, beauty,...from
　　　　vanishing away?
　　　　Ó is there no frowning of these wrinkles, rankèd
　　　　wrinkles deep,
　　　　Dówn? no waving off of these most mournful
　　　　messengers, still messengers, sad and stealing
　　　　　messengers of grey?

Much later in the nineteenth century, Gerard Manley Hopkins was also pushing intense poetic language beyond the limits of metrical verse, developing his own idiosyncratic metrical mode (and sometimes using his own scansion symbols, as in this example). He called it "sprung rhythm," and claimed that it could be scanned metrically. However, it often works best when read as a type of free verse. Although Hopkins often used long lines which owe something to Biblical verse, he exploited the power of the strong run-on even more fully than Blake.

(3)　　See, they return; ah, see the tentative
　　　　　　　Movements, and the slow feet,
　　　　　　　The trouble in the pace and the uncertain
　　　　　　　Wavering!　　　　　　　　　　　　　　　4

　　　　See, they return, one, and by one,
　　　　With fear, as half-awakened;
　　　　As if the snow should hesitate
　　　　And murmur in the wind,　　　　　　　　　　8
　　　　　　　And half turn back;
　　　　These were the "Wing'd-with-Awe,"
　　　　　　　Inviolable.

The use in free verse of shorter lines together with great variety in line-length became common in the twentieth century, the most profound influence being that of Ezra Pound. In this example, Pound uses the new-found liberty of rhythm and line-length to evoke the hesitant motion of the returning, enfeebled classical gods. He also begins to experiment with layout on the page: there is no way a reading could convey the relation of the different lines of this example. Layout later became a staple resource for him and for many other free verse poets.

```
(4)    Those who sharpen the teeth of the dog, meaning
       Death
       Those who glitter with the glory of the hummingbird, meaning
       Death                                                          4
       Those who sit in the sty of contentment, meaning
       Death
       Those who suffer the ecstasy of the animals, meaning
       Death                                                          8
```

T. S. Eliot employed a wide range of metrical and nonmetrical forms; here he combines the incantatory potential of strict parallelism (four sentences beginning and ending with the same words, and in the same relation to the lines of verse) with the focusing effect of a single word after a strong run-on. The long lines, as with much of Eliot's free verse, move on the edge of metricality: they could be scanned as five-beat stress verse, a rare form that does not encourage the perception of marked beats.

```
(5)    in this strong light
       the leafless beechtree
       shines like a cloud

       it seems to glow            4
       of itself
       with a soft stript light
       of love
       over the brittle           8
       grass
```

William Carlos Williams was also extremely influential in breaking up the movement of the sentence by visual cutting, and matching minimalist verse to miniaturist art. In some ways, this is the opposite of Blake's (or Whitman's) practice: instead of the verse line expanding to accommodate utterances too large and momentous for the metrical frame, it splinters into fragments to achieve a minute focus on the details that might be lost in a metrical progression. The run-on is, of course, crucial in this kind of verse, both heightening and violating the reader's sense of the continuity of the sentence.

```
(6)     I'm scared a lonely. Never see my son,
        easy be not to see anyone,
        combers out to sea
        know they're goin somewhere but not me.     4
        Got a little poison, got a little gun,
        I'm scared a lonely.
```

By the time John Berryman began a long poetic sequence in the 1950s, he had a vast stock of metrical and free verse precedents to draw on. In forging a repeatable form for the short poems that make up the sequence he drew on many of those models. This example – which constitutes the first third of one of the 18-line poems – moves between iambic pentameter (line 1), three-beat duple meter (line 3), an apparently six-beat line that thanks to its diction falls into a nursery-rhyme-like quadruple line with four main beats (line 5), a two-beat line (line 6), and two lines that do not fall into a meter (lines 2 and 4). The result of this constantly shifting movement is that no expectations for metrically organized beats are set up, and the verse remains "free." (Notice that, unusually for free verse, Berryman uses rhyme.)

```
(7)     earliest before sunrise    Last
        before sunset

        twilight   (between day
        and dark)                                    4

        is about to begin    And with time
        I could do it

        ends childhood
        Time an old bald thing   a servant          8
```

Susan Howe's poetry illustrates the potential that free verse possesses to fragment and dislocate the normal sequentiality of language, beyond even the techniques deployed by Pound and Williams. This extract, the first few lines of section 3 of Howes's *Pythagorean Silence*, uses the disposition of words on the page in combination with disruptions of syntax to suggest bursts of utterance interspersed with silences. The morsels of language demand maximal attention, and the poet's task is to make sure this attention is rewarded (not necessarily by the gratification of ordered meaning). These few lines cannot show how verbal threads interlace in a long poem, but they do indicate something of the resonating power phrases can have when the connectivity provided by syntax, phrasing, rhythm, and visual linearity is partly – though only partly – broken.

These examples all testify to the rhythmic potential that exists in the English language, quite apart from its readiness to embrace metrical patterns. It is a potential which is exploited in many different ways in the body of poetry we call "free verse," and in commenting on the rhythms of free verse no single approach is adequate. In this chapter, we shall consider briefly two ways of approaching the movement of free verse: metrical analysis and rhythmic analysis. In the following chapter, we shall consider phrasal analysis, which includes a way of registering the movement – so important in free verse – from one line to the next.

Metrical analysis

It may seem perverse to apply metrical analysis to verse that is avowedly nonmetrical, and it is certainly the case that such analysis is inappropriate for much free verse. But as long as song, popular rhymes, and advertising instill in the members of our culture, from an early age, an awareness of language's proclivity toward regular meters, poetry will always take up some relation to the fundamental rhythmic forms we have discussed. This relation may be one of straightforward rejection, in which case there is little more to be said, or it may be a more complex evoking of and dallying with the forms of regular meter, in which case the half-heard regular rhythms are an important part of the movement of the verse. (The examples by Pound, Eliot, and Berryman quoted earlier all make use of regular meters in this way.) We must remember, however, that the conditions which govern the emergence of beats in metrical patterns are very strict, and although it is not difficult to analyze lines of verse on paper as though they were metrical lines, it is another matter actually to *hear* a metrical movement. Much free verse may *look* like metrical verse, but this does not necessarily mean that it engages with the distinctive rhythmic experience we call meter.

Adrienne Rich's "Night Watch" is an example of a poem that derives its rhythmic quality from its existence on the borders of regular verse. Its rhythms move in and out of regularity, giving the poem a rather formal gait through which the metrical tradition of English verse can be heard, and connecting a highly personal experience with many earlier expressions of anguish and helplessness. If we detect echoes of Shakespeare, Tennyson, or Yeats in the poem, this is partly because the rhythm opens a channel of communication (though specific choices of words are always important too). The poem opens as follows:

(8)   And now, outside, the walls
        of black flint, eyeless.
        How pale in sleep you lie.
        Love: my love is just a breath   4
        blown on the pane and dissolved.
        Everything, even you,
        cries silently for help, the web
        of the spider is ripped with rain,   8
        the geese fly on into the black cloud.
        What can I do for you?
        what can I do for you?
        Can the touch of a finger mend   12
        what a finger's touch has broken?

The first line leads us immediately into the rhythmic world of regular meter:

        x   ⌣   x   ⌣   x   ⌣
        And now, outside, the walls

Not only does this line give us alternating unstressed and stressed syllables, but these syllables occur in rising phrases, making it a paradigmatic iambic trimeter. The run-on after "walls" is not strong enough to prevent the line from having its own integrity as a rhythmic unit.

We might contrast this with some of Rich's more clearly *nonmetrical* openings:

(9)   Two people in a room, speaking harshly.

(10)   My three sisters are sitting

(11)   In a bookstore on the East Side

The point is not that these lines cannot be scanned in terms of the possibilities of syllable-stress meter. It is that they do not *invite* a metrical reading as they begin the poem, because their disposition of stresses and phrasing encourages a more prosaic, speech-like rhythm.

However, a regular opening line need not be followed by a continued reinforcement of the metrical norms it seems to establish. "Night Watch" in fact breaks with the norm in its second line, whose most important rhythmic feature is its three successive stresses:

            /   /   /
        of black flint, eyeless.

It would be theoretically possible to scan these stresses as beats (separated by two virtual offbeats), sustaining the pattern of the three-beat line established by the first line, but this would imply that a much stronger metrical expectation had already been set up. We are more likely to feel that the meter has been suspended while the figure of the night as surrounding walls is developed in the style of a horror story, emphasized by the slow-moving sequence of stresses.

The iambic trimeter meter is then reasserted, in a line redolent of a long poetic tradition:

```
      x   ⌿   x   ⌿   x   ⌿
      How pale in sleep you lie.
```

Once again, the phrasing produces three clearly defined iambic groups, and this time the line is contained within a single sentence. Then the rhythm changes again, but this time the shift is to a pair of lines in different meters, both beginning and ending on a beat:

```
      ⌿   x   ⌿   x   ⌿   x   ⌿
      Love: my love is just a breath
```

```
      ⌿   x    x   ⌿   x    x   ⌿
      blown on the pane and dissolved.
```

The arresting image is given the force of an aphorism by its symmetrical rhythms, a four-beat duple line and then a three-beat triple line.

For most of this passage, stresses are separated by one or two unstressed syllables, and grouped by the line-divisions into threes or fours, thus keeping a connection with the most common metrical forms of four-beat verse. But no consistent pattern emerges, and the breaking of any incipient pattern is part of the rhythmic distinctiveness of the poem. Thus a light, regular, predominantly triple rhythm is set up in

```
                           x   ⌿
                           the web
```

```
      x    x   ⌿ x   x   ⌿      x    ⌿
      of the spider is ripped with rain,
```

only to be broken by the less metrical and more ominous line that follows:

```
      x   /      /  /   x   x   x   /      /
      the geese fly on into the black cloud.
```

It is crucial to understand why, in verse such as this, the irregularities are not experienced as variations in fundamentally metrical verse. The common metrical variations such as demotion, promotion, and inversion can be felt as such only when a sufficiently strong metrical expectation has been set up, and this happens very seldom in free verse. In the line just quoted, for instance, the reader is unlikely to experience "fly" as demoted or the second syllable of "into" as promoted, though the same phrases in regular verse would certainly work in that way. This is the same as saying that we don't experience fully formed beats in this line, which is why the line isn't scanned as metrical verse. We do, of course, experience the successive *stresses*, which contribute to the heavier, harsher quality of the line.

The lines that follow become more lyrical, in spite of the anguish they express, as though the helplessness of the speaker is in part that of being caught up in a pattern of events over which the individual has no control. This feeling emerges from the verbal repetitions and the more regular quality of the rhythm, with its strong suggestion of a triple movement:

```
 ∟  x  x  ∟  x   x
What can I do for you?

 ∟  x  x  ∟  x   x
what can I do for you?

 x   x  ∟   x  x  ∟  x   ∟
Can the touch of a finger mend

  x  x  ∟  x    ∟    x   ∟ x
what a finger's touch has broken?
```

Though these lines could never occur in a strictly metrical poem, they draw on the power of meter to heighten and control raw emotion.

The remainder of the poem continues to hover on the edge of metricality. In the following scansion I show a possible stressing for each line, and beats where there is some tendency for the line to fall into a regular meter:

```
   /  \    /    /     /
Blue-eyed now, yellow-haired,

   /         /   /
I stand in my old nightmare

 ∟        ∟      ∟
beside the track, while you,
```

16

```
    ⌒        ⌒        ⌒        ⌒
and over and over and always you

  /              /   \
plod into the deathcars.

  ⌒             ⌒
Sometimes you smile at me

  /       \     /
and I - I smile back at you.                    20

   ⌒       ⌒    x      ⌒      ⌒        ⌒
How sweet the odor of the station-master's roses!

   ⌒       ⌒     x      ⌒     x        ⌒
How pure, how poster-like the colors of this dream.
```

Notice how the chilling line "plod into the deathcars," which shifts the poem into a new register, gains some of its effectiveness from its resolute unmetricality after two lines which swing quite strongly with a regular rhythm. I have shown the two last lines as alexandrines (six-beat iambic lines), though they require careful reading to function in this way: if the unstressed syllables are slurred, the promoted offbeats will not emerge. This is not to say that an unmetrical reading is wrong, but that a metrical reading is possible – and very appropriate to the deceptive sweetness of the image.

Free verse poems can approach the movements of regular meter in a number of different ways (and different readers will hear these approaches in a variety of ways). By not wholly engaging with meter, such poems cannot avail themselves of its full capacity for expressive and memorable shapings of sound, but they may gain a heightened ability to capture the movements of thought, speech, and feeling that run through our daily lives.

EXERCISE

Metrical analysis

(1) Discuss the ways in which the following lines – the first section of "The Old Age of Michelangelo," by F. T. Prince – make use of free verse's capacity to exploit metrical rhythms.

```
Sometimes the light falls here too as at Florence
Circled by low hard hills, or in the quarry
Under its half-hewn cliffs, where that collection
```

```
Of pale rough blocks, still lying at all angles
  on the dust-white floor                              4
Waits, like a town of tombs.
                        I finish nothing I begin.
And the dream sleeps in the stone, to be unveiled
Or half-unveiled, the lurking nakedness;               8
Luminous as a grapeskin, the cold marble mass
Of melted skeins, chains, veils and veins,
Bosses and hollows, muscular convexities,
Supple heroic surfaces, tense drums                   12
And living knots and cords of love:
- Sleeps in the stone, and is unveiled
Or half-unveiled, the body's self a veil,
By the adze and the chisel, and the mind              16
Impelled by torment.
                      In the empty quarry
The light waits, and the tombs wait,
For the coming of a dream.                            20
```

Rhythmic analysis

There is no absolute division between the working (or the analysis) of meter and of rhythm – obviously, metrical patterning, when it occurs, is a central element in the rhythm of a poem. But in free verse poems which do not evoke the movements of meter, part of the dynamic texture of the poetry comes from the arrangement of stressed and unstressed syllables. The general dynamic texture of a free verse poem – the ease or difficulty with which it moves, the nearness or distance from the rhythms of speech (and of different kinds of speech), its moments of heightened attention and of relaxation – depends, among a number of other factors, upon the rhythmic movement of its syllables. And the poet can vary that texture as the poem proceeds, by controlling the placing of words and the lengths of the lines.

D. H. Lawrence's "Mountain Lion" is an example. The form which Lawrence uses is a highly variable one; line-lengths in this poem range from one word to twenty-one, and the rhythmic quality of the language keeps changing, without ever suggesting the regularity of meter. The speaker is in a party climbing into a Mexican canyon when they meet two men, one of whom reveals that the object he is carrying is the corpse of a mountain lion.

```
(12)    He smiles, foolishly, as if he were caught doing
        wrong.
        And we smile, foolishly, as if we didn't know.
        He is quite gentle and dark-faced.
```

The awkwardness of the encounter is enacted in part by the successive stresses of "smiles, foolishly," which cause the rhythm to pause, followed by a rapid movement with many unstressed syllables – a pattern that is then immediately repeated to suggest the mirroring of the discomfort between the two parties:

```
x    /      / x  x  x  x   x   x    /     xx
He smiles, foolishly, as if he were caught doing

   /
wrong.

x    /  /     / x   x  x  x   x   x x     /
And we smile, foolishly, as if we didn't know.
```

These lines could, of course, be read more slowly and deliberately, with more stressed syllables; but their great distance from a metrical pattern, the length of the lines, and their almost banal content, encourage a "prosaic" reading. (Note that "we" in the second line demands an emphatic stress, as the phrase is being contrasted with "He smiles," and that this, too, increases the awkwardness.)

The tone, and the rhythm, become more sober in the next line:

```
x x   /    /  x x   /    /
He is quite gentle and dark-faced.
```

Although "dark-faced" is a compound, where we might expect one of the stresses to be a secondary stress, the two words are equally important. The change of movement in this line marks a transition which is fully achieved in the lines that follow:

```
It is a mountain lion,
A long, long slim cat, yellow like a lioness.
Dead.
```

The shorter lines, as well as the deepening tone, encourage a much slower reading, and the stress-rhythm co-operates by increasing the proportion of stressed to unstressed syllables (the second line including a run of five successive stresses):

```
x  x  x  /  x   /x
It is a mountain lion,
```

```
  x  /      /     /   /    /  x   x   x  /x x
  A long,  long slim cat, yellow like a lioness.

     /
  Dead.
```

The slow, deliberate pace of the rhythm signals the impact of the spectacle on the poet's deeper feelings, not those he can express openly in a meeting with strangers but those he wishes to share with his readers. The two distinct rhythms – superficial human conversation with its rapid runs and awkward pauses, and the meditation of the poet with its many successive stresses – alternate once more in the lines that follow. First a line of conversation, then six lines of response, using unusually long series of monosyllabic adjectives to slow down the rhythm by means of repeated stresses:

```
  x    /     x   x   /  x    x  /       / x    /  x   x
  He trapped her this morning, he says, smiling foolishly.

  /   /   x   /
  Lift up her face,

  x   /      /      /      /   x    /
  Her round, bright face, bright as frost.

  x   /      /    \  x     /    x    /  /   /
  Her round, fine-fashioned head, with two dead ears;        4

  x     /   x   x   /  x      /   x  x   /      /
  And stripes in the brilliant frost of her face, sharp,

     /     /    /
    fine, dark rays,

  /    /    /    /  x   x  / x      /   x  x   /
  Dark, keen, fine rays in the brilliant frost of her face.

  /    x x   /    /
  Beautiful dead eyes.
```

The fifth and sixth lines give us no fewer than nine successive stresses, none of them likely to be subordinated to the others. Lawrence is here exploiting to the full the freedom that nonmetrical verse has to draw upon the rhythmic resources of syllables and stresses themselves, in order to bring before us as vividly as possible not just the beauty of the dead beast but the powerful emotions aroused by the encounter.

All free verse necessarily uses sequences of stressed and unstressed syllables, but only in some examples are these orchestrated to achieve specific
effects in the way that Lawrence does in this poem. It's always possible to
mark these sequences, of course, but it becomes a useful exercise only when
we can say what they contribute to the total working of the poem. The
rhythmic patterning of syllables – and its relation to metrical forms, if any –
needs to be considered in relation to the phrasal movement of the verse.
This is the topic of chapter 8, which will return to the analysis of free verse
in its final section.

EXERCISE

Rhythmic analysis

(2) Mark the stressed and unstressed syllables in the following lines,
which open Elizabeth Bishop's poem "A Cold Spring." Discuss the
contribution they make to the descriptive power of the poetry:

```
A cold spring:

The violet was flawed on the lawn.

For two weeks or more the trees hesitated;

the little leaves waited,                           4

carefully indicating their characteristics.

Finally a grave green dust

settled over your big and aimless hills.

One day, in a chill white blast of sunshine,        8

on the side of one a calf was born.

The mother stopped lowing

and took a long time eating the after-birth,

a wretched flag,                                    12

but the calf got up promptly

and seemed inclined to feel gay.
```

Summary

A. Free verse and metrical verse

Free verse, which is of many kinds, is verse that does not fall into a metrical pattern. It relies more heavily than metrical verse on visual layout. The rhythm and movement of free verse can be analyzed in three ways: metrically, rhythmically, and phrasally. These all interrelate. (Phrasal analysis is discussed in chapter 8.)

B. Metrical analysis

Metrical analysis can reveal the way in which some free verse poems maintain a relation to metrical verse, approaching and deviating from regular metrical patterns. In passages where a metrical pattern is fully realized, the reader perceives beats, and variations such as demotion and promotion are possible. In other passages there is only a slight feeling of metrical regularity.

C. Rhythmic analysis

Rhythmic analysis examines the disposition of stressed and unstressed syllables when they do not produce a regular meter.

Chapter 8

Phrasal movement

The importance of phrasing

In our discussion of English verse forms in the foregoing chapters, we have frequently noticed the important part played by syntax and meaning in the movement of poetry. Poetry is organized in sentences as well as rhythmic patterns, and these two modes of organization work together to produce a poem's uniquely configured progression through time. Grammatical and semantic properties contribute to our sense of stronger and weaker stresses; they play a crucial role in our sense of the divisions of verse, whether within the line or at its end; they affect the many decisions the reader takes as to pace, tone, and rhythmic regularity or irregularity. However, what we have noted so far only scratches the surface of a highly important and highly intricate aspect of poetic movement, and in this chapter we shall pursue the topic a little further.

We call this dimension of the movement of poetry *phrasing*, a word which refers both to syntax and to meaning, and which in its form ("phrasing" rather than "phrases") indicates the *dynamic* nature of the phenomenon it refers to. Alternatively, we use the term *phrasal movement*, to remind us that this property of verse interacts constantly with the property we have been concentrating on so far, rhythmic movement. Every example of language has a particular phrasing, just as it has a particular rhythm. In order to analyze phrasing, we need a set of tools different from those traditionally used in prosodic study. A great deal still needs to be done in developing such tools, and this chapter aims at nothing more than introducing a simple approach to one aspect of phrasing.

A poem's phrasing is an important part of its varying sense of pace and onward impetus, and of its different degrees and types of pause and closure. Like meter and rhythm, phrasing is not something we *add* to language but something that is already part of what we know and do when we speak and understand a language. What we are concerned with in this chapter is a method of *representing* this shared awareness so that it can be recorded on the page and talked about. When we refer to the "rhythm" of a particular poem, we are often referring – whether we know it or not – to its phrasing, and hence it is perfectly appropriate to use the word *rhythm* to include phrasing. However, for the sake of clarity, we shall distinguish between rhythmic movement – produced by the patterning of stressed and unstressed syllables in relation to the units of verse – and phrasal movement – produced by syntax and meaning.

Let us begin with a very simple example of a 4x4 stanza, indicating first its metrical rhythm:

```
        ∕  x   ∕  x   x   x   ∕
(1)     Lizzie Borden with an ax

        ∕   x   ∕  x   ∕  x   ∕
        Hit her father forty whacks.

        x    x  ∕   x   x  x   ∕
        When she saw what she had done,

        x  ∕   x   ∕  x   \  x ∕
        She hit her mother forty-one.
```

As we saw in chapter 3, the 4x4 formation works by producing forward movement over spans of different length at the same time. While we sense a single succession of sixteen beats from start to finish, we also sense shorter movements occurring within it in a hierarchic pattern: two eight-beat movements, four four-beat movements, eight two-beat movements, and sixteen single beats that alternate with offbeats. The sense of closure after sixteen beats is especially strong because all these rhythmic movements end at once.

To examine the phrasal movement of this poem we focus not on its metrical structure, but on the way the *words* of the poem relate to one another. Most words in poems (or any stretch of language) can be felt as participating in one of four basic types of movement: (1) they are part of a movement *toward* some point that lies ahead; (2) they are part of a movement *away from* some point that has already passed; (3) they are part of a relatively *static* moment from which something might develop; (4) they are part of a moment of *arrival* toward which the previous words have been moving. *Phrasal scansion*, as we will deploy it here, simply consists in notating a poem to show these different movements occurring over different spans.

Here is example (1) rewritten as prose, to make it easier to ignore the contribution made by meter and to concentrate on the phrasing:

```
(1a)    Lizzie Borden with an ax hit her father forty whacks.
        When she saw what she had done, she hit her mother
        forty-one.
```

The most obvious division of the example is into its two sentences. The first sentence taken on its own is a single statement, moving neither toward nor away from anything else in the passage. The second sentence, however, is meaningful only in relation to the first: it continues the narrative, and could be said to be an extension of the first sentence. The movement of its meaning is movement away from the initial assertion, as if it were looking over its shoulder at what went before. We can show the relation of the two sentences by means of a simple notation (since we are treating the example as prose, the line-division here has no significance):

```
STA───────────────────────────────────────── | EXT ─
Lizzie Borden with an ax hit her father forty whacks. When

─────────────────────────────────────────── |

she saw what she had done, she hit her mother forty-one.
```

The abbreviation STA marks the beginning of a unit that runs to the symbol |, and indicates that it is a *statement*. The abbreviation EXT marks the start of a second unit that again runs to the symbol |, and indicates that it is an *extension* of the previous statement.

If we examine the two parts into which the first sentence divides, we find a somewhat different relationship. The first unit, "Lizzie Borden with an ax," is not a self-sufficient statement; rather, it seems to be moving *toward* something, to be arousing expectations that its meaning will be made clear by what is to come. We term it an *anticipation*, and mark it ANT. The second unit – "hit her father forty whacks" – satisfies the expectation generated by the first unit, and gives us a feeling of *arrival*. We mark it ARR. Like a statement, it does not give the impression of moving toward or away from anything else, but the fact that it comes as a climax to an earlier movement gives it a distinctive quality. The second sentence follows exactly the same pattern. Here is the phrasal scansion for the half-sentences:

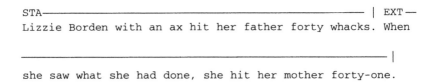

```
ANT ─────────────────── | ARR ─────────────────── | ANT ─
Lizzie Borden with an ax hit her father forty whacks. When

─────────────────────────┤ ARR ─────────────────── |
she saw what she had done, she hit her mother forty-one.
```

Each of these units divides into two further units, thanks to the organization of syntax and meaning. The first unit divides between the proper name "Lizzie Borden" and a descriptive phrase "with an ax" (this phrase actually describes the verb to follow, but its unusual placing in the sentence encourages us to take it in conjunction with the proper name). We can label the name STA because, although it is not a statement as such, it is self-sufficient and stationary, and does not move toward a goal. The descriptive phrase functions as an extension, moving away from the name as it tells us something about the person it names:

```
STA ──────────|EXT ───────|
Lizzie Borden with an ax
```

It is true that "with an ax" conveys a degree of anticipation – what did she do with the ax? But we have already recorded this anticipation in labeling the whole phrase ANT; we are concerned now only with the movement *within* its first segment. Our scansion demonstrates an important point: *phrasing is not simply a reflection of syntax.* We saw in chapter 2 how syntax, too, organizes sentences into hierarchic units, and in many cases these coincide with phrasal units. But there are numerous other factors at work in our preference for certain groupings of words over others – including the operation of meter, which here reinforces our tendency to divide the sentence after "ax," even though a purely syntactic analysis would be different.

The other three half-sentences move from anticipation to arrival. Here is the whole passage again, with these movements indicated:

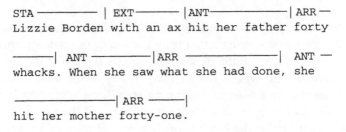

It might be argued that "hit her father" and "she hit her mother" are self-sufficient statements, not anticipations. This is correct if we take these statements by themselves, but in reading we are always both looking ahead and at the same time reinterpreting what has already passed. This means that it is important to consider the longer unit within which the shorter units occur. In these cases, "forty whacks" and "forty-one" function as a sort of second object of the verb "hit," and constitute the semantic climax of the sentences.

Now a crucial fact about phrasing is that, just like rhythmic movement in the 4x4 formation, it takes place over shorter and longer spans of the linguistic material *at the same time.* The movement within each sentence happens concurrently with the longer movement from one sentence to the next, and the same is true for the shorter divisions. We therefore need to show them all together in a single *phrasal scansion* to give an accurate picture of the passage's phrasal movement. By convention, we show the

longer movements *above* the shorter ones, and sometimes talk about"higher"
and "lower" levels. It is important, however, to remember that this
spatialization is purely arbitrary, and represents *simultaneous movements through
time.* We also number these levels, starting at 1 for the longest/highest; again
this is purely arbitrary and for convenience. Since the entire poem consists
of a single statement, a full phrasal scansion will show this statement as level
1. Each lower level shows a division into phrases of the same type – in this
case, level 2 shows sentences, level 3 shows the major subdivisions of the
sentences, and level 4 shows short phrases that are clearly unified.

```
1 STA ─────────────────────────────────────────────────────────────
2 STA ─────────────────────────────────────────────────── | EXT ─
3 ANT ───────────────────────── |ARR ──────────────────── | ANT ─
4 STA ───────── |EXT────────── |ANT ────────── |ARR ─────── | ANT ─
  Lizzie Borden with an ax hit her father forty whacks. When
```

```
  ──────────────────────────────────────────────────────────── |
  ──────────────────────────────────────────────────────────── |
  ────────────────────────────── | ARR ───────────────────── |
  ────────── |ARR────────────── | ANT ──────────── |ARR ─────── |
  she saw what she had done, she hit her mother forty-one.
```

   It is worth studying this scansion carefully in order to grasp what it tells
us. We can examine it starting either from the top or the bottom (though it
is usually easier to carry out a phrasal scansion by starting at the top, as we
have just done). The whole rhyme conveys the reader in a continuous
motion from start to finish: the beginning feels like a beginning (a proper
name about whom we are to be told something) and the end feels like an
end (the punch-line of the black joke). Within this movement, a sentence
begins and ends, leaving us a little puzzled by its baldly horrific content,
then another one begins, tells us more, and ends with the punch. Within the
first of these sentences, we begin with the arousal of expectation ("Lizzie
Borden with an ax") that is immediately, and darkly, fulfilled ("hit her father
forty whacks"). Within the second, we begin again with expectation aroused
("When she saw what she had done") followed by fulfillment ("She hit her
mother forty-one"). And within these four movements are further movements: statement and extension in the first and anticipation and arrival in
the others.
   If we start from the bottom, we note that short spans combine in pairs,
first a statement plus an extension then three instances of anticipations leading to arrivals; that these longer spans themselves combine in pairs, both
anticipations leading to arrivals; that these two spans themselves form a pair,
consisting of a statement plus an extension; and that this pair forms the

entire example, a single statement. In the context of phrasal analysis, we shall refer to units at all levels as *phrases*, giving the term a meaning that is wider than the one it has in linguistics. Thus the two sentences of this example constitute a single phrase, as does each of the subdivisions. When dealing with a particular level of the analysis, we can speak of the *subphrases* that make up the phrase. It must be remembered, though, that subphrases are themselves phrases at their own level; when we turn to examine them, we find that they, too, are made up of subphrases, until we reach the shortest phrases of our analysis. *Apart from the highest and the lowest levels, every phrase is also a subphrase and every subphrase is also a phrase.* When examining a phrasal scansion, each level should always be considered in relation to the levels above and below it – because that is how poetry happens, in a constant interrelated series of forward movements.

What does this scansion tell us about the way these two sentences work? First, the phrasal movement is strictly *duple*. Although it is possible for a phrase to be made up of three or four subphrases, this does not happen here. The duple phrasal movement gives the sentences a firmness and clarity that suits the absurd arithmetical logic of the reported actions. Second, the phrasal divisions occur in a clear pattern, which arises from the duple movement. We can observe this pattern by looking at the number of | symbols one above the other in the same scansion. The number of symbols reflects the strength of the closure – that is to say the degree to which we feel an ending and (if there is more to come) a new beginning. The pattern that emerges is 1, 2, 1, 3, 1, 2, 1, 4; that is, an alternation between weaker and stronger closures, with the stronger closures themselves alternating in strength to finish with the strongest. Third, there is a predominant movement of antici-pation to arrival at the lower two levels, giving the sentences a strong for-ward impetus. This is countered at the level of the sentences themselves; after the first sentence, we have no idea where we are going – hence the surprise effect of the second one.

These qualities of phrasal movement are processed by the reader at the same time as, and in close relation to, the rhythmic form of the stanza. To assess their importance in the poem, therefore, we need to show it in lines, with a metrical scansion showing stressed and unstressed syllables, beats and offbeats. It is also useful to show stress groups, which have a rhythmic qual-ity similar to that of phrases: unstressed syllables either anticipate a stressed syllable or extend it, and rising groups could be said to consist of one or more anticipations plus an arrival, while falling groups consist of a statement plus one or more extensions. Another connection between phrases and stress groups is that the boundaries of the lowest level of phrasing always coincide with stress group boundaries. However, stress groups are more closely linked to the sound pattern of English, and exist in a greater variety of types than phrases, so it is best to keep their identity separate.

The only addition to the phrasal scansion itself when we set the poem out as a poem is the symbol > at the end of some lines; this indicates that the phrase continues past the end of the line and onto the next one. Below the lowest level of phrasing are the indicators of stress groups, and below that the metrical scansion. (There is no need to show stressed and unstressed syllables in the stress groups since these are shown in the metrical scansion.)

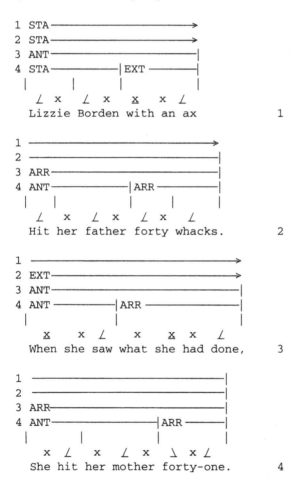

The scansion shows clearly how the phrasal movement coincides with and reinforces the metrical structure. The metrical divisions in the 4x4 formation correspond exactly with the vertical lines that indicate the hierarchy of phrasal divisions; the pattern in both is 1, 2, 1, 3, 1, 2, 1, 4, where 1 is the weakest and 4 is the strongest. Conversely, the strength of the run-on endings is shown by the number of > symbols; the sequence here is stronger, weaker, stronger, and none at all, which also mirrors the metrical structure of the 4x4 formation. The simple, regular, metrical pattern and rhyme scheme contribute their own forward momentum, and their own sense of closure at the end. Apart from the differing relations between phrases, the main source of variety in the movement of the poem is at the level of the stress groups: the poem moves from a rising rhythm to a mixed rhythm in the first half, and from a predominantly rising rhythm to a mixed rhythm in the second half. (Notice that the stress groups function as subdivisions of the shortest phrases; like phrases, they always occur within the longer units of the level above them.)

"Lizzie Borden" is highly typical of a large body of popular verse. In such verse the duple hierarchical organization of phrasing and of rhythm reinforce each other, and against this background the phrasal relations and stressgroups provide a continuously varying movement.

EXERCISE

Analyzing phrasal movement

(3) The following sentence has two meanings; give two phrasal scansions reflecting these meanings.

```
I warmly recommend this candidate with no

qualifications whatsoever.
```

(4) Scan the meter of the following stanza (the first stanza of "A Song," by Thomas Carew), indicate the stress groups, and then add a phrasal scansion on four or five levels. Examine the relation of the phrasing to the structure of the 4x4 formation.

```
Ask me no more where Jove bestows,

When June is past, the fading rose;

For in your beauty's orient deep,

These flowers, as in their causes, sleep.
```

(g) Above all, don't dawdle.

(h) He held out the cigar-case, and his visitor winced.

(i) Rounding the bend, before she could see what lay
     ahead, she had a premonition that the road was
     blocked.

(j) Three dusty elephants, several surprisingly dowdy
     peacocks, and a few fraying llamas were all that the
     park contained.

(2) Give a phrasal scansion of the following poem, showing four
levels of phrasing (including, at level 1, the whole poem). Consider
how the poem's phrasing contributes to its humor.

The Turtle

The turtle lives 'twixt plated decks

Which practically conceal its sex.

I think it clever of the turtle

In such a fix to be so fertile.

Analyzing phrasal movement in a poem

Phrasal analysis offers a striking illustration of the complexity of what we
do, without realizing it, when we read a poem attentively. In the previous
section we found a great deal to say about the phrasal movement of the very
simplest type of verse, a popular 4x4 stanza. There can be no prospect,
therefore, of analyzing fully a poem in the literary tradition in a short book
like this, nor of discussing all the intricacies of phrasal movement in English
and its relation to other features of language. But the principles implicit in
our discussion of "Lizzie Borden" underlie phrasing in every poem, and a
brief sketch of their operation in a literary example will serve as a sample of
what is possible on a larger scale.

The opening lines of Coleridge's poem "This Lime-Tree Bower My
Prison" are written in blank verse that presents no problems for metrical
scansion:

```
        /    x  x   /   x   /   x   x  x /
(2)    Well, they are gone, and here must I remain,

        x   /   \   / -  x   / x   x  x    /
       This lime-tree bower my prison! I have lost

        /  x   x   /  x    x   x   x    x    x
       Beauties and feelings, such as would have been

        \    /   x  x  x /  x    / -    x  /
       Most sweet to my remembrance even when age            4

        x   /    x   /   x   /  x    /   x   /
       Had dimmed mine eyes to blindness! They, meanwhile,

        /       x  x / x   /   x   /   x /
       Friends, whom I never more may meet again,

        x    / x  /    x /    x  /   \  /
       On springy heath, along the hill-top edge,

        / x  x   /  x   x   /   /    x   /
       Wander in gladness, and wind down, perchance,        8

        x   /   /   / x   /   x   /  x  /
       To that still roaring dell, of which I told...
```

As the scansion indicates, the meter is fairly regular, employing a number of the variations available to iambic verse to create a speech-like rhythm, including initial inversion ("Well, they are gone," "Beauties and feelings," "Wander in gladness"), rising inversion ("and wind down"), demotion ("Most sweet"), and promotion ("such as would have been" – a phrase which could in fact be read with very little stressing on any of its words without losing its metricality). But this metrical description does not go very far toward capturing the distinctiveness of these lines as an experience of movement, movement of thought and feeling realized through movement of language. Many readers have testified to the special quality of the opening of this poem, its blend of relaxation and tautness, the way it pulls the reader into the poem, the subtlety of its modulations of tone and attitude.

The speaker has been forced to remain at home (in a headnote Coleridge explains that the occasion of the poem was a domestic accident which confined him to his cottage), while his companions have set off without him on a walk he had been greatly looking forward to. The poem – which is 76 lines long – represents the thoughts that this "imprisonment" produces, leading from one to another in a sequence that is partly governed by reason, partly by emotion. Disappointment, anger, wry self-reflection, and self-pity play through the language, and one aspect of Coleridge's successful representation of this complex emotional drama is his handling, within the traditional blank verse scheme, of phrasing.

How do we go about analyzing the phrasal movement of Coleridge's lines? We can begin by reading the whole extract to establish whether it forms a single movement from start to finish. The answer is that it does. So we can mark the entire passage as a statement (STA) – by definition the only kind of phrase that can exist in isolation, since extensions, arrivals, and anticipations all depend on other phrases. We then ask what are the major sequences within that movement, and we find that they are the three sentences. This is not surprising, as there is usually a level at which phrasal movement and sentences coincide. The relation between these sentences (which, we may recall, we term *phrases* in so far as they participate in phrasal movement) is easy to detect: a statement is followed by two sentences of extension which develop the implications of that statement.

We are now in a position to indicate the two highest levels in the phrasing. (If you are carrying out a phrasal scansion yourself, it's wise to leave plenty of space between the highest levels and the lines of the poem.) What this scansion shows is that the onward movement of the lines is produced by a statement whose implications are gradually unfolded. (We might contrast this with the very different type of onward movement in which phrases of anticipation lead to an arrival.) This movement is strengthened by the relation between the phrasing and the lines of the meter: the run-on lines (indicated by > on the right) urge the reader over the metrical divisions at line-end; and the linear arrangement urges the reader over the major phrasal divisions, which occur within the line.

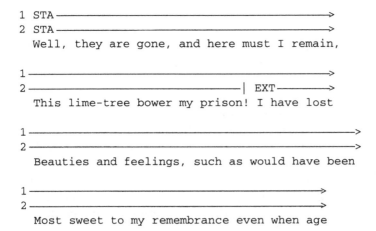

```
1 STA ─────────────────────────────────────────>
2 STA ─────────────────────────────────────────>
   Well, they are gone, and here must I remain,

1 ─────────────────────────────────────────────>
2 ──────────────────────────────| EXT──────────>
   This lime-tree bower my prison! I have lost

1 ─────────────────────────────────────────────>
2 ─────────────────────────────────────────────>
   Beauties and feelings, such as would have been

1 ─────────────────────────────────────────────>
2 ─────────────────────────────────────────────>
   Most sweet to my remembrance even when age        4
```

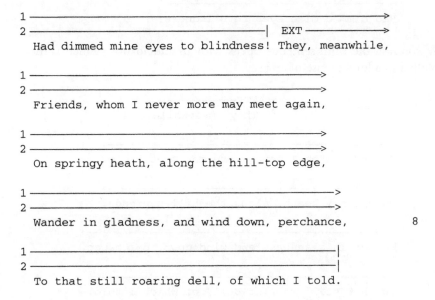

```
1 ──────────────────────────────────────────────>
2 ─────────────────────────────────────────│ EXT ────────────>
  Had  dimmed  mine  eyes  to  blindness!  They,  meanwhile,

1 ──────────────────────────────────────────>
2 ──────────────────────────────────────────>
  Friends,  whom  I  never  more  may  meet  again,

1 ──────────────────────────────────────────>
2 ──────────────────────────────────────────>
  On  springy  heath,  along  the  hill-top  edge,

1 ──────────────────────────────────────────────>
2 ──────────────────────────────────────────────>
  Wander  in  gladness,  and  wind  down,  perchance,         8

1 ──────────────────────────────────────────│
2 ──────────────────────────────────────────│
  To  that  still  roaring  dell,  of  which  I  told.
```

We now read the lines again, attending to the movement *within* each of the sentences. (Remember that phrases always run within the bounds of the higher phrases of which they are part.) The first sentence mirrors exactly the movement of the whole passage, beginning with a statement and following it by two movements of extension that spell out the consequences of that statement:

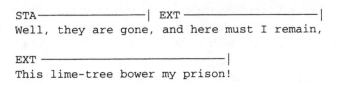

```
STA────────────────│ EXT ────────────────│
Well,  they  are  gone,  and  here  must  I  remain,

EXT ──────────────────────────│
This  lime-tree  bower  my  prison!
```

The second sentence also begins with a statement, followed this time by a single extension:

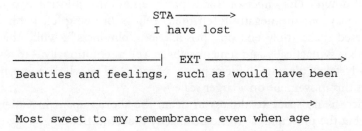

```
                      STA──────────>
                      I  have  lost

──────────────────────────│ EXT ────────────────────>
Beauties  and  feelings,  such  as  would  have  been

          ─────────────────────────────────────>

Most  sweet  to  my  remembrance  even  when  age
```

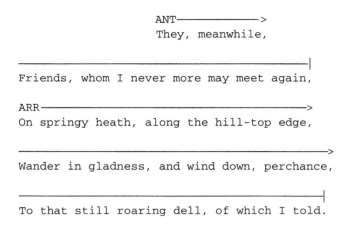

```
————————————————————————————|
Had dimmed mine eyes to blindness!
```

By contrast, the third sentence opens with an anticipation, which is then fulfilled in a long phrase of arrival:

```
                         ANT——————————->
                         They, meanwhile,

————————————————————————————————————|
Friends, whom I never more may meet again,

ARR——————————————————————————————————>
On springy heath, along the hill-top edge,

——————————————————————————————————————>
Wander in gladness, and wind down, perchance,

——————————————————————————————————————|
To that still roaring dell, of which I told.
```

When we first read these lines, we probably assume that the phrase "on springy heath, along the hill-top edge" refers to "meet again," and expresses the fear that the speaker may never in the future encounter his friends in his favorite places. As we read on, however, we may decide that the word "wander" needs to be supplemented by an indication of the *places* where the friends are wandering, so that the phrase in question goes with what follows rather than with what precedes it. One of the uses of phrasal scansion is that it can make clear a reader's decision in cases like this. The scansion above reflects the second reading, with its division coming after "meet again" and not after "edge."

The three sentences thus provide a modulation of the extract's overall movement from beginning to end. The first two consist of an unfolding of implications, while the third derives its drive from an anticipatory progress culminating in the imagined movements of the friends who "wander" and "wind down." The effect of this is partly emotional: the first two movements play out the negatively charged feelings of being left behind in a cloistered space (they end on "prison" and "blindness"), while the third ascends – syntactically and semantically as well as emotionally – to a vision of freely-taken pleasure in the expanses of nature. (The whole poem, in fact, enacts this movement on a larger scale.)

There is no space to discuss in detail the shorter spans in Coleridge's lines, but the principles at work are exactly the same. Before giving a possible phrasal scansion of the passage, there is one more feature to illustrate.

Sometimes a phrase is not subdivided at the level immediately below it (while other phrases at the same level are). When this happens, we leave a blank beneath it, to show that the phrasal movement is the same at both levels. Let us take as an example the phrase, "such as would have been/Most sweet to my remembrance!" The whole phrase divides into an anticipation and an arrival, but only the arrival is further subdivided at the level below. We show the phrasal movement at these two levels as follows:

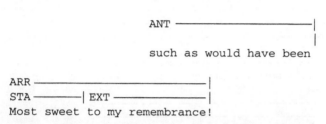

The anticipatory force of "such as would have been" remains intact at the lower level, giving it added strength. (We don't repeat "ANT" at this level, however, since what is being anticipated is the entire phrase "Most sweet to my remembrance," and not just its first subphrase.) When a phrase remains undivided for *several* levels, this indicates that it has particular prominence in the phrasal movement of the poem. As the scansion will show, an example in the Coleridge passage is "I have lost/Beauties and feelings."

The possible phrasal scansion of the passage given here extends to six levels. It would be possible to add further levels by scanning even smaller units. However, phrasing is not a very significant contributor to poetic movement below the lowest level shown here. More important at these levels are the movements within stress groups and, of course, the metrical rhythm. The number of levels shown in a scansion depends entirely on the particular poem: the more complex its phrasal movement, the more levels are needed to represent it.

```
1 STA ——————————————————————————————>
2 STA ——————————————————————————————>
3 STA ————————————| EXT ————————————>
4                 | STA ————————————|
5 ANT -| ARR ——————————|            |
6      |             | ANT ——————————|ARR —|
   Well, they are gone, and here must I remain,          1


1 ——————————————————————————————————>
2 ——————————————————————————| EXT ———>
3 ——————————————————————————| STA ———>
4 EXT ——————————————————————|       >
5                           |       >
6 ANT ——————————————|ARR ——————| ANT ———|
   This lime-tree bower my prison! I have lost          2


1 ———————————————————————————————————————>
2 ———————————————————————————————————————>
3 ————————————————————| EXT ——————————————>
4                     | STA ——————————————>
5                     | ANT ——————————————|
6 ARR ————————————————|                   |
   Beauties and feelings, such as would have been          3


1 ———————————————————————————————————————>
2 ———————————————————————————————————————>
3 ———————————————————————————————————————>
4 ——————————————————————————| EXT ————————>
5 ARR ——————————————————————|            >
6 STA ————————| EXT ——————————————| ANT ——————|
   Most sweet to my remembrance even when age          4


1 ————————————————————————————————————————————>
2 ————————————————————————————| EXT ——————————>
3 ————————————————————————————| ANT ——————————>
4 ————————————————————————————| STA ——————————>
5                             | STA —| EXT ———|
6 ARR ———————————————————| EXT ————————|     |      |
   Had dimmed mine eyes to blindness! They, meanwhile,          5


1 ———————————————————————————————————————>
2 ———————————————————————————————————————>
3 ——————————————————————————————————————|
4 ————————| EXT ——————————————————————|
5 EXT ——|                             |
6       | ANT ——————————————————|ARR ——————————|
   Friends, whom I never more may meet again,          6
```

```
1 ————————————————————————————————————>
2 ————————————————————————————————————>
3 ARR————————————————————————————————>
4 ANT————————————————————————————————|
5 STA———————————————| EXT———————————————|
6                   |                   |
   On springy heath, along the hill-top edge,      7


1 ————————————————————————————————————>
2 ————————————————————————————————————>
3 ————————————————————————————————————>
4 ARR————————————————| EXT———————————————>
5                    | ANT—————————| ANT—————————|
6 STA——| EXT—————————|             |             |
   Wander in gladness, and wind down, perchance,     8


1 —————————————————————————————————————|
2 —————————————————————————————————————|
3 —————————————————————————————————————|
4 ——————————————————————————| EXT—————————————|
5 ARR————————————————————————|             |
6                            |             |
   To that still roaring dell, of which I told...     9
```

Scanning the phrasal movement of these lines by Coleridge – like scanning their meter – is only the beginning of an analysis of their poetic operation. It provides the raw material for a critical discussion that would relate phrasing to rhythm and to the other features of the poem. We've already noted how the movement at levels 2 and 3 contributes to the tone and emotional coloring of the passage, its sense of confinement leading to imaginative liberation. The predominance of progressions from statements to extensions at the higher levels also contributes to the feeling of unforced and unpremeditated onward movement, and to a relaxed tone; to those qualities, in other words, which have led to the inclusion of this poem in the group of poems by Coleridge known as the "conversation poems." The shorter phrases, by contrast, include many ANT–ARR sequences, giving the poem an energetic forward drive at the lower levels.

Phrasal scansion also gives a much fuller indication of the operation of *closure* and *continuity* in verse, and Coleridge's lines are a good example. We've already noted how his placing of major phrasal divisions keeps us moving forwards, as the meter drives us over the phrasal breaks within the line and the phrases drive us over the metrical breaks at line-end. (This contrasts sharply with the mutual reinforcement between meter and phrasing in "Lizzie Borden.") More generally, in any stretch of language, there are moments when we feel strongly urged forward, others when we feel a strong sense of reaching an end, and many degrees in between these extremes.

Poets exploit these variations to give their verse the movement and emotional qualities they want – relaxed, urgent, insistent, song-like, sweeping in long waves or broken into short bursts, and so on. Phrasal scansion provides an understanding of this variety of movement: it arises from the fact that any closure, except the last, is accompanied by continuity at one or more higher levels.

One measure of closural strength is simply the number of levels at which a phrase-boundary (|) occurs. Thus in our scansion of the Coleridge passage we find that at the ends of the first two sentences phrase-boundaries occur at all levels except the highest, and that the third sentence ends with phrase-boundaries all the way up. By contrast, the syntactic break after "heath" in line 7 has a phrase-boundary at only the two lowest levels, a reflection of the feeling of incompleteness at this point.

The precise effect of these variations in closural strength and onward drive depends on their relation to the metrical line. Since the line-end is a place where closure is favored – the visual signal encourages us to pause, and if the poem is metrical there will be some degree of rhythmic closure at this point – it can reinforce the closural effect of phrasing. This kind of reinforcement happens most noticeably at the end of the passage; it happens also to some degree at the end of line 6, where we feel a slight breathing-space (though the two > symbols indicate that there is still some onward pressure). But if the phrasing of the poem strongly encourages forward movement at the same moment as the line comes to an end the effect is very different: metrical and visual norms are overridden by the demands of sense and syntax, as if the exigencies of feeling or thought were making themselves felt with particular urgency. In general, the phrasing of Coleridge's lines overrides line-ends. We can see this immediately from the number of > symbols in the scansion. Where there are five > symbols the onward drive is particularly strong; this happens at the ends of lines 2 and 4. At these points, we are encouraged to share the intensity of the sense of loss and frustration (and perhaps to register a touch of self-pity). At other line-ends there are usually four or three > symbols, showing a moderate degree of onward movement. In general, Coleridge's handling of line-ends helps to mute the insistence of the meter and to promote the sense of a speaking voice by highlighting the poem's phrasing.

Within the line, different degrees of closure have effects of another kind. In the passage by Coleridge, the strongest breaks (with five phrase-boundaries) occur within the line, and so do two of the three next strongest boundaries (with four phrase-boundaries). By placing these breaks within the line, Coleridge further strengthens the onward movement of the poem, and plays down any tendency for the meter to produce a regular line-by-line march. The strongest breaks in the lines fall, with one exception, near to the midpoint of the metrical structure – that is, after the second or the third beat. When the pentameter is divided in either of these two places, it has a balanced rhythm, possessing some of the qualities of the four-beat line divided in the middle (especially if one of the beats in the three-beat section is unstressed). The result of this tendency to use mid-line breaks is, once again, a certain relaxed formality. The nearest we come to a more disruptive break is line 6, which has a phrase-boundary at three levels after the first beat. This division throws weight onto the word "Friends," a word which is central to the poem's meditation, and which is also emphasized in the meter by an initial inversion.

The passage does not end with a full sense of conclusion, and the phrasing scansion shows why: it ends on a phrase that functions as an extension at levels 4, 5, and 6, where an arrival would give a stronger sense of closure. In fact, the sentence still has ten-and-a-half lines to go, lines made up of extensions at the higher levels with many anticipations and arrivals at the lower levels. The entire poem continues the subtle control of phrasing, playing both with and against the rhythm of the iambic pentameter.

EXERCISE

Analyzing phrasal movement

(3) The following sentence has two meanings; give two phrasal scansions reflecting these meanings.

```
I warmly recommend this candidate with no

qualifications whatsoever.
```

(4) Scan the meter of the following stanza (the first stanza of "A Song," by Thomas Carew), indicate the stress groups, and then add a phrasal scansion on four or five levels. Examine the relation of the phrasing to the structure of the 4x4 formation.

```
Ask me no more where Jove bestows,

When June is past, the fading rose;

For in your beauty's orient deep,

These flowers, as in their causes, sleep.
```

Some basic principles

Phrasal scansion is not an automatic reflection of any purely linguistic properties of the poem. It reflects a reader's sense of the way the poem goes – its high points, its unemphatic moments, its tonal variations, its shifts in feeling, its complex of meanings. A single phrasal scansion – such as the scansion above of the opening of "This Lime-Tree Bower My Prison" – is only one possible way of analyzing the movement implied by a given poem or passage. Other readers, reading the same lines, may well experience different patterns of anticipation and arrival, statement and extension, interrelating with one another in different ways. The value of a phrasal scansion is not that it specifies what *must* happen each time the lines are read, but that it shows how one understanding of the poem plays itself out in phrasal movements. Phrasing is not a question of consciously managing the voice in complicated patterns, but of the way the meanings and syntactic connections of the poem actually unfold in the reader's mind as he or she makes sense of the words. Phrasal movement is less determined by rules and conventions than metrical movement, and phrasal scansion is therefore an even less exact science – or rather, art – than that of metrical scansion.

However, there are a number of constraints on the way phrasing works that arise from the nature of the English language and of more general properties of phrasal movement. As a consequence of these constraints, the possible types of phrase are limited. There are only two types of two-unit phrase:

        ANT–ARR   STA–EXT

There are three types of three-unit phrase:

        ANT–ANT–ARR   ANT–ARR–EXT   STA–EXT–EXT

Four-unit phrases (which are much less common) are of four types:

        ANT–ANT–ANT–ARR   ANT–ANT–ARR–EXT

        ANT–ARR–EXT–EXT   STA–EXT–EXT–EXT

By examining these possible phrases, it is not difficult to get a sense of the constraints that operate. For example, one or more occurrences of ANT are always followed by ARR, and ARR is always preceded by one or more occurrences of ANT. STA is always followed by one or more occurrences of EXT (except when it labels the entire poem or passage). A third constraint is that only an anticipation (ANT) or an extension (EXT) can be repeated. In other words, once a statement (STA) has been made or an arrival (ARR) reached, something *different* has to happen – the phrase either ends or is extended.

For the most part, poetic phrasing employs only these nine different types of phrase in its multi-layered onward movement (or ten, if you include the single movement of the whole phrasal unit which we label "STA"). Most of the time only five of these will be found, since phrases usually consist of two or three subphrases. (The lines by Coleridge, in the scansion above, use just these five types.) Anything longer than four subphrases is very rare, though the examples of four-unit phrases above show how they could occur: by the addition of more ANT subphrases before an arrival and/or more EXT subphrases after an arrival or a statement.

The more levels of phrasing used in a scansion, the simpler the structure of the individual phrases (and the more accurate the reflection of the complex hierarchical movement of language). By starting with the longest phrase of any text, and asking, "Is the movement of this whole phrase produced by two or three subphrases?," and then moving to shorter and shorter phrases with the same question, it's not difficult to capture the hierarchic patterning that is characteristic of phrasing. To capture every nuance, however, might require so many levels of analysis that the usefulness of the scansion as a snapshot would be lost; we should therefore be prepared to simplify where necessary. The lowest level of the Coleridge scansion is something of a simplification, for instance, and could be re-analyzed into two or three levels. However, the gain in subtlety might well be canceled by the loss in clarity.

What is the longest stretch of verse that can be considered a single phrase, and subjected to a phrasal analysis? It's not possible to give a precise answer, since it depends on the movement of the particular poem as it is perceived by a reader. When we reach a long phrase which we do not experience as part of any larger movement we have reached the outer limit of phrasing. It may be a whole poem (if it is relatively short), it may be a single stanza, it may be a verse paragraph. Of course, if the longest phrase does not correspond to the whole poem there will still be *structural relations* over longer spans: interest in the events of the plot may continue to build up until the denouement, an enigma may be posed that drives the reader on to its solution, sections of a long poem will relate to each other in terms of theme and narrative; and so on. But these cannot be described in terms of the movement of the *language*. The dividing line is not easy to draw, but one test of whether a relation between parts of a poem involves phrasal movement is to read, or imagine reading, without any attempt to pronounce the words in real time: purely *structural* relations (which are relations of meaning) would still be felt, but the poem's *movement* would be lost.

EXERCISE

Basic principles

(5) Give a possible phrasal scansion of the following poem by Coventry Patmore. How does the poem's phrasing contribute to its effectiveness? How are the two sentences contrasted in their phrasal movement?

Magna est Veritas

Here, in this little Bay,

Full of tumultuous life and great repose,

Where, twice a day,

The purposeless, glad ocean comes and goes,   4

Under high cliffs, and far from the huge town,

I sit me down.

For want of me the world's course will not fail:

When all its work is done, the lie shall rot;   8

The truth is great, and shall prevail,

When none cares whether it prevail or not.

Phrasing in free verse

In the previous chapter, we examined two ways of approaching the movement of free verse, which we termed "metrical" (the relation of the lines to standard meters) and "rhythmic" (the patterning of stressed and unstressed syllables). Phrasal scansion gives us a third, and potentially more illuminating, way of analyzing the forms of free verse. Phrasing is an aspect of poetic form in which the distinction between metrical and free verse is relatively unimportant: exactly the same structures and processes are to be found in both kinds of verse – and in all uses of language. Of course, it makes a difference if phrasal movement occurs in conjunction with metrical movement, since the two are closely interrelated, but the analysis of the phrasal movement itself follows exactly the same principles.

Let us consider an example of free verse. Here is a poem by Oswald Mbuyiseni Mtshali, a black South African poet, written during one of the

harshest phases of the enforcement of apartheid in his country. It consists of
four sections which, although they have different numbers of lines, we can
call stanzas:

(3)   **Boy on a Swing**

```
Slowly he moves
to and fro, to and fro,
then faster and faster
he swishes up and down.              4

His blue shirt
billows in the breeze
like a tattered kite.

The world whirls by:                 8
east becomes west,
north turns to south;
the four cardinal points
meet in his head.                    12

    Mother!
Where did I come from?
When will I wear long trousers?
Why was my father jailed?            16
```

The poem is at once powerful and, it appears, quite simple. But poetry does
not move us just by means of straightforward statements. If the experience
of reading a poem is a surge of emotion, or a vivid flash of understanding, or
a sudden sense of empathy with another individual, this has happened
because the sequence of words has been crafted with particular effectiveness. Think of how many ways one could tell the brief narrative of a boy on
a swing asking his mother the typical questions of a child, and adding one
that is not typical – except for black children growing up in a country like
South Africa under apartheid. Most of those thousands of alternative pres-
entations would lack the force of this one, and although we cannot hope to
explain why this is so (if we could, computers would write better poems
than people) we can examine some of the contributing factors. In carrying
out such an examination, we not only come to a clearer understanding of
how poetry – and therefore language – works, but we increase our admira-
tion for this poem, and our capacity to be moved by it. Phrasal analysis is
one instrument in that process.

The whole poem is felt by the reader as a single continuous movement
from beginning to end; the highest level of phrasing is therefore the entire
work. Within this overarching phrase there are two distinct movements, the

first of which encompasses three stanzas describing the swinging and its effects, and the last of which comprises the last stanza with its direct speech and its three questions. What is the relation between these two long phrases? Although logically they are not connected, they present the boy's increasingly higher and faster swinging as a build-up to the shout of "Mother!" and the questions that follow. The two phrases therefore function as anticipation and arrival.

At the level below this, we register the great difference between these two movements. The first phrase divides easily into a statement (stanza 1) and two extensions (stanzas 2 and 3) that elaborate upon the initial description, each of these stanzas being one sentence. The second phrase is harder to analyze into its subphrases. Although syntactically it looks like an anticipation ("Mother!"), an arrival ("Where did I come from?") and two extensions, adding further questions ("When will I wear long trousers? Why was my father jailed?"), the emotional force of the entire poem is concentrated in that last question. (And it is increased if we place the poem in the context of South Africa in the 1970s.) It is more accurate, therefore, to show this sequence as three anticipations and an arrival, reflecting the way the two innocent questions lead up to the fraught one, whose impact on the reader comes precisely from the boy's equating it with the others as a natural condition of youthful existence.

We are in a position now to scan the three highest levels of phrasing. The scansion on pages 206–7 also includes three further levels, and an indication of stress groups, which we shall discuss in due course. A phrasal scansion like this is difficult to take in as a whole, especially if one is still learning to handle this type of analysis. It is best to focus on one or two levels at a time. The difference in movement between the first three stanzas and the last is evident at levels 4 and 5, the levels below the ones we have so far discussed. In the first three stanzas, the most common sequence is statement and extension. The only exceptions are two anticipation–arrival sequences: the increasing excitement of "then faster and faster | he swishes up and down" and the subsidiary climax of "the four cardinal points | meet in his head," which hints at a symbolic centrality for the apparently mundane scene. This predominantly calm movement contributes to the sense of normality, in spite of the disorienting experience described in the third stanza.

The final stanza, however, has no additional articulations at levels 4 and 5. What this means is that the movement of the third level (four sentences in the sequence ANT–ANT–ANT–ARR) is repeated and reinforced at these lower levels, whereas up to now the poem had introduced new complexities at these levels. To put it another way, the forcefulness of the final stanza stems in part from its sudden simplicity of movement – a movement that is strongly forward-driving. (Notice that if it were scanned in isolation, the six levels shown would be reduced to three. This indicates how important continuity and contrast are in phrasal movement: the quality of the last stanza is in large part a product of its relation to what has gone before.)

The scansion of level 6 shows how, at the level of shorter phrases, anticipation–arrival sequences become common (here syntactic relations, which usually involve many anticipations, play a greater part). The pattern is not random, however. The first two stanzas move forward primarily by means of statement–extension, reinforcing the calmness of the higher level. Stanza three is more energetically forward-moving, with a series of anticipation–arrival sequences ("The world – whirls by"; "east – becomes west"; "north – turns to south") followed by a reinforcement of the anticipation at a higher level of "the four cardinal points" and finally, within the higher-level arrival of "meet in his head," a slight slackening on a statement–extension sequence. Thus the boy's increasingly vigorous swinging, expressive of some unarticulated emotion, is felt partly through the increasing vigor of the poem's phrasal motion.

The sixth level of the scansion also shows that the intensity of the final stanza derives in part from its repeated pattern of expectation and climax within the lines. It would be possible to divide the questions in a number of different ways, but all of them would show a movement at low levels from anticipation to arrival, and a final arrival on the word "jailed," the word that shocks the reader into reinterpreting the whole poem. This word is an arrival at every level of phrasal movement – except, of course, the highest, which makes of the poem one long statement. Even at the highest level, the poem is perhaps exceptional: we might consider it a single lengthy anticipation, rather than a statement. That is to say, the poem moves toward a conclusion that it doesn't reach, ending instead on a question. The conclusion, the answer to the boy's last question, is for the reader to provide.

As always, the phrasal scansion shows clearly – by the number of arrows – the quality of the transitions between lines. The strongest end-stopping occurs after "meet in his head," where the poem pauses before it shifts into the unexpected direct speech of the last stanza. It is interesting to note that this strong end-stopping is preceded by one of the stronger run-ons, "the four cardinal points / meet...," giving this climactic phrase the additional forcefulness of a strong push over the line-division followed immediately by a strong conclusion. The strongest run-on in the poem, however, is from line 5 to line 6 ("His blue shirt / billows"), emphasizing the movement of the shirt.

Phrasing at the lower levels is articulated very closely with stress groups. One reason for the phrasing "east | becomes west" and "north | turns to south" is that the contrasting compass points take emphatic stress, which in turn produces stress groups that focus on "west" and "south" and

```
1 STA————————>              1 ————————————————>
2 ANT————————>              2 ————————————————>
3 STA————————>              3 ————————————————>
4 STA————————>              4 ————————————————|
5 STA————————|              5 EXT————————————|
6 ANT——|ARR————|            6 STA————————| EXT————|
  |  / x | x  /  |            | / x  |  /|  /|x    /|
    Slowly he moves    1       to and fro, to and fro,   2


1 ———————————————>          1 ———————————————>
2 ———————————————>          2 ———————————————>
3 ———————————————>          3 ——————————————|
4 EXT ——————————>           4 ——————————————|
5 ANT ——————————|           5 ARR——————————|
6 STA ———————— |EXT ———|    6 STA————————|EXT————|
  |  x  / x |x   /  x |       |  x  / x |/ | x   / |
   then faster and faster 3   he swishes up and down.   4


1 —————————>                1 ———————————>
2 —————————>                2 ———————————>
3 EXT ———————>              3 ———————————>
4                           4
5 STA ———————>              5 ——————————————|
6 ANT ———————|              6 ARR——— | EXT ————————|
  |  x   /  |  /  |           | / x |x   x  /  |
    His blue shirt     5       billows in the breeze   6


1 ——————————————>
2 ——————————————>
3 ——————————————|
4               |
5 EXT ——————————|
6               |
  | x   x  / x  | /  |
   like a tattered kite.   7
```

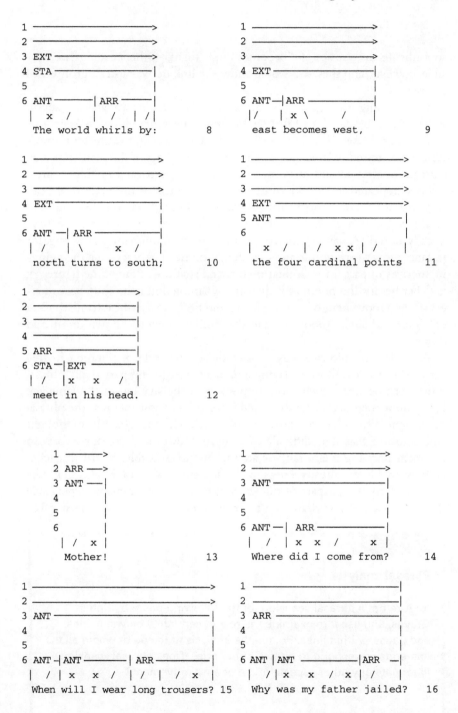

```
1 ─────────────>                    1 ──────────────>
2 ─────────────>                    2 ──────────────>
3 EXT ─────────>                    3 ──────────────>
4 STA ─────────|                    4 EXT ──────────|
5             |                     5             |
6 ANT ───| ARR ───|                 6 ANT ─|ARR ──────|
 | x /  |  /  | /|                   |/   | x \    /    |
   The world whirls by:    8          east becomes west,    9


1 ─────────────>                    1 ────────────────>
2 ─────────────>                    2 ────────────────>
3 ─────────────>                    3 ────────────────>
4 EXT ─────────|                    4 EXT ────────────>
5             |                     5 ANT ────────────|
6 ANT ─| ARR ──────|                6               |
 | /   | \    x /  |                 | x / | / x x | /    |
   north turns to south;    10        the four cardinal points    11


1 ──────────>
2 ──────────|
3 ──────────|
4 ──────────|
5 ARR ──────|
6 STA ─|EXT ──────|
 | / |x   x  /  |
   meet in his head.    12


        1 ────>                     1 ───────────────>
        2 ARR ──>                   2 ───────────────>
        3 ANT ─|                    3 ANT ───────────|
        4     |                     4               |
        5     |                     5               |
        6     |                     6 ANT ─| ARR ──────|
         | / x |                     | /   | x x /     x |
          Mother!    13               Where did I come from?    14


1 ────────────────>                 1 ───────────────|
2 ────────────────>                 2 ───────────────|
3 ANT ────────────|                 3 ARR ───────────|
4                |                  4               |
5                |                  5               |
6 ANT ─|ANT ──────| ARR ──────|     6 ANT |ANT ──────|ARR ─|
 | / |x   x / | / | / x |            | / |x   x / x | /    |
When will I wear long trousers? 15  Why was my father jailed?    16
```

subordinate the stresses of "becomes" and "turns." Other readings are possible, however, and they too would show the link between stress groups and phrases.

In discussing stress groups we are already introducing a *rhythmic* analysis, which could be developed further. We might note how line 2 is kept slow by its many stresses, and how line 3 speeds up because of the greater proportion of unstressed syllables. We might discuss the effect of the many repeated patterns of stressed and unstressed syllables – three stresses in "blue shirt / billows" repeated in "world whirls by," for instance, or the pattern of "east becomes west" and "north turns to south" echoing "Boy on a Swing" and confirmed in "meet in his head" (whose climactic phrasal role we have already noted). A *metrical* analysis would also be illuminating, showing, for instance, how the rhythmic appropriateness of the lines describing the swinging derives in part from familiar meters and rhythmic figures: the figure / x x / that begins the poem as it does many iambic lines; the four-beat nursery-rhyme movement of "to and fro, to and fro"; the two-beat triple rhythm of "faster and faster" modulating to the iambic trimeter "he swishes up and down."

A single example can only hint at the central role of phrasing in free verse. With metrical forms playing a reduced part (or no part at all), phrasal movement becomes even more important in the shaping of the language into potent, memorable, subtly varied verse. It is precisely because the phrasal movement of speech is so intimately connected with the dynamics of thought and emotion that it is difficult to analyze. However short our efforts to represent phrasing might fall, the attempt itself is valuable, in that it teaches us how much we already know without being aware of it. Phrasing, like meter and rhythm, is part of our daily experience of language, experience that poets have always drawn on to create memorable and moving words.

EXERCISE

Phrasal analysis

(6) Attempt a phrasal scansion for the following poem by Robert Graves, and use it to examine the role of continuity between lines, and pauses within lines. Pursue the analysis to the point where all the line-ends correspond to phrase-boundaries. Does phrasal scansion illuminate any other aspects of the poem's movement?

The Impossible

```
Dear love, since the impossible proves
  Our sole recourse from this distress,
Claim it: the ebony ritual-mask of no
  Cannot outstare a living yes.              4

Claim it without despond or hate
  Or greed; but in your gentler tone
Say: "This is ours, the impossible," and silence
  Will give consent it is ours alone.        8

The impossible has wild-cat claws
  Which you would rather meet and die
Than commit love to time's curative venom
  And break our oath; for so would I.        12
```

Summary

The *phrasal movement* (or *phrasing*) of a poem is the experience the reader has of moving toward points of arrival or away from points of departure. It occurs over spans of different length at the same time, most phrases being made up of shorter subphrases with their own patterns of movement. Phrases (which can be any length) are produced by syntax and meaning, and have a varying relation to the rhythm, sometimes reinforcing its movement, sometimes contradicting it.

A particular way of responding to the phrasal movement of a poem or a series of lines is shown in a *phrasal scansion*. It is arranged in *levels*, with the longest phrases at the top, showing the multi-layered character of phrasing. Phrasal scansion indicates degrees of *closure* and *continuity* at every point of the poem; this is especially significant at line-ends (where the greater the number of > symbols one above the other, the stronger the onward movement), and at major breaks within the line. A scansion may be more or less detailed (that is, show a greater or smaller number of levels), depending on the purpose it is serving.

There are four types of phrase: statement (STA), extension (EXT), anticipation (ANT), and arrival (ARR). These function together in a limited number of ways. Usually, the number of subphrases in any phrase is two, three, or four. At the lowest levels, the operation of stress groups and meter is more important than phrasal movement.

Phrasing plays a significant role in both metrical and free verse. In free verse, where there is no continuous metrical scheme, the movement of the poem is largely dependent on its phrasing.

Appendix 1

Scansion

Scanning poetry

To scan a poem is to give a visual representation of some aspects of its rhythmic movement. In scanning a poem, the purpose of the exercise should always be taken carefully into consideration – there is no single mode of scansion that meets all needs. Since there exist many different conventions of notation, it is important when scanning a poem to ensure that the meanings of the symbols are clear.

In dealing with mainstream English metrical verse (stress or syllable-stress), the simplest type of scansion is an indication of where the beats fall. It is best to do this by means of a notation that could not be mistaken as implying that these syllables are stressed, since they may not be. An underline above the first vowel of the relevant syllables is a straightforward notation:

(1)   Loose to the wind their airy garments flew,

Thin glittering textures of the filmy dew.

To someone who knows English and who is familiar with the working of English meter, this is actually all that is necessary to specify the metrical structure of these lines. Not only are the beats indicated; the scansion also shows what happens *between* the beats. There is no doubt that these are iambic pentameter lines, using some of the accepted variations from strict alternation.

However, we might want to include information about the offbeats in our scansion, especially if the meter involves us in making choices about the elision of syllables. We could mark syllables in offbeats with an asterisk:

Loose to the wind their airy garments flew,

Thin glittering textures of the filmy dew.

The scansion now explicitly shows the offbeats, indicating that one of them is a double offbeat (indicated by ★ ★). It also shows that the word "glittering" is to be pronounced as one syllable, not two, since there is no double offbeat marked above it. (We could also indicate the elision by a separate mark if we wished to.)

We have not yet indicated anything about how the lines are *performed*; the assumption is that they demand a normal prose pronunciation. A fuller scansion will show not only the metrical structure of the line, but will give some indication of how this structure is produced by the stress contour of the sequence of words itself, and will sometimes suggest preferable modes of performance. In the notation used

210

in this book, we mark stressed syllables that function as beats with an underlined slash, $\underline{/}$; unstressed syllables that function as beats (i.e. promoted syllables) with an underlined x, unstressed syllables in the offbeat with a plain x, and stressed syllables in the offbeat (i.e. demoted syllables) as a plain slash, /. There is no need for a special symbol for the offbeat; any symbol that is *not* underlined is part of an offbeat. We show an elided vowel by means of a hyphen, - (or better, an en-dash, –).

```
       /    x   x  /    x   / x  / x        /
(1)    Loose to the wind their airy garments flew,

       /    /  - x    / x    x    x  / x  /
       Thin glittering textures of the filmy dew.
```

One further convention is used: we show virtual beats and offbeats (see chapter 3) in square brackets:

```
       x   /  x   /    x  /[x]/  x   x   /
(2)    When lofty trees I see barren of leaves

(3)    Gather ye rosebuds while ye may,

       /    /  x    /   x  /x   [/]
       Old time is still a-flying
```

Since simpler forms of electronic transmission such as e-mail do not permit character formatting, an alternative notation for electronic purposes simply replaces the underlines with a B beneath the line:

```
       /    x   x  /    x   / x  / x        /
(1)    Loose to the wind their airy garments flew,
       B            B        B   B          B

       /    /  - x    / x    x    x  / x  /
       Thin glittering textures of the filmy dew.
       B            B        B    B        B
```

(See "Double-line scansion" below for a more fully-developed version of this notation.)

There are a number of ways in which the stress contour could be shown in more detail; in this book we have sometimes indicated when syllables receive a stress that is significantly less than full (secondary or subordinated stress) with a backslash, \:

```
       \    /  x    /   x  /x   [/]
       Old time is still a-flying
```

Other systems of notation exist to reveal the more complex stress-relations that occur in any English sentence. These more detailed systems don't show any more about the *meter*; what they capture are the many ways in which the same metrical lines can be performed. (In some types of verse – stress verse that demands a chanted reading, for instance – they may provide a misleading picture, since the stress contour of the language is deliberately simplified in performance.)

Reading a sequence of lines aloud while allowing the words to fall into a simple rhythm – and exaggerating it if necessary – is usually the best way of finding where the beats of a meter fall, and from there it is usually not difficult to complete a scansion in whatever detail is required. Sometimes, however, it will be difficult to get a particular poem to work in this way. The reason may of course be that it is in some type of free verse; but it is always worth counting the syllables of the lines before reaching that conclusion. If, for example, every line has ten or eleven syllables, it is likely (though not absolutely certain) that it is in iambic pentameter; this can then be tested in a reading. If the lines vary considerably in terms of their syllable-count, they may be in stress verse (although stress verse usually falls very easily into a strong rhythm), a more complex scheme of varied lines (in which case it is useful to find out if there is any pattern to the variation), or free verse. If the syllable-count is fixed, or varied according to a fixed pattern, and there is no way of reading the lines so that rhythmic beats emerge, the lines are an example of syllabic verse (or some idiosyncratic metrical scheme, such as an imitation of a classical meter).

Scansion can also show other features of rhythmic movement. In strongly rhythmic verse we may want to show more than a single level of metrical movement, and one way of doing this is using variable underlining of the beats (or for electronic purposes, b, B, B+ beneath the line). Virtual offbeats are not shown in this example for the sake of clarity:

(4)
```
        x      ╱   ╱   ╱   ╱   ╱  x   ╱ x   ╱  x x
        We're foot-slog-slog-slog-sloggin' over Africa –

     ╱   ╱   ╱   ╱   ╱  x   ╱ x   ╱  x x
     Foot–foot–foot–foot–sloggin' over Africa –

       ╱   ╱   ╱   ╱   ╱ x   ╱  x   ╱  x ╱
       (Boots–boots–boots–boots–movin' up and down again!)

          x      ╱  x  ╱   x    x   ╱  [ ╱  ╱  ╱]
          There's no discharge in the war!
```

Phrasing can also be indicated by means of scansion, again in varying degrees of detail; a simple system for doing so was introduced in chapter 8. (An even simpler reflection of one aspect of phrasing is to mark mid-line syntactic breaks and to note the occurrence of end-stopped and run-on lines.) More sophisticated systems reveal with more subtlety the complex phrasal relations that characterize any English utterance. Once again, these may or may not be significant in a given example; dull or clumsy verse can have metrical and phrasal patterns just as complex as moving or deft verse. Scansion is a critical art, requiring decisions to be made about what is important to poetic effect and what is irrelevant.

Single-line scansion

The single-line scansion used for most of the examples in this book gives all the necessary information above the line of verse. The symbols used are given in the box below:

Single-line scansion

Symbols

/	stressed syllable; in metrical verse, stressed syllable not functioning as a beat (i.e. demoted)
\	syllable with secondary or subordinated stress; in metrical verse, such a syllable not functioning as beat (i.e. demoted).
∠	stressed syllable functioning as a beat
⅃	syllable with secondary or subordinated stress functioning as a beat
x	unstressed syllable; in metrical verse, unstressed syllable functioning as an offbeat or part of an offbeat
x̱	unstressed syllable functioning as a beat (i.e. promoted)
–	elided syllable
[∠]	virtual beat
[x]	virtual offbeat
∠̲	primary beat in quadruple verse
a/	stress with alliteration (in alliterative verse)
|	division between phrases or stress groups
R	rising stress group
F	falling stress group
M	mixed or monosyllabic stress group
ANT	phrase of anticipation
ARR	phrase of arrival
STA	phrase of statement
EXT	phrase of extension
>	continuation of phrase over line-juncture

Double-line scansion

In the same author's more detailed study of rhythm and meter, *The Rhythms of English Poetry*, and some other works which have adopted its approach, an alternative scansion – which we can call *double-line scansion* – is used. Double-line scansion shows more unmistakably the distinction between, on the one hand, the metrical structure of beats and offbeats and, on the other, the pattern of stressed and unstressed syllables that determines the pronunciation of the words. It also explicitly marks double offbeats, and shows the pause (or "implied offbeat") which occurs between any pair of successive stressed beats which are not separated by a virtual offbeat. Inversion is therefore always signaled by the co-occurrence of a double offbeat and an implied or virtual offbeat (" and ^).

The main symbols are given in the box below (these have been adapted from *The Rhythms of English Poetry* to make them usable in electronic transmission).

Double-line scansion

Symbols

Above the line

+s	stressed syllable
-s	unstressed syllable
s	syllable with secondary stress
(s)	elision by the dropping of a vowel
^s	elision by the coalescence of two vowels

Below the line

B	beat
b	secondary beat in dipodic verse
~B	promoted syllable
o	offbeat
"	double offbeat
*	demoted syllable
[B]	virtual beat
[o]	virtual offbeat
^	implied offbeat

(*The Rhythms of English Poetry* does not distinguish between implied and virtual offbeats: both types are called "implied offbeats," while virtual beats are called "unrealized beats.")

The two modes of scansion can easily be converted. Here are the earlier examples notated with double-line scansion:

```
        +s   -s  -s +s      -s +s-s +s  -s      +s
(1)     Loose to the wind their airy garments flew,
        B         "     B    o  B  o B   o      B
```

```
+s    +s  (s)-s  +s  -s    -s    -s +s  -s +s
Thin glittering textures of the filmy dew.
 *     B    o    B   o   ~B    o  B  o  B
```

```
-s  +s -s  +s   -s +s  +s -s  -s   +s
(2)   When lofty trees I see barren of leaves
       o   B  o    B  o  B[o]B    "      B
```

(3)   Gather ye rosebuds while ye may,

```
s   +s  -s   +s  -s  +s-s
Old time is still a-flying
 *    B   o    B   o   Bo  [B]
```

When successive stressed beats occur without an intervening virtual offbeat, the
scansion shows an implied offbeat. Furthermore, the two major types of elision are
distinguished. The following example shows both of these:

```
^s +s (s)-s  +s-s    -s  +s     +s    -s +s
(5)   The adventurous Baron the bright locks admired
       o  B   o    B   "     B  ^ B  o  B
```

One of the advantages of double-line scansion is that it shows at a glance whether,
and how, a line meets the conditions that control the meter. An iambic pentameter
will always have five Bs below the line separated by one of the offbeat symbols (o, *,
", ^, [o]); it will usually have an offbeat symbol at the beginning and occasionally
one at the end. Inversion will always be marked by the co-occurrence of " and
either ^ or [o].

Double-line scansion also shows clearly above the line how the verse is to be
read. Its main disadvantages are that it is more laborious to write or type out, and
harder to take in at a single glance. But it is a good idea to practice converting the
single-line and double-line scansions into one another, and to develop the ability to
handle both.

Appendix 2

Glossary

This glossary lists two kinds of term: in **bold**, terms used in this book, and <u>underlined</u>, terms that may be encountered in other works on English rhythm and meter, and that are referred to only in passing in this book, if at all. It also indicates equivalences that exist within and between the two sets of terms. The same author's book *The Rhythms of English Poetry* (Longman, 1982), in which a fuller discussion of many of these terms may be found, is referred to as *REP*. Within the entries, **bold** or <u>underlined</u> type also indicates a cross-reference to another term listed in the glossary. (Note that entries are in the singular form, e.g. "foot," not "feet," and that cross-references may be combined, thus *four-beat stress-verse* refers to both *four-beat verse* and *stress-verse*.) Where appropriate, a brief definition is given, but for further information the index (which lists all the words in bold) should be used. For the terms "rhythm" and "meter," see chapter 1.

<u>accent</u>   Not always used in the same way, but most often equivalent to **stress**. Occasionally equivalent to **emphatic stress.** May be used to refer to the means whereby certain **syllables** are made prominent in *any* language (not necessarily by means of stress). It is also sometimes used to mean **beat**, though this can be misleading.

<u>accentual meter</u>   Usually equivalent to **stress meter**, or both **stress meter** and **strong-stress meter**.

<u>accentual-syllabic meter</u>   Equivalent to **syllable–stress meter.**

actual beat, actual offbeat   A **beat** or **offbeat** that is realized in language. Contrasted with **virtual beat, virtual offbeat**.

alexandrine   Six-beat **line** or meter; same as **hexameter**.

alliteration; alliterative verse   The repetition of initial sounds of words; verse which uses alliteration systematically.

<u>anacrusis</u>   The syllables occurring before the first **beat** in a **line**.

<u>anapest; anapestic verse</u> (also <u>anapaest;</u> <u>anapaestic verse</u>)   A **foot** of three syllables, x x /; verse based on this foot. See **triple meter**.

anticipation (ANT)   In **phrasing**, the quality of movement in a **phrase** leading up to another phrase, the **arrival**.

arrival (ARR)   In **phrasing**, the quality of movement in a **phrase** which is led up to by an **anticipation**.

ballad stanza, <u>ballad meter</u>   A variant of the **4x4 formation** with **virtual beats** at the end of the second and fourth **lines** (4.3.4.3). The same **stanza** is called **common measure** in the classification of hymns. May be in **stress meter** or **syllable–stress meter**. (Ballads are usually in stress meter.)

beat   The main rhythmic pulse in

216

metrical verse. May be an **actual beat** or **virtual beat**. Sometimes called <u>ictus</u>, sometimes called (and confused with) **stress** (as in <u>four-stress verse</u>). Shown in **scansion** as underlining: $\underline{/}$, $\underline{x}$.

<u>binary meter</u> Equivalent to **duple meter**.

blank verse Unrhymed **iambic pentameter**.

blurring In **syllable-stress meter**, a reduction in the contrast between **beat** and **offbeat**. Sometimes called <u>hovering accent</u>.

break A syntactic division, registered mentally in reading and sometimes vocally (by means of a **pause**). Often, but not always, indicated by punctuation, breaks are of differing strength, and are an important element of **phrasing**. When occurring within the **line**, a break is sometimes called a <u>caesura</u>.

Burns stanza A variant of the **4x4 formation**, 4.4.4.2.4.2 in **iambic meter**.

<u>caesura</u> A **break** occurring within a **line**. In classical prosody it refers to a specifically metrical requirement, but in accounts of English verse it usually refers to a feature of the syntax as it relates to the meter.

<u>catalectic</u> Lacking the final **syllable**. Used in **foot-prosody** of **hepta-syllabic** lines, for instance.

<u>clitic group</u>, <u>clitic phrase</u> Equivalent to **stress group**.

<u>closed couplet</u> A rhymed **couplet** which coincides with an important syntactic unit.

common measure, <u>common meter</u> A hymn **stanza**, equivalent to the **ballad stanza**.

compensation The addition or omission of a **syllable** in order to maintain the syllable-count in **syllable-stress verse**. It occurs as part of an **inversion**, after an **offbeat** syllable has been omitted or added.

complexity The degree to which a line of metrical verse varies from the most regular realization of the meter. Same as **tension**; see also **variation**.

<u>contraction</u> The dropping of a **syllable** indicated by an apostrophe: "'twas," "Heav'n."

contrastive stress An **emphatic stress** given to a **syllable** as a result of a contrast between two words.

couplet A metrical form with two rhymed **lines**, usually of the same length.

<u>dactyl</u>; <u>dactylic verse</u> A **foot** of three syllables, / x x; verse based on such a foot. See **triple meter**.

<u>decasyllabic</u> Having ten **syllables**. Usually refers to **iambic pentameter**.

demoted stress, demoted syllable See **demotion**. In **duple verse**, equivalent to **stressed offbeat**.

demotion The functioning of a **stressed syllable** as an **offbeat** or part of an offbeat. Occurs in the **rhythmic figures** $\underline{/}$ / $\underline{/}$ and / $\underline{/}$ (at the beginning of the line).

<u>dimeter</u> A **two-beat line** or meter. In **foot-prosody**, a line of two **feet**, or verse made up of such lines.

<u>dipodic verse</u>; <u>dipodic rhythm</u> Equivalent to **quadruple verse**; **quadruple rhythm**.

division See **metrical division**.

<u>dolnik</u>, <u>dol'nik</u> Equivalent to **four-beat stress verse**: a term from Russian prosody, sometimes applied to English verse.

<u>double inversion</u> A metrical **varia-**

tion in **iambic verse**, in which the **compensation** for an omitted or added **offbeat syllable** occurs after another **beat**: x / / x / x x / (double falling inversion) or / x x / x / / x (double rising inversion). Theoretically possible in **trochaic verse** too. Also called <u>postponed pairing</u> (see *REP*).

double-line scansion   A method of **scansion** which shows the relevant linguistic features of the verse (**stressed** and **unstressed syllables**, **elision**) on a line above it, and the metrical structure (**beats** and **offbeats, promotion, demotion, inversion**) on a line below it. (This method is used in *REP*.) See also **single-line scansion**.

double offbeat   Two **syllables** functioning as an **offbeat**. In **stress verse** double offbeats occur freely; in **duple syllable-stress verse** they occur in **inversions** and, in some metrical styles, as **free double offbeats**; and in **triple verse** they occur regularly. In **foot-prosody**, a double offbeat may be scanned as part of an **inversion** or a **substitution**. Shown in **scansion** as x x, or, with **demotion**, x / or / x.

<u>double rhyme</u>   Equivalent to **duple rhyme**. See also <u>feminine rhyme</u>.

duple ending; duple rhyme   A line-ending on a **single offbeat**; a line-ending of this type with **rhyme**. Also called <u>feminine ending</u>; <u>feminine rhyme</u>, and <u>double rhyme</u>.

duple meter; duple rhythm; duple verse   A meter with predominantly **single offbeats**; the rhythm which this meter produces; verse written in this meter.

duple rhyme   See **duple ending**.

eights and sevens   A **four-beat meter** using lines of eight and seven **syllables**.

elision   The dropping of a **syllable** in pronunciation. Shown in **scansion** as −.

emphasis, emphatic stress   An increase in stress on a specific **syllable** for semantic reasons. Also called <u>rhetorical stress</u>.

end-stopped line   A **line** which ends with a significant syntactic **break**.

<u>enjambment</u>   Equivalent to **run-on**.

<u>even position</u>   In some metrical theories, the place in the **line** occupied by a **beat** in **iambic verse** and by an **offbeat** in **trochaic verse**. No equivalent in this book. In **iambic verse**, also called <u>strong position</u>.

extension (EXT)   In **phrasing**, the quality of movement in a **phrase** prolonging, or moving away from, a **phrase** which is a **statement** or an **arrival**.

falling inversion   A **variation** in **syllable-stress meter** which reverses an **unstressed** and a following **stressed syllable**. Produces the **rhythmic figure** / x x / (when it occurs with a **virtual offbeat**) or / / x x (when it occurs without a virtual offbeat). See also **initial inversion**.

<u>falling meter</u>   In **foot-prosody**, sometimes used of meters based on **trochaic** or <u>dactylic</u> feet. No equivalent in this book.

falling rhythm   A rhythm in which **falling stress groups** predominate.

falling stress group   A **stress group** that begins with a **full stress**.

feminine ending; feminine rhyme
Equivalent to **duple ending; duple
rhyme**.

**five-beat line, five-beat meter,
five-beat verse, five-beat
rhythm**   A **line** or meter with five
actual beats. One of the major
types of English metrical verse,
almost always in the form of **iambic
pentameter**.

five-stress line, five-stress verse, five-
stress meter   Sometimes used,
misleadingly, for **five-beat line**, etc.

foot   A theoretical division of a
metrical **line**. The feet in a line are
units of the same type, each with
one **syllable** that takes a **beat** and
one or more that make up an
offbeat.

foot-prosody   A traditional system
of **scansion** derived from classical
prosody and applied to **syllable-
stress verse**. Foot-prosody divides
the metrical **line** into **feet**.

**four-beat line, four-beat meter,
four-beat verse, four-beat
rhythm**   A **line**, meter, type of
verse or rhythm based on units of
four **beats**, one of which may be
virtual. One of the major types of
English metrical verse, occurring in
both **stress verse** and **syllable-
stress verse**. See also **tetrameter**.

**four-by-four formation, 4x4
formation**   A very common
metrical structure of sixteen **beats**,
in which **four-beat lines** tend to be
divided into two-beat **half-lines**,
and to join together in pairs. The
basis of the **ballad stanza** or
common measure and the **iambic
tetrameter quatrain**, among many
other forms.

four-stress line, four-stress verse, four-
stress meter   Sometimes used,
misleadingly, for **four-beat line**,
etc.

fourteener   A variant of the **ballad
stanza** in **syllable-stress meter**,
with the 4.3.4.3 form becoming two
lines: 7.7.

free double offbeat   In **syllable-
stress verse**, a **double offbeat**
occurring outside an **inversion**; that
is, without any **compensation** to
preserve the syllable-count.

free verse   Used of all types of **verse**
without a regular metrical form.
Same as **nonmetrical** verse.

full stress   The **stress** on a monosyllabic word, or the **main stress** of
a polysyllabic word (in contrast to
secondary stress). May be a
subordinated stress.

generative metrics   An approach to
meter based on generative linguistics.
Generative metrics seeks to define
the limits of metricality.

half-line   A metrical subdivision of a
line, usually a two-beat unit in a
four-beat line.

hemistich   Equivalent to **half-line**.

heptameter   A seven-beat **line** or
meter. Examples are the **fourteener**
and the second line of the **poulter's
measure couplet**. Usually has one
virtual beat, making it a double
four-beat unit. In **foot-prosody**, a
line of seven **feet**, or verse made up
of such lines.

heptasyllable, heptasyllabic   A
syllable-stress meter with seven
syllables and four **beats** per **line**.

hexameter   A six-beat **line** or meter;
same as **alexandrine**. Sometimes has
two **virtual beats**, making it two
four-beat units. See also **poulter's
measure**. In **foot-prosody**, a line

of six **feet**, or verse made up of such lines.

hovering   Rough equivalent of **blurring** (as in "hovering accent").

iamb   A two-syllable metrical **foot**, x /.

iambic meter; **iambic verse**   A **duple syllable-stress meter**, normally beginning on an **offbeat** and ending on a **beat**; verse in this meter. In **foot-prosody**, divided into iambs.

iambic pentameter   Equivalent to **five-beat iambic meter**. Very common meter in English literary verse.

iambic tetrameter   Equivalent to **four-beat iambic meter**. Very common meter in English verse.

iambic verse   See **iambic meter**.

ictus   Equivalent to **beat**; used sometimes in **foot-prosody**.

implied offbeat   In **double-line scansion**, a **pause** between successive **stresses** not separated by a **virtual offbeat**. (See *REP*.)

indefinite stress   In **double-line scansion**, a **syllable** that can function either as **stressed** or as **unstressed**. Roughly equivalent to **secondary stress**. (See *REP*.)

initial inversion   A **falling inversion** that occurs at the beginning of an **iambic line**, producing the **rhythmic figure** / x x /.

inversion   A **variation** in **syllable-stress meter**, which effectively switches a pair of **syllables**, an expected x / becoming / x and vice versa. See **falling inversion, initial inversion, rising inversion**.

isochrony; isochronous   Equivalent to **stress-timing; stress-timed**..

limerick   A variant of the **4x4 formation**, with lines of 3.3.2.2.3

actual beats in **triple meter**.

line   Strictly, a segment of a poem determined by layout on the page (or by a performance which reflects that layout). In metrical verse, used more loosely of a segment of the metrical structure normally laid out as a single line on the page – as in **four-beat line, five-beat line**.

line-juncture   The transition from the end of one **line** to the beginning of another.

long measure   A hymn **stanza**: the **4x4 formation** with no **virtual beats**, 4.4.4.4.

main stress   In a polysyllabic word, the strongest **stress** (contrasted with one or more **secondary stresses**). Always a **full stress**. Also called primary stress.

masculine ending; masculine rhyme   Equivalent to **single ending; single rhyme**.

measure   Used in some prosodic systems of a segment of metrical verse consisting of a **beat** and all **syllables** before the next beat.

metrical division   A point at which a metrical unit ends (usually followed by the beginning of the next metrical unit). Part of the **metrical hierarchy**.

metrical hierarchy   The organization of metrical units in levels, with shorter spans combining to make longer spans. Especially marked in the **4x4 formation**.

metrical set   The expectations established by a meter and affecting the way in which the verse is perceived and read. (See *REP*.)

mixed stress group   A **stress group** which neither begins nor ends with a **full stress**.

monometer   A one-beat **line** or
   meter. In **foot-prosody**, a line of
   one **foot**, or verse made up of such
   lines.
monosyllabic stress group   A
   stress group consisting of a single
   stressed syllable.

nonmetrical verse   Same as **free
   verse**.

octameter   An eight-beat **line** or
   meter. Usually divides into two
   four-beat units. In **foot-prosody**,
   a line of eight **feet**, or verse made up
   of such lines.
octave   A set of eight rhymed **lines**.
   Used most often of the first part of a
   sonnet.
octosyllabic meter, octosyllabics   A
   meter based on an eight-syllable
   line, usually **iambic tetrameter**.
odd position   In some metrical
   theories, the place in the **line**
   normally occupied by an **offbeat** in
   iambic verse and by a **beat** in
   trochaic verse. No equivalent in
   this book. In **iambic verse**, also
   called weak position.
offbeat   A weak pulse between,
   before, or after the **beats** of a meter.
   May be a **single offbeat** or a
   double offbeat, and may be an
   actual offbeat or a **virtual offbeat**. (In **double-line scansion**,
   may also be an **implied offbeat**: see
   REP.) Shown in **scansion** by
   absence of underlining. Possible
   offbeats are x, x x, /, x /, / x.
ottava rima   A **stanza** of **iambic
   pentameter lines** rhyming
   abababcc.

pairing   In **double-line scansion**,
   equivalent to **inversion**. (See *REP*.)

pause   A brief silence or a lengthened
   syllable in the performance of
   verse. A pause may be produced by
   a syntactic **break** alone, a significant
   division of the verse (most often a
   line-juncture), or both together. In
   the first case, a pause momentarily
   suspends the meter; in the second
   and third cases it usually reinforces it
   (especially if it coincides with a
   virtual beat and/or **offbeat**). (In
   music, a pause always implies a
   suspension, in contrast to a rest.)
   When it is caused by a syntactic
   break within the **line**, it is sometimes called a caesura.
pentameter   A **five-beat line** or
   meter (with no **virtual beats**).
   Almost always **iambic pentameter**.
   A staple **line** in English literary
   verse. In **foot-prosody**, a line of
   five **feet**, or verse made up of such
   lines.
phrasal movement   Same as
   phrasing.
phrase   A unit of meaning in a
   poem, functioning as part of a
   phrasing hierarchy.
phrasing   The movement of a poem
   produced by syntax and meaning.
   Same as **phrasal movement**.
phrasing hierarchy   The simultaneous movement over spans of different length that constitutes a poem's
   phrasing.
poulter's measure   A variant of the
   4x4 formation in **syllable-stress
   meter**, with **lines** of 6 and 7 **beats**.
   It has two **virtual beats** in the first
   line and one in the second, making
   it a version of the 3.3.4.3 or **short
   measure stanza**.
primary beat   The stronger beat in
   quadruple verse.
primary stress   Equivalent to **main
   stress**.

prolongation   A phrasal movement of **anticipation** and **arrival**, or **statement** and **extension**.

promoted syllable   See **promotion**. Same as **unstressed beat**.

promotion   The functioning of an **unstressed syllable** as a **beat**. Occurs in the **rhythmic figures** x x̲ x, x x̲ (at the end of the line), and x̲ x (at the beginning of the line).

pyrrhic   A foot of two syllables, x x.

quadruple verse; quadruple rhythm Verse in which the beats are perceived as alternating between **primary beats** and **secondary beats**; the rhythm of this verse. Always part of a **4x4 formation**. Also called dipodic rhythm.

quantity; quantitative verse   A property of **syllables** in the classical languages upon which meter was based, with no obvious equivalent in English; **verse** based on quantity.

quatrain   A four-line **stanza**, or part of a stanza, usually rhymed.

regular verse; regularity   Verse that satisfies the expectations aroused by a meter without using many **variations**; the quality of movement of such verse. Regularity is contrasted with **tension** or **complexity**.

relative stress   The comparison of adjoining **syllables** in terms of their actual **stress**. Less important than syntactic relations between syllables, or the rhythm of the **line** as a whole, but a dogma of some twentieth-century approaches to meter.

rest   A segment of meter not realized in language, consisting of one or more **virtual beats** and/or **offbeats**. See also **pause**.

reversed foot   Equivalent to inversion, when it occurs within the bounds of a **foot**.

rhetorical stress   Equivalent to **emphatic stress** and **contrastive stress**.

rhyme   The repetition of the **stressed** vowel of a word and any sounds that follow it, in conjunction with a difference in the consonant immediately preceding it.

rhythmic figure   A discrete pattern of **stressed** and **unstressed** syllables in a particular relation to a series of **beats**. See **demotion**, **promotion, initial inversion, rising inversion, falling inversion**.

rising inversion   A **variation** in **syllable-stress meter** which reverses a **stressed** and a following **unstressed syllable**. Produces the **rhythmic figure** x x / / (when it occurs, as it usually does, without a **virtual offbeat**), or x x / (when it occurs with a virtual offbeat).

rising meter   In **foot-prosody**, sometimes used of meters based on **iambic** or anapestic **feet**. No equivalent in this book.

rising rhythm   A rhythm in which **rising stress groups** predominate.

rising stress group   A **stress group** which ends with a **full stress**.

run-on   Syntactic continuation across **line-juncture**. Also called enjambment.

scansion   A graphic representation of a poem's metrical, rhythmic, and/or phrasal movement. See **single-line scansion** and **double-line scansion**.

secondary beat   The weaker **beat** in **quadruple verse**.

secondary stress   In a word of two or more **syllables**, a stress on a syllable or syllables other than the **main stress** (which is always a **full**

stress). Shown in **scansion** as \. See also **sub-ordinated stress.**

septet   A **stanza** of seven **lines**.

sestet   A **stanza** of six **lines**, or a set of six rhymed lines forming the second part of a sonnet.

short measure   A hymn **stanza**: the **4x4 formation** with **virtual beats** at the ends of three of the lines, 3.3.4.3. See also **limerick** and **poulter's measure**.

single ending; single rhyme   Line-ending on a **beat**; line-ending of this type with **rhyme**. Also called masculine ending; masculine rhyme.

single-line scansion   A method of **scansion**, used in this book, which shows both the relevant linguistic features of the verse (**stressed** and **unstressed syllables, elision**) and its metrical structure (**beats** and **offbeats, promotion, demotion, inversion**) on a single line above the verse.

single offbeat   One syllable function-ing as an **offbeat**. Shown in **scan-sion** as x, \ or /.

single rhyme   See **single ending**.

six-beat line   Same as **alexandrine, hexameter**.

sonnet   A fourteen-line form, made up of an **octave** and a **sestet**, usually in **iambic pentameter** and employing one of a number of fixed rhyme-schemes.

Spenserian stanza   A **stanza** of nine **lines** rhyming ababbcbcc. The first eight lines are **iambic pentameter**, the last is an iambic **hexameter**.

spondee, spondaic   A **foot** of two syllables, / /.

sprung rhythm   A type of meter devised by Gerard Manley Hopkins. Most examples are best read as **free verse**.

stanza   A repeated grouping of **lines**, often with an identical rhyme-scheme. To be distinguished from a **verse paragraph**.

statement (STA)   In **phrasing**, the quality of movement in a **phrase** that is self-sufficient.

stress; stressed syllable   Additional energy in the production of a **syllable**; a syllable which is given this extra force. See also **full stress, main stress, secondary stress, subordinated stress, emphatic stress, contrastive stress**. Also called accent.

stressed offbeat; stressed offbeat syllable   Equivalent to **demoted stress** or **demoted syllable**.

stress group   A word or group of words consisting of one **full stress** and one or more weaker **syllables** attached to it. Also called clitic group or clitic phrase.

stress maximum   Used in generative metrics of a particularly prominent **stress**. No equivalent in this book.

stress meter; stress verse   A meter based on a count of **beats** in relation to the **line** and the **syntax**, allowing **syllables** in the **offbeat** to vary within limits; verse in this meter. Usually in **four-beat meter**.

stress-syllable meter   Equivalent to **syllable-stress meter**, accentual-syllabic meter, syllabotonic meter.

stress-timing; stress-timed   The tendency of the **stresses** in a lan-guage like English to fall at intervals felt to be roughly equal; having this property. Also called isochrony; isochronous.

stress verse   See **stress meter**.

strict stress-meter   Equivalent to **stress meter**.

strong position   In some accounts of meter, the place in the **line** occupied by a **beat**. No equivalent in this book. In **iambic verse**, also called even position.

strong-stress meter; strong-stress verse   A meter which requires a special performance to produce **beats** on four **stresses** in each **line**; verse in this meter. Also called accentual meter; sometimes called **stress meter**.

subordinated stress; subordination   A **full stress** which is felt as somewhat weaker than a nearby stress within the same syntactic unit; the process whereby this happens. Shown in **scansion**, if necessary, as \. See also **secondary stress**.

subphrase   One of the units into which a **phrase** is divided at the next lowest level of the **phrasing hierarchy**. At its own level, each subphrase is itself a phrase, and at every level but the lowest is divided into further subphrases.

substitution   In **foot-prosody**, the replacement of the expected **foot** by another one. No equivalent in this book.

syllabic meter; syllabic verse   A meter based on the number of **syllables** in the **line**, without any control of the **stresses**; verse in this meter.

syllable   The smallest rhythmic unit of English.

syllable-stress meter; syllable-stress verse   A meter based on the number of **beats** and **syllables**, in relation to the **line** and the **syntax**; verse in this meter. Also called accentual-syllabic meter, stress-syllable meter, syllabo-tonic meter.

syllable-timed   Used to describe a language in which the dominant rhythmic unit is the **syllable** (unlike English, in which the dominant rhythmic unit is **stress**).

syllabotonic meter   Equivalent to **syllable-stress meter**.

tension   Same as **complexity**.

tercet   A stanza of three **lines**.

ternary meter   Equivalent to **triple meter**.

terza rima   A continuous verse form in which **lines** occur in threes, rhyming aba bcb cdc, etc.

tetrameter   A **line** or meter with four **actual beats**. In **foot-prosody**, a line of four **feet**, or verse made up of such lines.

three-beat line   A line with three **actual beats**. In some verse, it is in effect a **four-beat line** with one **virtual beat**. Also called trimeter.

three-stress line   Sometimes used, misleadingly, for **three-beat line**.

trimeter   A **line** or meter with three **actual beats**. In **foot-prosody**, a line of three **feet**, or verse made up of such lines.

triple ending; triple rhyme   Line-ending on a **double offbeat**; line-ending of this type with **rhyme**.

triple inversion   A rare metrical **variation** in **iambic verse**, in which the **compensation** for an omitted or added **offbeat syllable** occurs after two further **beats**: x $\angle$ $\angle$ x $\angle$ x $\angle$ x x $\angle$ (triple falling inversion) or $\angle$ x x $\angle$ x $\angle$ x $\angle$ $\angle$ x (triple rising inversion).

triple meter; triple rhythm; triple verse   A meter with predominantly **double offbeats**; the rhythm which this meter produces; verse written in this meter.

triple rhyme   See **triple ending**.

trochaic meter, trochaic verse   A **duple syllable-stress meter**, normally beginning on a **beat** and ending on an **offbeat**. In **foot-prosody**, divided into <u>trochees</u>.

<u>trochee</u>   A two-syllable metrical **foot**, / x.

two-beat line   A **line** with two **actual beats**. Also called <u>dimeter</u>.

<u>unrealized beat</u>   Equivalent to **virtual beat**. (See *REP*.)

unstressed beat   Same as **promoted syllable**.

unstressed syllable   A syllable that has neither **full** nor **secondary stress**. Shown in **scansion** as x.

variation   An acceptable deviation from the expected pattern of **stressed** and **unstressed syllables** in a particular meter.

verse   Language which is distinguished from prose by being governed by an additional principle or principles (e.g. division into **lines**, use of meter, occurrence of **rhymes**). Some-times used as equivalent for line or (in more general discussion of poetry) **stanza**.

verse paragraph   An irregular division of a poem, signaled on the page by space and/or other paragraph marker. Characteristic of both **blank verse** and **free verse**. Contrasted with **stanza**.

virtual beat   A **beat** that is not realized in language, but experienced by the reader as part of the **4x4 formation**. Contrasted with **actual beat**. Shown in **scansion** as [/].

virtual offbeat   An **offbeat** that is not realized in language, but experienced by the reader. Shown in scansion as [x].

<u>weak position</u>   In some accounts of meter, the place in the **line** occupied by an **offbeat**. No equivalent in this book. In **iambic verse**, equivalent to <u>odd position</u>.

Appendix 3

Sources of examples

The following is a list of the sources of the examples used in this book. Examples not listed here are invented.

Chapter 1

1 William Wordsworth, *The Prelude* (1805 version), Book 1, lines 1–4
2 Walt Whitman, *Song of Myself,* lines 167–70
3 Denise Levertov, "Matins"
4 William Blake, *Poems from the Notebook, 1791–2*
5 William Carlos Williams, "The Dance"
6 G. K. Chesterton, "Lepanto"
7 Wallace Stevens, "Peter Quince at the Clavier"
8 Philip Larkin, "Church Going"
9 John Milton, "On the Late Massacre in Piedmont"
10 Thomas Hardy, "During Wind and Rain"
11 John Dryden, "Song for St Cecilia's Day"
12 Edmund Spenser, *The Faerie Queene*, Book 1, canto 9, stanza 40
13 John Milton, *Paradise Lost,* Book 1, lines 1–2
14 George Herbert, "Virtue"

Chapter 2

1 H. D., *The Flowering of the Rod*, 4
2 William Shakespeare, *The Tempest,* Act 5, scene 1, line 94
3 William Wordsworth, "Composed upon Westminster Bridge, September 3, 1802"
4 Alfred Tennyson, "Break, break, break"
5 Jane Austen, *Pride and Prejudice*
6 Charlotte Perkins Gilman, *The Yellow Wallpaper*

Exercises

1 Theodore Roethke, "Frau Bauman, Frau Schmidt, and Frau Schwartze"
2a Samuel Johnson, *Preface to Shakespeare*
2b Samuel Johnson, "The Vanity of Human Wishes," lines 315–18
2c James Joyce, *A Portrait of the Artist as a Young Man*
4 John Ashbery, "The New Spirit," *Three Poems*
6a William Wordsworth, *The Prelude* (1850 version), Book 12, lines 225–30
6b Flannery O'Connor, "Good Country People"
6c Henry Wadsworth Longfellow, *The Song of Hiawatha*, Introduction
6d Charles Dickens, *A Christmas Carol*

Chapter 3

1 Nursery rhyme
5 Traditional

6 Traditional
7 Traditional
8 Traditional
9 Thomas Hardy, "The Little Old Table"

Exercises

1a–c Nursery rhymes
2 J. K. Stephen, "After the Golden Wedding" (embedded in invented prose)
3 Langston Hughes, "Motto"
4 Henry Howard, Earl of Surrey, "Good ladies, you that have your pleasure in exile"

Chapter 4

1 William Butler Yeats, "Into the Twilight"
2 Louis Untermeyer, "Song Tournament: New Style"
3 Ditto
4 Traditional
5 Traditional
6 Gerard Manley Hopkins, "Inversnaid"
7 Traditional
8 Traditional
9 Robert Browning, "Youth and Art"
10 William Wordsworth, *The Waggoner*, Book 3, lines 110–11
12 Samuel Taylor Coleridge, "Christabel"
13 Thomas Hardy, "Rain on a Grave"
14 Traditional
15 Robert Frost, "The Thatch"
16 Traditional
17 Nursery rhyme
18 Traditional
19 Traditional
20 Traditional
21 Traditional

22 Sir Walter Scott, "Young Lochinvar"
23 Traditional
24 Algernon Charles Swinburne, "A Forsaken Garden"
25 Traditional
26 Nursery rhyme
27 Nursery rhyme
28 W. H. Auden, *The Age of Anxiety*
29 "The Seafarer," translated by Michael Alexander
30 *Sir Gawain and the Green Knight*, translated by Marie Borroff
31 E. Sermon and P. Smith, "It's My Thing"
32 Matt Dike, Mike Ross, Tony Smith, and Marvin Young, "Wild Thing"

Exercises

1 George Gordon, Lord Byron, *The Siege of Corinth*, lines 698–703
2 Lewis Carroll, "The Hunting of the Snark," lines 1–4
3 Robert Browning, "Meeting at Night"
4 John Keats, "La Belle Dame sans Merci"
5 Rudyard Kipling, "Gentlemen-Rankers"
6a William Blake, "Nurse's Song," from *Songs of Innocence*
6b William Blake, "London," from *Songs of Experience*
7 Traditional
8 Robert Browning, "A Woman's Last Word"
9 E. Fletcher, S. Robinson, C. Chase and M. Glover, "The Message"

Chapter 5

1 Traditional "Love is Teasing"
2 Karl Shapiro, "Elegy Written on a Frontporch"

3 Thom Gunn, "'Blackie, the Electric Rembrandt'"
4 John Betjeman, "Church of England Thoughts Occasioned by Hearing the Bells of Magdalen Tower"
5 W. H. Auden, "Lullaby"
6 Jonathan Swift, "Stella's Birthday, 1727"
7 John Dryden, *Absalom and Achitophel*, lines 1–4
8 William Shakespeare, Sonnet 87
9 George Gordon, Lord Byron, *Don Juan*, Canto 11, stanza 60
10 Robert Louis Stevenson, "Good and Bad Children," *A Child's Garden of Verses*
11 Charles Kingsley, "Airly Beacon"
12 John Milton, "L'Allegro," lines 19–22
13 John Clare, "Song: I Hid My Love"
14 Edward Lear, "Incidents in the Life of My Uncle Arly"
15 Anne Bradstreet, "The Flesh and the Spirit"
16 Robert Lowell, "Mr Edwards and the Spider"
17 Elizabeth Barrett Browning, "Grief"
18 John Keats, "Ode to a Nightingale"
19 George Gordon, Lord Byron, *Don Juan*, Canto 1, stanza 103
20 William Shakespeare, Sonnet 2
21 Andrew Marvell, "The Garden"
22 Andrew Marvell, "Damon the Mower"
23 Christopher Marlowe, *Dr Faustus*, Act 5, scene 2, lines 153–4
24 Robert Browning, "The Bishop Orders His Tomb at Saint Praxed's Church," lines 52-5
25 Percy Bysshe Shelley, "Adonais," stanza 35
26 Alfred Tennyson, *In Memoriam*, 54
27 W. B. Yeats, "A Dialogue of Self and Soul"
28 Emily Dickinson, "Because I could not stop for Death"
29 William Shakespeare, Sonnet 66
30 William Shakespeare, "The Phoenix and the Turtle"
31 Richard Lovelace, "To Althea, from Prison"
32 Matthew Arnold, "Stanzas from the Grande Chartreuse," lines 175–80
33 William Wordsworth, "Strange fits of passion have I known"
34 William Wordsworth, *The Prelude* (1850 version), Book 4, lines 326–7
35 William Shakespeare, *The Merchant of Venice*, Act 5, scene 1, lines 89–91
36 John Keats, "Ode to a Nightingale"
37 Andrew Marvell, "The Garden"
38 John Keats, "Ode on a Grecian Urn"
39 Alfred Tennyson, *Idylls of the King*, "The Passing of Arthur," lines 89–91
40 Alexander Pope, *The Dunciad in Four Books*, Book 2, lines 387–8
41 John Donne, Holy Sonnet: "At the round earth's imagined corners, blow"
42 Percy Bysshe Shelley, "Epipsychidion," lines 437–9
43 Percy Bysshe Shelley, "The Sensitive Plant," Part 3, line 15
44 Samuel Johnson, "The Vanity of Human Wishes," lines 61–2
45 Alexander Pope, *The Rape of the Lock*, Canto 2, lines 121–2
46 Matthew Arnold, "Stanzas from the Grande Chartreuse," line 209
47 Sir Philip Sidney, *Astrophil and Stella*, sonnet 20
48 James Thomson, *The Seasons*, "Summer," lines 1379–81
49 Alexander Pope, "Epistle to Burlington," lines 143–4
50 W. B. Yeats, "Among School Children"
51 Alexander Pope, "Epistle to Bathurst," lines 169–70
52 Alexander Pope, "Epistle to Bathurst," lines 113–14
53 Alexander Pope, "Epistle to Bathurst," lines 21–2

54 Alexander Pope, "Epistle to Arbuthnot," line 28

55 Jonathan Swift, "A Description of a City Shower"

56 Alexander Pope, "Epistle to Bathurst," lines 149–50

57 Alexander Pope, "Epistle to Bathurst," lines 47–8

58 Alexander Pope, "Epistle to Bathurst," lines 133–4

59 William Wordsworth, *The Prelude* (1805 version), Book 7, line 667

60 William Shakespeare, Sonnet 42

61 William Shakespeare, Sonnet 29

62 William Wordsworth, *The Prelude* (1850 version), Book 11, lines 136–7

63 William Shakespeare, *The Tempest*, Epilogue

64 William Wordsworth, "The Reverie of Poor Susan"

65 George Gordon, Lord Byron, "Stanzas Written on the Road between Florence and Pisa"

66 Thomas Hardy, "The Voice"

67 Ralph Waldo Emerson, "The Snow-Storm"

68 John Keats, "To Autumn"

69 Robert Devereux, Earl of Essex, "Change thy mind since she doth change"

70 Michael Drayton, *Idea*, Sonnet 61, "Since there's no help, come let us kiss and part"

71 John Keats, "Ode to a Nightingale"

72 Thomas Gray, "Elegy Written in a Country Churchyard"

73 Thomas Gray, "Ode on the Death of a Favourite Cat"

74 William Shakespeare, *A Midsummer Night's Dream*, Act 1, scene 1, lines 232–3.

75 William Shakespeare, *A Midsummer Night's Dream*, Act 2, scene 2, line 121

76 William Shakespeare, Sonnet 19

77 George Gordon, Lord Byron, "The Destruction of Sennacherib"

78 Thomas Hood, "The Bridge of Sighs"

79 William Shakespeare, *The Tempest*, Act V, scene 1, line 93

80 Robert Browning, "How They Brought the Good News from Ghent to Aix"

Exercises

1a Alfred Tennyson, "The Lady of Shalott"

1b Edward Fitzgerald, "Rubáiyát of Omar Khayyám," stanzas 56–7

1c W. H. Auden, "In Memory of W. B. Yeats"

2 Sir Thomas Wyatt, "All heavy minds"

3 Sir John Betjeman, "Slough"

4 William Shakespeare, *Romeo and Juliet*, Act 2, scene 2, lines 2–10

5 John Milton, *Paradise Lost*, Book 4, lines 797–803

6 Matthew Arnold, "The Scholar-Gipsy"

7 Percy Bysshe Shelley, "Adonais," stanza 24

8 W. B. Yeats, "Meditations in Time of Civil War"

9 Samuel Johnson, "On the Death of Dr Robert Levet"

10 John Donne, "The Flea"

11 Percy Bysshe Shelley, *Queen Mab*, Book 8, lines 166–80 (altered)

12 Robert Browning, *The Ring and the Book*, Book 1, lines 91–109

13 Thomas Moore, "Dear Harp of my Country!"

14 Sir Philip Sidney, *Astrophil and Stella*, sonnet 20

Chapter 6

1 A. E. Housman, "The mill-stream, now that noises cease"

2 Emily Dickinson, "It was not Death, for I stood up"
3 Robert Burns, "To a Mouse"
4 Sir John Suckling, "Out upon it, I have loved"
5 Edgar Allan Poe, "The Raven"
6 Robert Browning, "A Toccata of Galuppi's"
7 Sir Thomas Wyatt, "With serving still"
8 Jonathan Swift, "Stella's Birthday, 1721"
9 W. H. Auden, "Shorts"
10 W. B. Yeats, "On a Political Prisoner"
11 Henry Vaughan, "Regeneration"
12 W. H. Auden, "Precious Five"
13 Sir Philip Sidney, *Astrophil and Stella*, sonnet 1
14 Traditional
15 Traditional, rewritten
16 Alexander Pope, "The First Epistle of the Second Book of Horace Imitated," lines 201–4
17 Andrew Marvell, "The Mower Against Gardens"
18 William Shakespeare, Sonnet 73
19 Katherine Philips, "Orinda upon Little Hector Philips"
20 John Milton, *Paradise Lost*, Book 1, lines 663–9
21 William Shakespeare, *King Lear*, Act 1, scene 2, lines 1–6

Exercises

1 Robert Herrick, "To Music, to Becalm His Fever"
2a Wilfred Owen, "Exposure"
2b Edward Thomas, "The Other"
3 Robert Herrick, "Corinna's Going A-Maying"

Chapter 7

1 William Blake, *Jerusalem*, Chapter 3, plate 67, lines 47–51
2 Gerard Manley Hopkins, "The Leaden Echo"
3 Ezra Pound, "The Return"
4 T. S. Eliot, "Marina"
5 William Carlos Williams, "The Descent of Winter"
6 John Berryman, *The Dream Songs*, poem 40
7 Susan Howe, *Pythagorean Silence*, 3.
8 Adrienne Rich, "Night Watch"
9 Adrienne Rich, "Novella"
10 Adrienne Rich, "Women"
11 Adrienne Rich, "Burning Oneself In"
12 D. H. Lawrence, "Mountain Lion"

Exercises

1 F. T. Prince, "The Old Age of Michelangelo"
2 Elizabeth Bishop, "A Cold Spring"

Chapter 8

1 Traditional
2 Samuel Taylor Coleridge, "This Lime-Tree Bower My Prison"
3 Oswald Mbuyiseni Mtshali, "Boy on a Swing"

Exercises

2 Ogden Nash, "The Turtle"
4 Thomas Carew, "A Song"
5 Coventry Patmore, "Magna est Veritas"
6 Robert Graves, "The Impossible"

Appendix 1: Scansion

1 Alexander Pope, *The Rape of the Lock,* Canto 2, lines 63–4
2 William Shakespeare, Sonnet 12

3 Robert Herrick, "To the Virgins, to Make Much of Time"
4 Rudyard Kipling, "Boots (Infantry Columns)"
5 Alexander Pope, *The Rape of the Lock*, Canto 2, lines 29–30

Suggested responses to the exercises

The following are suggested responses to those exercises and parts of exercises which call for scansion and other types of marking. In consulting them, readers should remember that there is often no single correct solution; what is represented here may be one possibility among many.

Chapter 2

Page 23

<table>
<tr><td>(1)</td><td>Gone the three ancient ladies</td><td>4</td></tr>
<tr><td></td><td>Who creaked on the greenhouse ladders,</td><td>6</td></tr>
<tr><td></td><td>Reaching up white strings</td><td>3</td></tr>
<tr><td></td><td>To wind, to wind</td><td>2</td></tr>
<tr><td></td><td>The sweet-pea tendrils, the smilax,</td><td>5</td></tr>
<tr><td></td><td>Nasturtiums, the climbing</td><td>1</td></tr>
<tr><td></td><td>Roses, to straighten</td><td>2</td></tr>
<tr><td></td><td>Carnations, red</td><td>1</td></tr>
<tr><td></td><td>Chrysanthemums; the stiff</td><td>1</td></tr>
<tr><td></td><td>Stems, jointed like corn,</td><td>5</td></tr>
<tr><td></td><td>They tied and tucked,-</td><td>7</td></tr>
<tr><td></td><td>These nurses of nobody else.</td><td></td></tr>
</table>

Page 25

(2)

```
          s   s  s  s    s   s     s      s   s s s    s s     s     s
(a)     A quibble is to Shakespeare what luminous vapours are to
```

```
      s   s s s     s s s     s s s     s s s       s  s
      the traveller: he follows it at all adventures; it is
```

```
      s   s  s     s  s   s    s   s  s     s   s s s     s  s
      sure to lead him out of his way and sure to engulf him in
```

```
        s   s
      the mire.
```

```
      s  s       s       s       s     s s s     s   s
(b)   In life's last scene what prodigies surprise,
```

```
      s    s     s    s     s     s  s     s     s   s
      Fears of the brave, and follies of the wise?
```

```
        s   s        s          s       s   s     s   s s      s
      From Marlb'rough's eyes the streams of dotage flow,
```

```
      s      s   s  s     s   s     s   s     s  s
      And Swift expires a driv'ler and a show.
```

The apostrophes in "Marlb'rough's" and "driv'ler" indicate that these
words are contracted, and their longer forms cannot be used here.

```
        s s s   s   s s   s   s s s   s   s     s     s s
(c)   The box of pawntickets at his elbow had just been rifled
```

```
      s    s s    s  s s s     s  s s s  s   s     s      s s
      and he took up idly one after another in his greasy
```

```
        s s      s   s s      s    s s        s     s     s s
      fingers the blue and white dockets, scrawled and sanded
```

```
      s      s      s    s s      s   s    s    s    s s s   s s
      and creased and bearing the name of the pledger as Daly
```

```
      s   s s s
      or MacEvoy.
```

Page 34

```
        /  x     x /     /  \     /  x   x /      /  x
(3)   rocket  divine  tree-root  restful  unhinged  gladly
```

```
        x  /
      consign
```

```
       /  x  x   x /    x   \ x   /     x / x      /   \ x
      terribly  delightful  understand  relation  dog-lover
```

```
      \      /  x
      topsy-turvy

      \  x  /  x     \  x  / x x    \  x / x x   /  x  \  x x
      intermission  multiplicity  reprehensibly  dairy-manager

          /      /  x   x   /    /    /    x    x   /   x
(4)   Quick thinking on your part saved us from such a

      \ x  x / x    /       /      x  /  x x  /        x
      melodramatic end, though: you merely restored the

      x /  x   x    x  x  / x x x   /x x     x  /  x x    x
      dimension of the exploratory dialogue, conducted in the

      / x x  /    x    x    /  x /   x    /   x   x  / x
      general interest, and we resumed our roles of progressive

        /  x   x    /   x   x   x /   x   /
      thinkers and builders of the art of love.

                        \      /       \     /            \
(5)   They lingered, half chastened, half glad, in the cool

         /          \    /      \    /                  \
      shadow of the old barn; the day's happenings needed much

         /
      thought.
```

The contrast between "chastened" and "glad" may result in emphatic stresses on these words, and in a weakening of the repeated "half."

Page 40

(6)
Order of regularity: c, d, a, b.

```
        x   x / x   /      x  /      x   /  x x x  / x
(a)   I remember well, that once, while yet my inexperienced

         /   x    /   x  /   x   / x    x    /    /    x
      hand could scarcely hold a bridle, with proud hopes I

        /   x   x   x   /  x    x /     x  /    x  /  x
      mounted, and we journeyed towards the hills: an ancient

        /  x   x   x   /  x    /      x  x   x   /  x  / x x
      servant of my father's house was with me, my encourager
```

```
x      /
and guide.
```

From Wordsworth's *Prelude*; alternating rhythm with some variations (verse set out as prose).

```
       x  x   / x   x   x   x   / x   \ x/ x x   x
(b)    He  was gazing at her with open curiosity, with
```

```
       \ x / x     x   x   /   /   x   x  /   x  / x  / x x
       fascination, like a child watching a new fantastic animal
```

```
       x    x  /   x    x x    /   x  x  x   x  x   /  x   /
       at the zoo, and he was breathing as if he had run a great
```

```
       /  x    x  /    x
       distance to reach her.
```

From Flannery O'Connor, "Good Country People"; rhythmically irregular (prose).

```
       |  /     x |/   x|  /   | x    / x   |  /   | x
(c)    Should you ask me, whence these stories?  Whence these
```

```
       / x   |x    x / x  | x     x / x  |x   x / x |
       legends and traditions, with the odors of the forest,
```

```
       x     x / |x   / |x  / x | x     x / x  | / |
       with the dew and damp of meadows, with the curling smoke
```

```
       x  / x | x    x / x |x   / | / x  | x    x
       of wigwams, with the rushing of great rivers, with their
```

```
       /  x | \ x / x   | x    x    /  | x \ x / x   | x
       frequent repetitions, and their wild reverberations, as
```

```
       x   / x |x    x / x   |
       of thunder in the mountains?
```

From Longfellow, *Hiawatha*, Introduction; strongly alternating (verse set out as prose). Note the tendency to stress many of the syllables marked here as unstressed. Four rising groups, three falling groups, fourteen mixed groups, and three monosyllables. The rhythm is predominantly mixed, countering the natural preference of the language for a rising rhythm.

```
       |x  / x|  /  |x / | x    /   | x   / |x / x| /x |
(d)    In easy state upon this couch, there sat a jolly Giant,
```

```
       / xx  | x / |   x / |x   / x | /  | x   / | x
       glorious to see; who bore a glowing torch, in shape not
```

```
x / |  / x | /  | x   / |x / |  \   / | x
unlike Plenty's horn, and held it up, high up, on

   /  | x  x  x   / x | /  | x| / |
Scrooge, as he came peeping round the door.
```

Dickens, *A Christmas Carol* (prose); alternating rhythm. Many readers will pronounce "unlike" with stress on the first syllable to keep the rhythm regular. Eleven rising groups, three falling groups, four mixed groups, and three monosyllabic groups. The rhythm is strongly rising, enhancing the natural preference of the language.

Chapter 3

Page 47

(1)
(a)
```
Georgie Porgie, pudding and pie,
   B       B        B          B

Kissed the girls and made them cry;
   B          B         B        B

When the boys came out to play,
   B     B      B     B

Georgie Porgie ran away.
   B       B     B    B
```

(b)
```
To market, to market, a gallop, a trot;
    B          B          B         B

To buy some meat to put in the pot;
    B        B        B         B

Threepence a quarter, a groat a side,
    B           B         B       B

If it hadn't been killed it must have died.
       B          B          B         B
```

(c)
```
The cock's in the woodpile a-blowing his horn,
     B          B              B          B

The bull's in the barn a-threshing of corn,
     B          B          B          B

The maids in the meadows are making of hay,
     B          B            B         B
```

```
The ducks in the river are swimming away.
    B            B           B        B
```

Page 53

(2)
```
She does not always see the point
    B        B      B      B
```

```
Of little jests her husband makes,
    B      B       B       B
```

```
And, when the world is out of joint,
     B        B       B      B
```

```
She makes a hundred small mistakes.
    B        B        B      B
```

Page 57

(3)
```
I play it cool and dig all jive –
    B       B       B      B
```

```
That's the reason I stay alive.
  B         B        B    B
```

```
My motto, as I live and learn
   B     B   B    B
```

```
Is Dig and be dug in return.
   B         B  B    B
```

The main syntactic division of the third line is after one beat, not the usual two.

Page 61

(4)
The poem is an example of *poulter's measure*, in which the 3.3.4.3 stanza becomes 6.7, with virtual beats after the units of three.

```
But you whom love hath bound, by order of desire,
    B          B         B  [B]  B      B      B   [B]
```

```
To love your lords, whose good deserts none other would
   B         B          B      B          B      B
```

```
require,
   B   [B]
```

```
Come you yet once again, and set your foot by mine,
      B      B      B  [B]   B           B         B      [B]

Whose woeful plight, and sorrows great, no tongue may
      B        B          B           B       B

well define.
  B     B         [B]
```

Chapter 4

Page 66

```
        /              /              /              /
(1)    The steeds are all bridled, and snort to the rein;
        B              B              B              B

    /          /            /            /
   Curved is each neck, and flowing each mane;
    B          B            B            B

    /          /            /            /
   White is the foam of their champ on the bit;
    B          B              B            B

       /           /            /            /
   The spears are uplifted; the matches are lit;          4
        B           B            B            B

       /           /            /            /
   The cannon are pointed, and ready to roar,
        B           B            B          B

       /           /            /            /
   And crush the wall they have crumbled before.
        B           B              B            B
```

```
        ∠              ∠              ∠              ∠
   The steeds are all bridled, and snort to the rein;

    ∠          ∠            ∠            ∠
   Curved is each neck, and flowing each mane;

    ∠          ∠            ∠            ∠
   White is the foam of their champ on the bit;

       ∠           ∠            ∠            ∠
   The spears are uplifted; the matches are lit;          4
```

```
       ∠          ∠           ∠          ∠
   The cannon are pointed, and ready to roar,

       ∠          ∠               ∠          ∠
   And crush the wall they have crumbled before.
```

Page 69

```
       x    x  ∠   x  x  ∠       x  ∠  x     ∠
(2)   "Just the place for a Snark!" the Bellman cried,

       x   x  ∠  x   x   ∠   x    ∠    [x  ∠]
      As he landed his crew with care;

       x  ∠  x   x    ∠  x    x  ∠  x     x  ∠
      Supporting each man on the top of the tide

       x  x  ∠  x  x   ∠    x   x   ∠   [x  ∠]
      By a finger entwined in his hair.
```

Page 74

```
       x   x  ∠   x   ∠    /    ∠  x   ∠
(3)   Then a mile of warm sea-scented beach;

        /   ∠    x   ∠   x   x  ∠  x  ∠
      Three fields to cross till a farm appears;

      x  ∠  x   x  ∠    x   ∠    /      ∠
      A tap at the pane, the quick sharp scratch

      x      ∠[x] ∠   x  x  ∠   x   ∠
      And blue spurt of a lighted match,                    4

      x    x  ∠    /   ∠     x   x   ∠  x   ∠
      And a voice less loud, through its joys and fears,

        x    x  ∠  /    ∠  x   ∠    x  ∠
      Than the two hearts beating each to each!
```

The scansion of "sea-scented" given here reflects a pronunciation that gives both parts of the compound equal weight. It would be closer to normal pronunciation – but more disruptive of the rhythm – to put the main stress on "sea":

```
       x   x  ∠    x    ∠ [x] ∠   \  x    ∠
      Then a mile of warm sea-scented beach
```

Page 77

```
        x  ∠  x  ∠    x     ∠   x  ∠
(4)     O what can ail thee, knight at arms,

        x ∠  x    ∠  x  ∠ x x
        Alone and palely loitering?

         x  ∠    x  ∠ x    x    x ∠
        The sedge has wither'd from the lake,

        x    ∠ /    ∠   [x ∠ x ∠]
        And no birds sing.                    4


        x   ∠  x  ∠    x     ∠   x  ∠
        O what can ail thee, knight at arms,

         x ∠ x  x   x  ∠   x \
        So haggard and so woe-begone?

         x   ∠  x     ∠ x x x   ∠
        The squirrel's granary is full,

        x    x  ∠ x     ∠   [x ∠ x ∠]
        And the harvest's done.               8
```

The virtual beats shown after the last line reflect the feeling the reader has of a long pause, though it's unlikely that they would be experienced as distinct beats.

Page 79

```
        x        ∠      ∠    ∠     x      ∠        ∠
(5)     If the home we never write to, and the oaths we never

          ∠
        keep,

        [∠]   ∠      ∠      ∠     x      ∠     [∠ ∠]
        And all we know most distant and most dear,

        [∠] ∠       ∠    ∠    ∠    ∠      ∠
        Across the snoring barrack-room return to break our

          ∠
        sleep,

        x      ∠    x    ∠     ∠       ∠ [∠ ∠]
        Can you blame us if we soak ourselves in beer?        4
```

```
    x      ∠      ∠      ∠      x      ∠
When the drunken comrade mutters and the great

          ∠         ∠
    guard-lantern gutters

    x      ∠    x      ∠        ∠      ∠  [∠  ∠]
And the horror of our fall is written plain,

  ∠    ∠      ∠      ∠      x      ∠      ∠
Every secret, self-revealing on the aching whitewashed

     ∠
    ceiling,

    x      ∠    x      ∠        ∠        ∠  [∠  ∠]
Do you wonder that we drug ourselves from pain?        8
```

Page 82

(6)

(a) Triple verse:

```
    x    x ∠ x  x    ∠  x  x    ∠    x    x  ∠
When the voices of children are heard on the green,

x    ∠  x  x    ∠  x    x ∠  [x  x  ∠]
And laughing is heard on the hill,

  x  ∠    x  x  ∠    x  ∠  x  ∠
My heart is at rest within my breast,

x    ∠ x    x    ∠  x    ∠  [x  x  ∠]
And everything else is still.
```

(b) Duple verse:

```
x  ∠  x    x    x    ∠  x      ∠
I wander through each chartered street,

  ∠    x    x  ∠ x    ∠    x    ∠
Near where the chartered Thames does flow,

x    ∠  x ∠  x ∠  x ∠
And mark in every face I meet

  ∠  x  ∠  x    ∠  x  ∠
Marks of weakness, marks of woe.
```

Page 85

(7)

```
x  /    \  x  /  x    x  /    x x  /
A sweet-scented Courtier did give me a Kiss,
```

```
x    / x    x  /  x    x  /  x    x  /
And promis'd me Mountains if I would be his,
```

```
x  /    x  x /    x    x x  x  x    /
But I'll not believe him, for it is too true,
```

```
x   /  x    x  / x    x   /    x    x  /
Some courtiers do promise much more than they do.    4
```

```
x  /  x  x /    x  x    /  x  x  /
My Thing is my own, and I'll keep it so still,
```

```
x / x   /    / x  x  /  x    x  /
Yet other young Lasses may do what they will.
```

The swing of the triple rhythm is not hindered by these instances of demotion and promotion.

Page 87

(8)

```
| / |  x   / x  |  / x  |      MMF
  See the creature stalking
```

```
|  / | x   / |               MR
  While we speak!
```

```
| / |x   / | x / x |          MRM
  Hush and hide the talking,
```

```
|  / |x   / |                MR
  Cheek on cheek!                    4
```

```
|  / | x / |x   / x |          MRM
  What so false as truth is,
```

```
| /   | x  / |                MR
  False to thee?
```

```
| / | x / x  | / x |  MMF
  Where the serpent's tooth is
```

```
| / | x  / |                MR
  Shun the tree —                    8
```

```
|  /  |  x / x |  /  x  |        MMF
Where the apple reddens
```

```
| / x |  /|                      FM
Never pry —
```

```
|  /  | x  /  |x   / x  |        MRM
Lest we lose our Edens,
```

```
|/  |x  /|                       MR
Eve and I.                              12
```

Eight rising groups, four falling groups, eighteen mixed or monosyllabic groups. Although short lines beginning on the beat often produce falling rhythms, all but one line in this example begin with a monosyllabic group, making possible a preponderance of mixed and rising rhythms.

Page 95

(9)

```
        ∠        ∠           ∠        ∠
A child is born with no state of mind
```

```
    ∠           ∠       ∠ ∠
Blind to the ways of mankind
```

```
        ∠           ∠           ∠        ∠
God is smiling on you but he's frowning too
```

```
        ∠           ∠         ∠        ∠
Because only God knows what you go through      4
```

```
        ∠           ∠           ∠       ∠
You grow in the ghetto, living second rate
```

```
        ∠           ∠     ∠            ∠
And your eyes will sing a song of deep hate
```

```
        ∠           ∠       ∠         ∠
The place that you play and where you stay
```

```
        ∠         ∠       ∠   ∠
Looks like one great big alleyway.              8
```

These marks show the placing of the beats in the performance by Grandmaster Flash and the Furious Five; however, the same words allow a number of different arrangements of beats.

Chapter 5

Page 105

(1)

(a)
```
      /x    /   x    / x    /
      Lying, robed in snowy white

      x   /   x   /   x   /   x    /
      That loosely flew to left and right –

      x   /    x /   x   /  x    /
      The leaves upon her falling light –

      x̱       x  / x  x̱    x  /
      Through the noises of the night          4

       x   /  x   /   x  / x x̱
      She floated down to Camelot.
```

The lines are in "eights and sevens"; that is, a mixture of iambic tetrameters and heptasyllabic lines (there are no trochaic lines, unlike the example from "L'Allegro" discussed earlier). The 4.4.4.4.4 stanza is a 4x4 formation with an additional four-beat line.

(b)
```
      x     /    x  x̱    x    / x   x̱   x    /
      Oh, Thou, who didst with Pitfall and with Gin

      x /   x  /  x  x̱   x _ / x   x̱
      Beset the Road I was to wander in,

       x   /   x   x̱     x \ x / x    /
      Thou wilt not with Predestination round

      x  /   x  x̱   x  /   x  /   x  /
      Enmesh me, and impute my Fall to Sin?         4


      x    ·/    x / x   / x  /      x    /
      Oh, Thou, who Man of baser Earth didst make,

      x    x̱  x  / x   x̱    x /   x   /
      And who with Eden didst devise the Snake;

       x   /   x  /   x   /   x  /   x  /
      For all the Sin wherewith the Face of Man

      x   / x     /   x /  x   /   x   /
      Is blacken'd, Man's forgiveness give – and take! 8
```

Iambic pentameters, in 5.5.5.5 stanzas.

(c)
```
x̱    x   ⌐   x    x̱    x   ⌐    [x]
In the nightmare of the dark

⌐    x  ⌐   x   ⌐  x     ⌐     [x]
All the dogs of Europe bark,

x̱      x  ⌐ x    ⌐ x      ⌐    [x]
And the living nations wait,

⌐     x  ⌐  x    x̱  x     ⌐    [x]
Each sequestered in its hate;         4


x̱  x   ⌐  x̱x̱    x   ⌐    [x]
Intellectual disgrace

 ⌐      x  ⌐  x  ⌐ x    ⌐    [x]
Stares from every human face,

x̱      x  ⌐   x    ⌐ x  ⌐    [x]
And the seas of pity lie

⌐     x     ⌐ x  x̱   x     ⌐   [x]
Locked and frozen in each eye.        8
```

Heptasyllabic lines, in 4.4.4.4 stanzas (i.e., 4x4 formation with no virtual beats).

Page 108

(2)
```
|x    ⌐  x| ⌐   |
All heavy minds                    MM

| x  ⌐  | x  ⌐  |  x      ⌐  |
Do seek to ease their charge,   RRR

|x      ⌐ |  x   ⌐  |  x   ⌐  |
And that that most them binds   RRR

| x  ⌐ |x    ⌐  |
To let at large.                RR    4


|  x    ⌐|  x     ⌐|
Then why should I               RR

| \   ⌐  |  x  x̱   x  ⌐   |
Hold pain within my heart       RR
```

```
|x    ∠ | x    ∠ |x  ∠|
And may my tune apply            RRR

 | x ∠  | x   ∠ |
  To ease my smart?              RR    8


 | x  ∠   x | ∠ |
  My faithful lute               MM

|x ∠  | x     ∠ | x  ∠ |
Alone shall hear me plain,       RRR

 | x  ∠  |\   ∠ x | ∠ |
 For else all other suit         RMM

|x    ∠ | x   ∠ |
  Is clean in vain.              RR    12
```

The rhythm is overwhelmingly rising; only lines 1, 9, and 11 resist this movement, and are thus given added emphasis. (The meter is regular iambic pentameter, divided 2:3 and 3:2; this, incidentally, is a meter Wyatt is often said to have been unable to master!)

Page 114

(3)

```
  /     ∠  x ∠    x    ∠  x    ∠
  Come, friendly bombs, and fall on Slough

 x  x x    ∠   x   ∠ x     ∠
 It isn't fit for humans now,

   x    x x    ∠   x   ∠   x ∠
 There isn't grass to graze a cow

        /   ∠ x    ∠
        Swarm over, Death!                        4


   /      ∠    x    ∠   x   ∠  x \
   Come, bombs, and blow to smithereens

   x  ∠   x  \ x       ∠    x ∠
   Those air-conditioned, bright canteens,

   /      ∠   /    ∠   /    ∠   /    ∠
   Tinned fruit, tinned meat, tinned milk, tinned beans

        /      ∠    /     ∠
        Tinned minds, tinned breath.              8
```

```
        x   /    x   /      x    / x  / x    /
(4)     But soft, what light through yonder window breaks?

        x  x   x  /   x    / x x    x  /
        It is the east and Juliet is the sun.

        x /    /   /  x    /    x /  x     /
        Arise, fair sun, and kill the envious moon,

         x  x  x  / x  /  x    /    x     /
        Who is already sick and pale with grief          4

         x    /   x   /   x    /   x   /    x    /
        That thou, her maid, art far more fair than she.

         x  /  x   /   x     x x  /  xx
        Be not her maid since she is envious;

         x  /  x   /  x x   x   /   x     /
        Her vestal livery is but sick and green,

        x    /   x   /    x  /  x    /   x /
        And none but fools do wear it; cast it off.       8

        x  x   x  / x  /  x  x   x  /
        It is my lady, O, it is my love!
```

Note that "envious" is pronounced once with two syllables and once with three; and "Juliet" and "livery," which could have three syllables, have two. See the section on "Elision" in chapter 5.

Page 119

(5)

```
        x / x    /  x  / x   / x    /
        So saying, on he led his radiant files,

        /   x    x  /  [x] /   x    x  /    x /
        Dazzling the moon; these to the bower direct

        x   /   x    /   x   /     x    /   x   /
        In search of whom they sought: him there they found

        /   x   x  /  [x] /  x   x  /   x  /
        Squat like a toad, close at the ear of Eve;       4

        x / x    x  x   /  x   /   x /
        Assaying by his devilish art to reach
```

```
    x  ∟  x   x   x   ∟    x   x    x  ∟
    The organs of her fancy, and with them forge
```

```
    x  ∟ x    x   x  ∟  [x] ∟  x    x    ∟
    Illusions as he list, phantasms and dreams...
```

Five falling inversions (boxed here), two of them initial inversions. (Note that "radiant," "bower," "devilish" and "fancy, and" are pronounced with two syllables; see the section on "Elision" in chapter 5.)

Page 122

(6)

```
     ∟   x   x   ∟   x    x  ∟ [x] ∟   \     ∟
     Screen'd is this nook o'er the high, half-reaped field,
```

```
     x   ∟   x   ∟  \    ∟ x    ∟  x  ∟
     And here till sundown, shepherd! will I be.
```

```
        x    x   ∟  ∟   x   ∟ x   ∟  x   ∟
        Through the thick corn the scarlet poppies peep,
```

```
     x   x    ∟   ∟   x   ∟   x    ∟   x  ∟
     And round green roots and yellowing stalks I see    4
```

```
        /    ∟   x  ∟ x  x  x   ∟   x    ∟
        Pale pink convolvulus in tendrils creep;
```

```
        x   ∟   \     ∟  x    ∟
        And air-swept lindens yield
```

```
        x    ∟   x   ∟ x   ∟   x    ∟ x    ∟
        Their scent, and rustle down their perfumed showers
```

```
        x    ∟  x   x  ∟   ∟      x   x x   ∟
        Of bloom on the bent grass where I am laid,
   8
```

```
        x    ∟   x   x   x ∟  x   ∟   x    ∟
        And bower me from the August sun with shade;
```

```
        x   x  ∟   ∟ x    ∟   x  ∟ x    ∟
        And the eye travels down to Oxford's towers.
```

The meter is iambic pentameter, with one line of iambic trimeter (see chapter 6). There are five rising inversions, shaded here. The first has a virtual offbeat, producing a different rhythmic figure. (Note that "yellowing" and "bower" are pronounced with two syllables; "showers" and "towers" could be pronounced with either one or two.)

Page 125

(7)

```
∟   x   x   ∟ x   ∟ x x    x   ∟
Out of her secret Paradise she sped,

    x    ∟   x   ∟ x   ∟    x    ∟   x    ∟
Through camps and cities rough with stone, and steel,

    x   ∟ x   ∟      x   x  x  ∟ x   ∟
And human hearts, which to her aery tread

∟  x   /   ∟  x    x  x  ∟ x x
Yielding not, wounded the invisible                        4

∟   x   x   ∟ x   ∟    x ∟    x   ∟
Palms of her tender feet where'er they fell:

    x   ∟ x   ∟      x   ∟   x   ∟   x    ∟
And barbèd tongues, and thoughts more sharp than they,

∟    x  /   ∟   x   ∟ x   ∟    x ∟
Rent the soft Form they never could repel,

    x  ∟ x   ∟   x    x ∟   ∟   x  ∟
Whose sacred blood, like the young tears of May,         8

∟   x   x ∟ x    ∟      x  \ x ∟ x    ∟
Paved with eternal flowers that undeserving way.
```

The meter is iambic pentameter with a final six-beat line or alexandrine (Spenserian stanza). Lines 4 and 7 begin with sequences that have to be read as double offbeats with demotion to sustain the meter; this happens easily in line 7 ("Rent the soft form," where "soft" is subordinated to "form"), but is very difficult in line 4, where "not" attracts a beat to itself, threatening to disrupt the line.

Page 130

(8)

```
/    ∟    /    ∟      x  ∟ x   x   x   ∟
Mere dreams, mere dreams! Yet Homer had not sung

x   x  x   ∟    x   ∟ x    x ∟    ∟
Had he not found it certain beyond dreams
```

```
x  ∠   x    ∠    /    ∠   x ∠   x     ∠
That out of life's own self-delight had sprung

(x)x ∠   x     ∠ (x)x    ∠    x    ∠  x  ∠
The abounding glittering jet; though now it seems      4

x  x   x    ∠ (x) x   ∠   x ∠    \    ∠
As if some marvellous empty sea-shell flung

∠  x   (x)x  ∠   ∠   x   x ∠     ∠
Out of the obscure dark of the rich streams,

x   ∠ x  ∠  x    x    x ∠  x    x
And not a fountain, were the symbol which

    ∠ x    (x)x ∠(x)x    ∠ x x    x  ∠
Shadows the inherited glory of the rich.                8
```

The meter is iambic pentameter. All the additional syllables could be elided, and in most readings they would be at least partially elided. (Note that in line 6, the additional syllable makes a double offbeat into a triple offbeat; if we do not elide the vowels of "the ob-" the metrical alternations will tend to promote "the" and produce an extra beat. However, this elision makes the line one syllable short.)

(9)

```
    x   ∠  x   ∠ x   ∠    x ∠
When fainting Nature called for aid,

    x    ∠ - x   ∠    x ∠    x  ∠
And hovering Death prepared the blow,

   x   ∠ - x    ∠ x x  x   ∠
His vigorous remedy displayed

    x  ∠ -  x ∠  x  ∠   x   ∠
The power of art without the show.           4

                    . . .

    x   ∠ x   ∠     x    ∠ x  ∠
His virtues walked their narrow round,

     x   ∠ x  ∠    x   ∠  x  ∠
Nor made a pause, nor left a void;

 x    ∠   - x ∠ x   ∠  x   ∠
And sure the Eternal Master found

    x  ∠  x  ∠ x   ∠   x  ∠
The single talent well employed.             4
```

Page 134

(10)

```
 /   x   x   /   x   /   x   /
Mark but this flea, and mark in this,

 x   /   x   x̱   x   x̱   x /-   x /
How little that which thou deniest me is;

 /  x   \     /     x   /   \      /
Me it sucked first, and now sucks thee,

 x   x̱   x    /  x    /   /    /  x   /
And in this flea our two bloods mingled be.
```

The lines alternate between four-beat and five-beat duple verse. It is in the third line that the contrasts between "Me" and "thee" and between "first" and "now" invite emphatic stresses which carry the line's four beats, while the repeated "sucked" and "sucks" are subordinated.

Page 135

(11)

line 3: The successive stresses of "blue mists" are not preceded or followed by a double offbeat, as is required in syllable-stress verse. (After two further beats, there is a double offbeat that compensates for the loss of the earlier syllable, so the line could be said to hover on the borders of metricality.) The scansion shows this accurately.

line 5: The line has six beats instead of five. The scansion shows this accurately.

line 6: The scansion is somewhat misleading in that it shows the demotion of "storms." Demotion in the double offbeat of an initial inversion usually involves a subordinated stress.

line 8: The line has four beats instead of five. The scansion is misleading in that it shows a promotion on "his," even though the conditions for promotion are not met.

line 9: The line has four beats instead of five. The scansion shows this accurately.

line 11: The line has six full stresses, none of which can be easily demoted. The scansion is misleading in that it shows the demotion of "prized." (Demotion in double offbeats within the line almost always occurs in the rhythmic figure / x / / after a syntactic break; moreover, the word "prized" requires a full stress because of its importance in the meaning of the sentence.)

line 13: The line is in triple rhythm, with a virtual offbeat at the syntactic break. The scansion shows this accurately.

Shelley's original lines are as follows:

```
         x      /   /      x      - x / x   / x    \
line 3: Where blue mists through the unmoving atmosphere
```

```
         x  ∠ - x  \ x ∠ x     x̲     x  ∠
line 5:  Unnatural vegetation, where the land
```

```
            ∠    x   /  ∠   x     ∠ x  x̲   x ∠
line 6:  Teemed with all earthquake, tempest and disease,
```

```
         x   ∠    x  x̲  x  ∠   x   ∠   x     ∠
line 8:  Had crushed him to his country's bloodstained dust;
```

```
         x  ∠ x  ∠ x   x̲   x  ∠  x  ∠
line 9:  Or he was bartered for the fame of power,
```

```
            /    ∠ x  ∠   x  ∠ x x  x   ∠
line 11: Makes human will an article of trade;
```

```
         x    ∠    x  ∠ x   ∠   x   x̲  x ∠
line 13: And dragged to distant isles, where to the sound
```

Page 136

(12)

```
                    x   ∠ x x̲  x ∠          1 promotion
                    That memorable day,
```

```
  ∠   x   x ∠    x ∠ x   ∠    x  ∠          1 initial inversion
(June was the month, Lorenzo named the Square)
```

```
x  ∠   x  ∠ x x  x  \ x ∠    x   ∠          1 free double offbeat
I leaned a little and overlooked my prize
```

```
  x  x ∠  ∠ x   x̲    x  ∠ x  ∠             1 rising inversion
By the low railing round the fountain-source      1 promotion          4
```

```
  ∠   x  x  ∠ x   x̲  x  x  ∠  x ∠           1 initial inversion
Close to the statue, where a step descends:       1 promotion
```

```
  x    ∠    x ∠ x  ∠ x  x   ∠   x   ∠       1 free double offbeat
While clinked the cans of copper, as stooped and rose
```

```
  ∠  \  x  ∠   x  ∠    x  x  ∠  ∠           1 initial inversion with
Thick-ankled girls who brimmed them, and made place   demotion, 1 rising
                                                       inversion
```

```
  x  ∠ x  \[x] ∠  x  \    ∠ x  ∠            1 falling inversion with
For marketmen glad to pitch basket down,           demotion             8
```

```
  ∠ x  /  ∠ x  ∠   x  ∠    x ∠             1 initial inversion with
Dip a broad melon-leaf that holds the wet,         demotion
```

```
x   ∠   x  ∠ x   ∠   x  ∠ x ∠
And whisk their faded fresh. And on I read
```

```
  ∠ x  x   x̲   x  ∠   /  ∠ x x̲            1 initial inversion
Presently, though my path grew perilous            2 promotions, 1 demotion
```

```
x  ∠   x ∠    \     ∠  \   ∠   x   ∠
Between the outspread straw-work, piles of plait        2 demotions              12


∠   x  x   ∠  x   ∠   x     ∠  /  ∠
Soon to be flapping, each o'er two black eyes           1 initial inversion, 1
                                                        demotion


x    ∠   x  ∠ x  ∠   x  ∠  x  ∠
And swathe of Tuscan hair, on festas fine:


 x    ∠  \ x    ∠   x  ∠  [x] ∠ x  x   ∠     1 demotion, 1 free double
Through fire-irons, tribes of tongs, shovels in sheaves, offbeat, 1 falling
                                                         inversion
∠ x x   ∠   x     ∠  x    \    x ∠        1 initial inversion
Skeleton bedsteads, wardrobe-drawers agape,                              16


∠  x  /   ∠   /   ∠   x   ∠  x   ∠       1 initial inversion with
Rows of tall slim brass lamps with dangling gear,-      demotion, 1 other demotion


x   ∠   /   ∠   x  ∠ -x  x   x  ∠        1 demotion
And worse, cast clothes a-sweetening in the sun:        1 promotion


∠  x   x  ∠   x ∠   x  ∠   x  ∠          1 initial inversion
None of them took my eye from off my prize.
```

This is not the only possible reading of the passage, especially of the more complex lines. The line which borders most closely on unmetricality is line 8; the reading given here requires a rather artificial stress on "-men," followed by a break which is acceptable but not indicated by punctuation, and the demotion of "pitch." On the other hand, if "-men" is unstressed (producing a double offbeat), the compensation for the double offbeat does not occur until after another beat, and both "pitch" and "basket" have to be strongly stressed to effect that compensation:

```
      x   ∠ x  x    ∠   x  ∠    ∠  x   ∠
      For marketmen glad to pitch basket down
```

The first reading works quite well if the line's emphasis is put on "glad," an emphasis which is rhetorically appropriate.

Another highly irregular line is 17, where the scansion shown for the first part of the line has to be imposed on the words. It is probably better to read "tall slim brass lamps" without trying to become conscious of the beat – as a suspension of the meter, in other words.

Other quite irregular lines are 7, 9, 11, and 15.

Page 139

(13)

```
      /    ∠  x   x ∠   x  x   ∠  x   x ∠    x
      Dear Harp of my Country! in darkness I found thee,
```

```
x  ∠   /  x  ∠ x   x  ∠  x    x  ∠  [x]
The cold chain of silence had hung o'er thee long,
```

```
x   ∠ x  x ∠  /  x   ∠   x x ∠    x
When proudly, my own Island Harp, I unbound thee,
```

```
x   ∠  x   x  ∠   x  /    ∠ x  x   ∠ [x]
And gave all thy chords to light, freedom, and song!
```

Apart from the initial demotion of "Dear," all the demotions occur on syllables that demand a stress at least as strong as their neighbors; this produces eddies of resistance against the triple swing of the meter.

Page 144

(14)

```
| /   / | x  /    |x / | x  /  | /      /|
Fly, fly, my friends! I have my death wound – fly!
```

```
| /   / | x  /  | x  /  |x   / |x / |
See there that boy, that murthring boy I say,
```

```
|  x  x |x   /  | | /  x | /   /  | x   / |
Who like a thief, hid in dark bush doth lie,
```

```
| x    / |x /| x  / | x   / |x  / |
Till bloody bullet get him wrongful prey.                    4
```

```
| /  / |x    /| x  / |x   /  | x     /|
So tyrant he no fitter place could spy,
```

```
| x   x| /    /|x  x | x  / |x   / |
Nor so fair level in so secret stay,
```

```
|x    x | /    /  | x   /  | x  /  |x / |
As that sweet black which veils the heavenly eye:
```

```
| /   x |/   x | x   / | x  /  | x   /|
There himself with his shot he close doth lay.              8
```

The regular foot is the iambic foot, and the following substitute feet occur:
line 1: spondee (2)
line 2: spondee
line 3: pyrrhic, trochee, spondee
line 5: spondee
line 6: pyrrhic (2), spondee
line 7: pyrrhic, spondee
line 8: trochee (2) (see "double inversion" in Glossary)

Chapter 6

Page 153

(1)

```
    /        /        /        /
Charm me asleep, and melt me so

        /    /      /      [/]
  With thy delicious numbers;

        /     /       /       /
  That being ravished, hence I go

      /     /    /      [/]
  Away in easy slumbers.                    4

/          /        /        /
Ease my sick head, and make my bed,

        /     x       /     [/]
  Thou power that canst sever

      /      /        /        /
From me this ill: and quickly still


        /      /      /    [/]
  Though thou not kill my fever.        8
```

As the scansion shows, the stanza is made up of two 4x4 formations in the ballad-stanza pattern, 4.3.4.3. The strongest run-on is from line 7 to line 8 (in the original layout), since it goes across the pause associated with a virtual beat.

Page 158

(2)

```
      x    /    /    x    x  /  - x    /    /    /     x
(a)   Our brains ache, in the merciless iced East winds that

      /  x
   knive us...

      / x    x  /   x /    x /      x  /   x   / x
   Wearied we keep awake because the night is silent...

      /     /  x    /    x  /   x    / - x x    x  / -x
   Low, drooping flares confuse our memory of the salient...
```

```
  ⌐ x    x ⌐ x     ⌐  x    ⌐ x    ⌐ -x    ⌐  x
Worried by silence, sentries whisper, curious, nervous, 4

          x   ⌐ x    ⌐ x
        But nothing happens.
```

The meter is six-beat iambic (alexandrine or hexameter) with duple endings, plus a two-beat closing line (dimeter); there is no regular pause after three beats to suggest four-beat units with virtual beats. The imperfect duple rhymes, arranged *abba*, also militate against the 4x4 movement.

```
        x  ⌐ x   ⌐ x     ⌐  x  x̲
(b)     The forest ended. Glad I was

        x  ⌐   x ⌐    x   ⌐    x ⌐
        To feel the light, and hear the hum

        x  ⌐   x    ⌐    x  ⌐x    ⌐
        Of bees, and smell the drying grass

        x    x  ⌐  ⌐    x ⌐   x  x   ⌐
        And the sweet mint, because I had come        4

         x x  ⌐  x   ⌐ x    x̲    x ⌐
        To an end of forest, and because

        ⌐   x    x   ⌐  x  ⌐     x  ⌐
        Here was both road and inn, the sum

        x   ⌐   /   ⌐ x    x̲    x   ⌐
        Of what's not forest. But 'twas here

         x  ⌐    x x̲ x  x̲  x   ⌐
        They asked me if I did not pass        8

        ⌐  x  x   ⌐  /    ⌐  /    ⌐
        Yesterday this way. "Not you? Queer."

        ⌐   x   x   ⌐   x    x  ⌐  ⌐
        "Who then? and slept here?" I felt fear.
```

Despite a fairly regular iambic tetrameter rhythm (the last two lines being the only two that are difficult to read with a regular rhythm), an elaborate rhyme scheme (*abababcacc*), and frequent divisions of the lines into two-beat half-lines, the syntactic units contradict the 4x4 formation strongly enough to reduce it to a faint presence.

Page 165

(3)

```
 /   x  x   /     x    x x   x x      /
Come let us go, while we are in our prime,

x   /   x /  x    /  x x    x  /
And take the harmless folly of the time.

  x   x      /  /   x /   x    /
We shall grow old apace and die

   x /    x   /   x   / x  x
Before we know our liberty.                    4

   x    /   x    /    x  x    /   /
Our life is short, and our days run

   x  /   x / x    x     x  /
As fast away as does the sun;

 /     x  x /  x    x  x   /  x   /
And, as a vapour, or a drop of rain,

 /     /    x   /    x  /    x /
Once lost, can ne'er be found again:           8

   /   x  x   /  x  / x    /
So when or you or I are made

x  /  x   /    x    /  x     /
A fable, song, or fleeting shade,

  /    /   /    / x   /   x /
All love, all liking, all delight

   /     /    x   /  x  /   x    /
Lies drowned with us in endless night.         12

  x    x    /   /     x   / x   x   x / x
Then while time serves, and we are but decaying,

 /     x  x /  x   /    /    / x  / x
Come, my Corinna, come, let's go a-Maying.
```

The longer lines are iambic pentameter, the shorter lines are iambic tetrameter. Inversions are marked by shading.

Chapter 7

Page 176

(1)
The following scansion shows the entire lines most easily accommodated to a duple meter (mostly iambic pentameter). Other lines have metrical portions, and there are sequences that fall into a triple rhythm.

```
             Sometimes the light falls here too as at Florence

             /   x   x   /   /   /     x   x   x  /  x
             Circled by low hard hills, or in the quarry

             /  x  x   /   \   /     x   x   x /  x
             Under its half-hewn cliffs, where that collection

             Of pale rough blocks, still lying at all angles on the

              dust-white floor                                    4

             /    x   x  /  x   /
             Waits, like a town of tombs.

                            x  / x   /  x   /  x \
                            I finish nothing I begin.

             x    x   /   /   x   x   /   x  x x  /
             And the dream sleeps in the stone, to be unveiled

             x   /  x  /      x  / x    / x  x
             Or half-unveiled, the lurking nakedness;           8

             Luminous as a grapeskin, the cold marble mass

             Of melted skeins, chains, veils and veins,

             /  x  x    /  x     /  x x   x  / x x
             Bosses and hollows, muscular convexities,

             /   x  x /x   /  x x    /     /
             Supple heroic surfaces, tense drums               12

             x   / x    /  x   /   x  /
             And living knots and cords of love:

                 /   x   x  /   x  x   x  /
             — Sleeps in the stone, and is unveiled
```

```
x  �ட  x  ⌟        x  ⌟ x    ⌟   x  ⌟
Or half-unveiled, the body's self a veil,

By the adze and the chisel, and the mind               16

x  ⌟     x  ⌟  x
Impelled by torment.

                  x̱    x ⌟  x   ⌟ x
                  In the empty quarry

The light waits, and the tombs wait,

For the coming of a dream.                             20
```

Page 180

(2)

```
        x  /        /
        A cold spring:

         x  /x x   x    /    x    x  /
        The violet was flawed on the lawn.

         x    /  /   x   /    x   /    / x \ x
        For two weeks or more the trees hesitated;

         x  / x   /       / x
        the little leaves waited,                       4

         /  x  x /  x \ x     x     \ x  x / x
        carefully indicating their characteristics.

         / x  x x   /     /    /
        Finally a grave green dust

         /   x  / x   x   / x  / x   /
        settled over your big and aimless hills.

         /   /   x x   /    /    /  x   /   \
        One day, in a chill white blast of sunshine,    8

        x   x  / x  /  x  /    x   /
        on the side of one a calf was born.

           x  / x   /       / x
        The mother stopped lowing

        x   /  x  /   /  / x    x / x   /
        and took a long time eating the after-birth,
```

```
x   /   x   /
a wretched flag,                              12


  x    x  /   \  /   /    x
but the calf got up promptly


 x    /    x   /    x  /    /
and seemed inclined to feel gay.
```

Chapter 8

Page 189

(1)

(a)
```
ANT————————————————————————————| ARR————————
When she found that she had time to spare, she made a

————————————————————————|
quick call to the optician.
```

(b)
```
STA————————————— | EXT——————————————————————— |
Spring at last - late and feeble, but still spring.
```

(c)
```
STA ——————————————————————————— | EXT ——————————————
The long steady drive had made him dozy, but a glimpse of

————————————————————————————————————————————|
Michelle waiting in the lounge was enough to wake him up.
```

(d)
```
ANT ———————————————————————————————————| ARR—
Nothing in my life had prepared me for this moment: a

———————————————————————|
real choice of occupation.
```

(e)
```
STA—————————| EXT—————————————————————————— |
Darkness fell before there was time to finish the job.
```

(f)
```
STA—————————| EXT—————————————|
They cursed like highwaymen.
```

(g)
```
ANT ——————| ARR———————————|
Above all, don't dawdle.
```

(h)
```
STA ———————————————————————| EXT————————————————— |
He held out the cigar-case, and his visitor winced.
```

ANT ———————————————————————————————————|
(i) Rounding the bend, before she could see what lay ahead,

ARR ——————————————————————————————|
she had a premonition that the road was blocked.

ANT ————————————————————————————————
(j) Three dusty elephants, several surprisingly dowdy

————————————————————————————| ARR ————————————————
peacocks, and a few fraying llamas were all that the park

—————————|
contained.

(2)

```
1  STA ————————————————————————————————————>
2  STA ————————————————————————————————————>
3  STA ——————————————————————————————————|
4  ANT ——————————————| ARR ————————————————|
   The turtle lives 'twixt plated decks     1

1  ——————————————————————————————————————>
2  ——————————————————————————————————————|
3  EXT ————————————————————————————————————|
4  ANT ————————————————| ARR ————————————————|
   Which practically conceal its sex.       2

1  ——————————————————————————————————————>
2  EXT ——————————————————————————————————>
3  ANT ——————————————————————————————————|
4  ANT ————————————————— |ARR ————————————————|
   I think it clever of the turtle          3

1  ——————————————————————————————————————|
2  ——————————————————————————————————————|
3  ARR ——————————————————————————————————|
4  ANT ——————————————| ARR ————————————————|
   In such a fix to be so fertile.          4
```

Page 199

(3)
(a)
```
1  STA ——————————————————————————————————————| EXT ——
2  ANT ——————————————————————| ARR ————————————————|
   I warmly recommend this candidate with no

1  ——————————————————————————————————————|
2                                          |
   qualifications whatsoever.
```

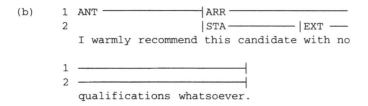

```
(b)    1 ANT ─────────────────┤ARR ──────────────────────
       2                       │STA ───────────┤EXT ──────
         I warmly recommend this candidate with no

       1 ──────────────────────────────────┤
       2 ──────────────────────────────────┤
         qualifications whatsoever.
```

In (a), the sentence is divided into a statement – "I warmly recommend this candidate" – and an extension which elaborates, positively, on the recommendation. In (b), the sentence begins with an anticipation – "I warmly recommend" – followed by an arrival that describes the candidate in negative terms.

(4)

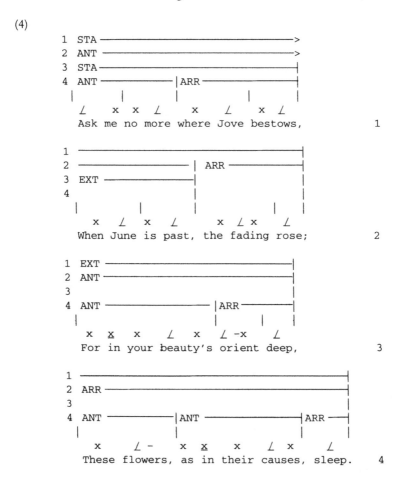

```
       1 STA ──────────────────────────────────────>
       2 ANT ──────────────────────────────────────>
       3 STA ──────────────────────────────────┤
       4 ANT ──────────────┤ARR ────────────────┤
         │         │         │         │         │
         ∠    x   x   ∠   x    ∠    x   ∠
         Ask me no more where Jove bestows,              1

       1 ──────────────────────────────────────────┤
       2 ──────────────────────┤ ARR ──────────────┤
       3 EXT ───────────────────┤                    │
       4                         │                    │
         │         │         │              │   │
           x   ∠  x   ∠        x  ∠ x     ∠
         When June is past, the fading rose;            2

       1 EXT ────────────────────────────────────┤
       2 ANT ────────────────────────────────────┤
       3                                           │
       4 ANT ───────────────────────┤ARR ─────────┤
         │                           │     │       │
           x   x   x     ∠   x     ∠ -x    ∠
         For in your beauty's orient deep,              3

       1 ──────────────────────────────────────────┤
       2 ARR ──────────────────────────────────────┤
       3                                             │
       4 ANT ────────────────┤ANT ─────────────────┤ARR ──┤
         │                    │                      │     │
           x        ∠ -     x   x    x    ∠   x      ∠
         These flowers, as in their causes, sleep.      4
```

Page 202

(5)

The following is only one of several possible ways of analyzing the poem. Any phrasal scansion should show that the first sentence is a single long unit divided only at the lower levels (and therefore having strong line-to-line continuity), while the second sentence is divided at high levels into a series of units (and has strong end-stopping).

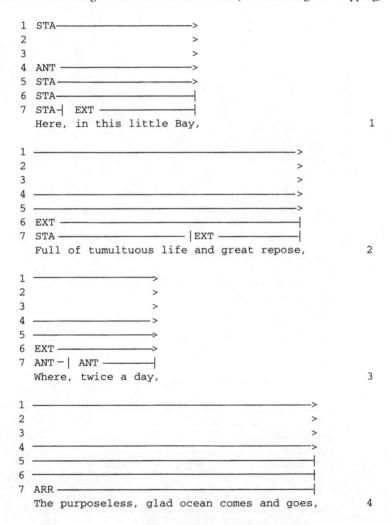

```
1 ──────────────────────────────────────────>
2                                           >
3 ──────────────────────────────────────    >
4 ──────────────────────────────────────────|
5 EXT ─────────────| EXT ─────────────────|
6                  |                       |
7                  |                       |
    Under high cliffs, and far from the huge town,     5


1 ─────────────|
2              |
3              |
4 ARR ─────────|
5              |
6              |
7              |
    I sit me down.                                     6


1 EXT ────────────────────────────────────────>
2 ANT ────────────────────────────────────────|
3                                              |
4                                              |
5 ANT ─────────────|ARR ──────────────────────|
6                  |                           |
7                  |                           |
    For want of me the world's course will not fail:   7


1 ──────────────────────────────────────────>
2 ARR ────────────────────────────────────────>
3 STA ────────────────────────────────────────|
4                                              |
5 ANT ───────────────────| ARR ───────────────|
6                        |                     |
7                        |                     |
    When all its work is done, the lie shall rot;      8


1 ──────────────────────────────────────>
2 ──────────────────────────────────────>
3 EXT ────────────────────────────────────>
4 STA ────────────────────────────────────|
5 STA─────────────────| EXT ───────────────|
6                     |                     |
7                     |                     |
    The truth is great, and shall prevail,             9
```

```
1 ─────────────────────────────────────|
2 ─────────────────────────────────────|
3 ─────────────────────────────────────|
4 EXT ───────────────────────────────|
5                                       |
6                                       |
7 ANT ──────────────| ARR───────────────|
```
When none cares whether it prevail or not.   10

Page 208

(6)

```
1 STA───────────────────────────────────>
2 STA───────────────────────────────────>
3 ANT ──────────────────────────────────>
4 ANT ───────| ARR ─────────────────────>
5            | ANT ─────────────────────|
6            | ANT ──────────────| ARR──|
```
Dear love, since the impossible proves   1

```
1 ───────────────────────────────────>
2 ───────────────────────────────────>
3 ─────────────────────────────────|
4 ─────────────────────────────────|
5 ARR───────────────────────────────|
6 ANT ──────────────| ARR ───────────|
```
Our sole recourse from this distress,   2

```
1 ─────────────────────────────────────>
2 ───────| EXT ─────────────────────────>
3 ARR ──────|                            >
4           |                            >
5           | STA ─────────────────────|
6           | ANT ──────────────| ARR ─|
```
Claim it: the ebony ritual-mask of no   3

```
1 ─────────────────────────────────|
2 ─────────────────────────────────|
3                                    |
4                                    |
5 EXT ───────────────────────────────|
6 ANT ──────────────| ARR ───────────|
```
Cannot outstare a living yes.   4

```
1  EXT ──────────────────────────────>
2  STA ──────────────────────────────>
3                                    >
4                                    >
5  STA ──────| EXT ──────────────────>
6           | ANT ──| ARR ──| EXT ──|
   Claim it without despond or hate                    5


1  ─────────────────────────────────>
2  ──────── | EXT ────────────────────>
3          | STA────────────────────>
4          | ANT ────────────────────>
5  ──────── | ANT ────────────────────|
6  EXT──────|                         |
   Or greed; but in your gentler tone                  6


1  ───────────────────────────────────────>
2  ───────────────────────────────────────>
3  ──────────────────────────── | EXT ──────>
4  ──── | ARR ──────────────────────|        >
5  ARR | ANT ──────────── | ARR──────────| ANT──────────>
6      |                |             | STA────────|
   Say: "This is ours, the impossible," and silence   7


1  ───────────────────────────────|
2  ───────────────────────────────|
3  ──────────────────────────────|
4                                 |
5  ──────────────────── | ARR────────────|
6  EXT───────────────────| STA──────── | EXT─|
   Will give consent it is ours alone.                8


1  EXT────────────────────────────────>
2  STA────────────────────────────────>
3  STA────────────────────────────────|
4                                     |
5                                     |
6  STA──────────── | EXT────────────────|
   The impossible has wild-cat claws              9


1  ─────────────────────────────────→
2  ─────────────────────────────────→
3  EXT ──────────────────────────────→
4  ANT ──────────────────────────────|
5                                    |
6  ANT ──────────────────── | ARR────────|
   Which you would rather meet and die          10
```

```
1  ───────────────────────────────────────────>
2  ───────────────────────────────────────────>
3  ───────────────────────────────────────────>
4  ARR ────────────────────────────────────────|
5                                               |
6  ANT ──────────────── |ARR ──────────────────|
   Than  commit  love  to  time's  curative  venom          11


1  ──────────────────────────────────────|
2  ──────────────────── |EXT ─────────────|
3  ────────────────────|                  |
4  EXT ────────────────|                  |
5                       |                  |
6                       |                  |
   And  break  our  oath;  for  so  would  I.             12
```

Index

For a list, not indexed here, of definitions and terminological equivalents, see Appendix 2. For authors of examples cited, also not indexed here, see Appendix 3. Page-references to passages in which important terms are defined or explained are given in bold type.

CPSIA information can be obtained
at www.ICGtesting.com
Printed in the USA
LVHW091744170820
663417LV00003B/357